# Justice and the Ethics of Legal Interpretation



*Justice and the Ethics of Legal Interpretation* addresses how it is that legal texts – laws, statutes and regulations – can, and do, have meaning. Conventionally, legal decisions are justified with reference to language. However, since language is always open to interpretation, and so cannot fully justify any legal decision, there is a responsibility that is inherent in legal interpretation itself. In this book, Susanna Lindroos-Hovinheimo uncovers and analyses this responsibility – which, she argues, is not limited by the text that is being interpreted (and through its mediation, by the legal system). It is not simply a responsibility to read well; it implies a responsibility for the effects of the interpretation in a particular situation and with regard to those whose case is being decided. Ultimately, it is a responsibility to do justice. It is these two aspects of responsibility that are conceptualised here as the two key dimensions of the ethics of legal interpretation: the textual and the situational. Drawing on the work of Wittgenstein, Gadamer, Derrida and Levinas, *Justice and the Ethics of Legal Interpretation* offers a fresh approach to long-standing questions about language and meaning in law. It will be of enormous value to those with interests in jurisprudence and legal theory.

**Susanna Lindroos-Hovinheimo** is a researcher at the University of Helsinki. Her research includes philosophy of language, ethics, and political theory, especially theories of responsibility and justice. She has published several articles on legal interpretation.

# Justice and the Ethics of Legal Interpretation

Susanna Lindroos-Hovinheimo

Routledge
Taylor & Francis Group
LONDON AND NEW YORK

First published 2012
by Routledge
2 Park Square, Milton Park, Abingdon, Oxon, OX14 4RN

Simultaneously published in the USA and Canada
by Routledge
711 Third Avenue, New York, NY 10017

A GlassHouse Book

*Routledge is an imprint of the Taylor & Francis Group, an informa business*



First issued in paperback 2013



*British Library Cataloguing in Publication Data*
A catalogue record for this book is available from the British Library

*Library of Congress Cataloging in Publication Data*
Lindroos-Hovinheimo, Susanna.
Justice and the ethics of legal interpretation / Susanna Lindroos-Hovinheimo.
p. cm.
Includes bibliographical references.
ISBN 978-0-203-12798-8 (ebk)
1. Law--Interpretation and construction. 2. Law--Philosophy. I. Title.
K290.L56 2012
340'.1--dc23
2011033909

ISBN 978-0-415-68892-5 (hbk)
ISBN 978-0-203-12798-8 (ebk)
ISBN 978-0-415-72019-9 (pbk)

Typeset in Times New Roman
by Saxon Graphics Ltd, Derby DE21 4SZ

# Justice and the Ethics of Legal Interpretation

Susanna Lindroos-Hovinheimo

Routledge
Taylor & Francis Group
LONDON AND NEW YORK

First published 2012
by Routledge
2 Park Square, Milton Park, Abingdon, Oxon, OX14 4RN

Simultaneously published in the USA and Canada
by Routledge
711 Third Avenue, New York, NY 10017

A GlassHouse Book

*Routledge is an imprint of the Taylor & Francis Group, an informa business*



First issued in paperback 2013



*British Library Cataloguing in Publication Data*
A catalogue record for this book is available from the British Library

*Library of Congress Cataloging in Publication Data*
Lindroos-Hovinheimo, Susanna.
Justice and the ethics of legal interpretation / Susanna Lindroos-Hovinheimo.
p. cm.
Includes bibliographical references.
ISBN 978-0-203-12798-8 (ebk)
1. Law--Interpretation and construction. 2. Law--Philosophy. I. Title.
K290.L56 2012
340'.1--dc23
2011033909

ISBN 978-0-415-68892-5 (hbk)
ISBN 978-0-203-12798-8 (ebk)
ISBN 978-0-415-72019-9 (pbk)

Typeset in Times New Roman
by Saxon Graphics Ltd, Derby DE21 4SZ

"Far from being 'indeterminate' or 'nihilistic', however, or a matter of wanton free play or arbitrary choice, each reading is, strictly speaking, ethical, in the sense that it *has* to take place, by an implacable necessity, as the response to a categorical demand, and in the sense that the reader *must* take responsibility for it and for its consequences in the personal, social, and political worlds."

(J. Hillis Miller)

"At some point, and perhaps you were trying to provoke me, you said that if we practice close reading we will never act. On the contrary, I would assume that political, ethical and juridical responsibility requires a task of infinite close reading."

(Jacques Derrida)

# Contents

# Acknowledgements

I would like to express my gratitude to Desmond Manderson for his very helpful comments on drafts of this book. I have been fortunate to discuss these ideas with many other people as well, of whom I want to thank especially Kaarlo Tuori, Ari Hirvonen, Samuli Hurri, Toomas Kotkas and Jacques de Ville. I am grateful to Colin Perrin, Melanie Fortmann-Brown and Jessica Moody at Routledge for their great help. Lastly, I want to express my gratitude to my family and Petra for their unwavering support.

# Introduction: post-semantic interpretation

This book is about meaning in law. The question is how legal texts, for instance laws, statutes and regulations, can and do have meaning. It is argued here that an answer to this question compels us to think about ethics, but ethics itself is not the actual topic of this book. This is not a book about ethics and law but about legal interpretation. Nevertheless, it seems that thinking about meaning in law we are at some point necessarily directed to questions concerning ethics as well. Thus, the aim is not to discuss the complicated relationship between law and ethics or morality. Our primary interest is not the often debated question of whether law is fundamentally good or bad or the other classic problem of whether law and ethics are essentially distinct or overlapping fields. These issues are touched upon because of the openings that the problems of legal meaning lead to, but they are not the primary focus of the book.

The primary focus is legal interpretation. Questions that are asked are: How is it done, and how should it be done? The natural presupposition is that at the core of the problem lies language because it is the medium of law. Language makes legal interpretation difficult as it holds no definite meanings. No utterance has only one exact meaning, and texts can always be interpreted in several ways. This leads to the idea that we cannot decide what the meaning of a text is by looking at language alone. Language itself does not provide us with criteria for good or bad interpretations. Still, we do think that good and bad interpretations exist. How can that be? Often one interpretation seems wrong and another seems right, or at least better. Legal theory is permeated by the search for some criteria by which we could distinguish good and bad, better and worse interpretations.

The difficult nature of language seems to be a problem for law. Traditionally, we have been looking for a way to justify legal decisions and uphold legal certainty through reference to language, but this approach is highly problematic. If we loosen the tight theoretical bond between semantics and legal interpretation, we might come to see things differently. Separating law and semantics does not necessarily lead to a catastrophe. It does not mean that anything goes. Even if legal meanings cannot be pinpointed directly on the meaning of words, this does not mean that it is at the arbitrary will of the judge to use their power any way that they like, nor that there would be no criteria whatsoever for legal interpretation. Nor, it must be noted, does it mean that we abandon semantics altogether either. However, there is certainly a need to think and rethink the relationship between law and language, and the 'post-semantics' developed here is an attempt at such a reconfiguration.

If legal interpretation cannot be based on the meaning of words, on what can it be based? When the theoretical connection between semantics and legal meaning is loosened and we realise that language cannot be a means of justifying legal decisions, the consequence is that the responsibility inherent in legal decisions can be seen in full. This approach to legal interpretation is to be preferred for several reasons. First, the way the correctness of interpretation has been tied to semantics is problematic, and upholding this legal fiction is an obscure and misleading strategy. It may be a way of concealing what is actually done when legal texts are interpreted, or it may be part of a more general ideology about the role of law in society or the separation of powers. Be that as it may, it is not a working theory today, when most practicing lawyers and theorists alike agree on the ambiguities of linguistic meaning. Second, by acknowledging the responsibility of interpretation we do something important because we underline the accountability of legal decision-making.

This leads us to search for ways to analyse and explain the responsibility of interpretation. The responsibility of the legal interpreter is above all legal but also ethical and social. The main argument is that this responsibility contains a responsibility towards the text that is interpreted (and, through the mediation of the text, towards the legal system as well), but not only this. It is not simply a responsibility to read and read well, but transcends this to concern a broader plain. It includes responsibility for the interpretation decision with its effects in a particular situation and with regard to the people whose case is decided. Ultimately, it is a responsibility to do justice. These two aspects of responsibility are conceptualised here as the two dimensions of the ethics of legal interpretation: the textual and the situational.

This book is divided into five chapters. The interconnectedness between law and language and some of the problems that this causes are first introduced. It becomes evident that legal meaning cannot be linked directly to semantics, but in order to understand how language still has to be at the centre of law we must study theories of language and meaning in detail. This is done in Chapters 1 and 2. The conclusions drawn give a picture of the problems involved in defining meanings, but they also give us some hope for finding solutions. But, in order to understand legal interpretation, we also have to understand interpretation in general, not only the subtleties of linguistic meaning. Hence, theories of interpretation are studied in Chapter 3, focusing first on hermeneutic theories with the aim of shedding light on the process of interpretation as human action. The reading of hermeneutics offered here may not be the most conventional one as it accentuates ethical factors at play in understanding and interpretation. Through hermeneutics we approach deconstruction, which is a different kind of theory dealing partly with the same issues. At this point we realise that even though both theories of language and theories of interpretation enable tentative insights into legal interpretation, none of these theories provide sufficient answers to the questions posed here. We are brought to consider questions regarding the ethics of language and reading, and need to study in more detail whether and how the criteria for good interpretation can be understood as ethical. This is done in Chapter 4. If ethics is relevant for interpretation, then what does this mean for law? Here we face more general questions regarding the connections between legal interpretation and justice, which are studied in Chapter 5. Ultimately, it is the question of justice that stands out as the leading theme of this whole project.

The overall aim of the book is therefore to study certain theories of language, interpretation and legal interpretation, and find a theoretical frame that can explain how interpretation is done, how it can be done and how it should best be done in the legal field. This is neither a legal dogmatic nor an empirical study. Instead, it can be best described as philosophical. I feel very strongly that this kind of intellectual exercise is needed in law. Law should study its own premises, its presuppositions and its underlying presumptions in order better to understand what lawyers do, how and why. This kind of research comes very close to research on what the law is because of the central role that legal interpretation and decision-making play in law. However, the ontology of law falls outside the interests of this book as it concentrates on asking how meaning is constructed in the legal sphere. To narrow down the scope, it is necessary to focus mainly on interpretation by judges and courts. But the argument does not commit itself to any particular legal system, although the legal background of the writer can perhaps be surmised from the text. The aim is to find a wider perspective, something general that can be said about meaning in law. Thus, the research subject is vague (and according to some views, maybe too vague). However, this reflects the subject matter well: legal meaning is vague in many ways.

Philosophical research can seldom aspire to very direct practical usage but should rather be seen as a means of self-reflection. This is its purpose and also its strength: to open new ways of thinking and provide food for thought, to add to the self-understanding of lawyers. Of course, on a sociological level, one could also argue that the theory which we choose to believe in does, indeed, have practical consequences for how we see the law and our own role in it. Daily legal life operates always under some theoretical presuppositions, both explicit and implicit. This makes research into the presuppositions and premises underlying legal interpretation all the more important.

The conceptions presented in this book have strong roots in Ludwig Wittgenstein's later work. The basic understanding of language and meaning are highly influenced by his views. But the argument is not committed to merely a single philosophical tradition. It is argued here that the picture of language that we can draw from a reading of Wittgenstein's texts can be counterpointed in interesting ways by Jacques Derrida's ideas on language and meaning. Wittgenstein and Derrida should not be seen as each other's opponents even though they are usually classified in different philosophical traditions. Their views on meaning and language can be read to complement each other. While points of difference certainly exist between the two philosophers, enough similarity remains to allow juxtaposition. But the shift from one to the other does involve a shift in style and a leap in ways of expression, which the reader will soon discover.

Through a discussion of Wittgenstein's and Derrida's thoughts, a view on meaning can be developed that can be used as a starting point when considering legal interpretation. It is not claimed that this is the only plausible view on meaning, but it might be the best and most realistic one that we have in contemporary philosophy. However, the problem that lies at the heart of this book, the question of meaning in law, is not solved by the theories put forward by these philosophers. Vagueness and undecidability always haunt meaning, as is shown in the analysis of these philosophers. This causes severe problems for legal interpretation, problems that can only be unravelled through a shift in focus, which takes place towards the end of this book.

Derrida's writings function as an interesting contrast to hermeneutic theories. Here the core question of how legal texts have meaning appears in a different light. I argue that the seed to an answer lies in the inter-personal and situated activity of interpretation and communication, an idea that can be discerned in Wittgenstein, Derrida and Hans-Georg Gadamer. Meaning can be understood as interchange and a coming together of people. Its home is in communication, and this way we are naturally led to think about the relations of people and also ethics. As *the other person* sneaks into the discussion of meaning, the whole field of ethics is opened. It is approached in this book through a reading of Emmanuel Levinas's work. His theory of ethics and language, focusing on topics such as otherness, friendship and hospitality, provides possibilities for answering some of the questions posed here. However, when we talk of responsibility, we move inside a normativity, where ethics and politics come together in many ways. Especially in the field of law we are not only confronted with the other person but with innumerable people who place claims on the law that can be understood as political just as well as ethical.

## The uncertainty of legal interpretation

In a paper presented in 1989, Michel Rosenfeld gives a bleak diagnosis: legal interpretation finds itself in a crisis. This crisis can be understood as having very long roots, but it has been a pressing issue in legal theory through the latter half of the twentieth century. Rosenfeld describes it as a loss of faith in 'objective criteria permitting the ascription of distinct and transparent meanings to legal texts' (Rosenfeld 1992: 152; see, also, Rosenfeld 1998). This manifests itself in many ways, for instance in the dissolution of any consensus concerning values, the inescapable indeterminacy of legal rules, and the belief that all dispositions concerning legal issues are political and subjective.[1] The reasons for the crisis are many.

1 See, also, for example Timothy Endicott on the connections between (linguistic) vagueness and the impossibility of the rule of law in Endicott 2000.

How can it be resolved? According to Rosenfeld, there cannot be an easy solution. Importantly, there cannot be a return to the narrow understanding of interpretation, where meaning is defined as the original intent of the legislator or party drawing up a contract. Approaches that stress the interpreting community or extra-legal values are equally problematic.[2] What, then, can resolve the crisis of legal interpretation?

The question at issue is intertwined with the question of how to understand the relationship between law and politics. Rosenfeld concentrates on showing that law, even in the crisis in which it finds itself, cannot be reduced to politics. Law can, through its interpretive deeds, sustain an identity of its own, and this way the crisis of interpretation can be overcome. In contrast to politics, which focuses on the self before the other, and ethics, which lifts the other before the self, law strikes a balance between these two positions (Rosenfeld 1992: 167). Rosenfeld's idea is that the logic of law is neither the egoism of politics nor the altruism of ethics, but something in between. And law can uphold this logic through its interpretive deeds. The crisis of legal interpretation, which turns into a general crisis of law, can be overcome by holding on to exactly what seems to be the problem: interpretation. The definition of the crisis is that the identity of law is about to disappear, that law is turning into politics (nobody seems to be afraid that law would turn into ethics; perhaps that is an impossible idea). The promise of a future for law is in its being true to itself, that is, its character as interpretation.

The crisis of legal interpretation is one reason for the presence of so much general scepticism and even nihilism in legal theory. Quite a few writers claim that law is a failure and merely an irresponsible system of repression. Some of these ideas are discussed below.[3] What has provoked these attitudes towards law is of course not only the crisis of meaning. They can also be understood as reactions caused by general disappointment. Simon Critchley describes nihilism, referring to Nietzsche as the uncanniest of guests, who arrives when faith in meaning has been lost. Nihilism is the breakdown of the order of meaning, where what we previously imagined as a basis for valuation has been lost. It involves a sense of meaninglessness, which can even lead to despair. The philosopher's task is to resist nihilism and its paralysing indifference. Thus Critchley defines philosophy as the thinking through of the fact that the basis of meaning has become meaningless (Critchley 2007a: 2). This is the task set in this book as

2 Rosenfeld himself thinks that deconstruction may be a way of overcoming the crisis. He maintains that deconstruction can be a method of interpretation; it can stand up to the challenge of the indeterminacy of meaning. Interpretation as a rewriting of a text is subject to constraints. These constraints do not, however, dictate a single determinate meaning. Rather, they open and close different paths, which legitimate certain meanings and bar others (see Rosenfeld 1992: 163–165).

3 What will not be directly approached here are the anarchist and Marxist critical traditions, which are in themselves interesting and deserve proper attention that unfortunately cannot be given here.

well.[4] Losing certainty does not mean that meaning has been lost completely. Meaning exists and there can be good interpretations, but what these are needs to be rethought.

Legal interpretation was a much studied field especially in the 1980s and 1990s. In contrast with earlier Western legal theory, which had to a large extent concerned questions regarding the nature of law, the 1980s saw a turn to methodological questions. Law became first and foremost a linguistic construction, and new kinds of theories emerged, including new perspectives.[5] Ronald Dworkin became famous for underlining the nature of law as an interpretive practice. However, around the turn of the century, interest in questions concerning legal interpretation declined. But the questions have not been solved.

Deconstruction has undeniably had an impact on legal thinking, especially in pointing out the problems connected to language that partly lead to the idea of crisis as a loss of foundation for legal meaning. The view of language which deconstruction holds meant in the Anglophone world that the connection between text and decision had to be thought anew. This fostered nihilistic announcements about interpretation by some legal realists. Loss of meaning threatened lawyers (see Goodrich *et al.* 2008b: 3). This book inquires into the nature of language and meaning, not only to explore failures and threats but also to seek out possibilities. Deconstruction is one important theoretical horizon in this endeavour, but it is not the only one.

Before I go into the problems of legal interpretation in more detail, a few words are needed on what it means here. Legal theory habitually talks about legal interpretation as distinct from application of legal norms and often also as distinct from legal reasoning and legal argumentation.[6] A rough understanding of the matter could be that what distinguishes legal interpretation from application is that legal interpretation is performed in order to deduce a legal norm from a legal text while

4 Critchley is not primarily concerned with nihilism, however, but with political disappointment. Political disappointment arises from the realisation that the world is violently unjust and provokes the question of what justice might be in such a world. He distinguishes it from nihilism, which he defines as a reaction to a disappointment of a religious nature. According to him, the two are intermixed and, indeed, one can say that they both figure in the background of the issues discussed in this book (see Critchley 2007a: 3).

5 Costas Douzinas and Ronnie Warrington claimed at the beginning of the 1990s that the importation of semiotics, literary theory and hermeneutics into jurisprudence helped a field that was plagued by 'largely irrelevant and irredeemably boring debates of the 60s and 70s between positivism, analytical moral philosophy and various shades of sociology of law'. They refer to Ronald Dworkin and Stanley Fish as two examples of orthodox jurisprudence that have embraced the new theoretical standpoint and to Peter Goodrich as an example of a more critical approach also inspired by literary theory and hermeneutics. However, Douzinas and Warrington say that in focusing uncritically on meaning, the violent nature of law is neglected (Douzinas and Warrington 1991: 115–117).

6 Sometimes, however, legal reasoning, interpretation and even application are used more or less interchangeably.

application is the activity of deciding how that norm should be applied in a particular situation. However, hermeneutics shows us, as we shall see, that a sharp distinction cannot be upheld because interpretation of a legal text in order to find out what the law commands is done with a particular or hypothetical case in mind.

In order to understand the reasons for the so-called crisis of legal interpretation, we need to take a step back and consider the problems connected with the difficult relationship between law and language. Often, all problems of legal interpretation are seen as problems concerning the meaning of expressions. However simplified this picture is, we must nevertheless accept that a close link between law and language does exist. How close this link is, and whether it is the most important thing to consider when we try to solve problems of interpretation, is another question. The old but still influential idea that legal interpretation should be based on general usage of language functions as a good introduction to these issues. This standard or method of interpretation has been called 'linguistic', 'grammatical' or 'semantic' interpretation. We can examine what kind of linguistic and philosophical presuppositions underlie this idea.

Consider the famous rule that forbids you to take a vehicle into a park (see Hart 1958).[7] The use of linguistic arguments entails that we should study what the word 'vehicle' means if we want to know whether we are allowed to take our skateboard inside the park walls. The decision as to whether or not skateboards are allowed rests on the meaning of the utterance 'vehicles are forbidden in this park'. This way the obedience conditions, that is, the conditions under which we can say that somebody obeyed the rule, depend on the meaning of the sentence. It seems that the notion of linguistic arguments is quite ambiguous up to a point where it is doubtful what such arguments actually entail. The 'plain meaning of words' (MacCormick 2005: 125) is one definition of what linguistic arguments are, which implies that they refer to literal meaning.[8] The idea is that we can find help in interpreting legal texts by studying what the literal or standard meaning of a word or utterance is. This way the choices on what the meaning of a legal text is and what the text commands in a certain situation are also justified by reference to the meaning of words. But what is involved in this justification?

Certain restrictions have been postulated by legal theorists for the application of linguistic arguments. First of all, the text has to be intelligible in ordinary language. Even if it is, many factors can still weaken the force of the argument. The background linguistic conventions may not wholly exclude other meanings. The way the words are used in the text, may cast doubt on the appropriateness of

7 In this classic article Hart discusses what objects are to be held as 'vehicles' and thus denied entry to the park. He asks if toy automobiles are to be called 'vehicles' for the purpose of the rule or not. Thus the formulation of the problem is quite interesting, as it concentrates on the meaning of the word 'vehicle'.

8 Literal meaning is used as an argument also in interpretation of EC law (see Bengoetxea 1993: 234–237). See, also, Paunio and Lindroos-Hovinheimo 2010 on a critique of this.

the meaning that those words have in similar sentences in ordinary life. Where the term is vague, an argument based on ordinary or technical meaning may be weak, as is the case when the text is old, and so on. Nevertheless, it has been concluded that 'the argument from ordinary meaning and the argument from technical meaning have in many settings perfectly clear conditions and consequences of application for resolving interpretational problems in law' (MacCormick and Summers 1996: 512–513).

An obvious problem with linguistic arguments is that if we see the literal or standard meaning of words as a tool that can help a judge to interpret a legal text, then the judge should have a means of checking what the literal meaning of a word *really* is. This idea supposes that words have meaning in themselves, as if a meaning were given to them from the skies above or from the 'thing itself'.

What is interesting about the notion of linguistic arguments is that it is difficult to see how they can work in practice, how they facilitate the work of a judge trying to solve a case. If the judge has doubts about how to interpret an utterance in a legal text, what are they to do? If the utterance is vague in the sense that it includes a word that is evaluative, such as 'reasonable', then what help is it to them to use the 'literal meaning' of the word as a starting point? It is of no use to look in a dictionary because the dictionary cannot solve this question. It only gives examples on what words mean or how they are often used, but it says nothing of what the word means *in this text*. It is of no use to know what 'reasonable' means literally when you have to decide on what is reasonable in this particular case according to this legal text. And even when the dictionary gives just one meaning in one word for a word, the judge also has to interpret this new word.

## Legal interpretation and values

According to Neil MacCormick, the 'enterprise of explicating and expounding criteria and forms of good legal reasoning has to be in the context of fundamental values that we impute to legal order' (MacCormick 2005: 1). There is no getting around the fact that the fundamental values of law have to be taken into account when we try to decide what good legal reasoning or legal interpretation is like. The criteria for legal reasoning are closely connected with the fundamental values of the legal system. The quality of reasoning can be measured only against criteria that necessarily involve an understanding of the fundamental values of law.

A starting point in this book is that we need a way to evaluate and criticise interpretations of legal texts. Most importantly, we have to be able to debate the meaning ascribed to a legal text. This has to do with broader and fundamental questions of the role of law in society. Law is expressed in texts[9] in order to place some limits to the meaning that it can have. Both citizens and actors in the legal

9 The texts of law need not necessarily be written, they can also be oral.

field need some understanding of what the law requires and what it allows. To express legal norms in texts is a way of defining the content of law. And the reason we interpret the texts is that we want to know what they command in specific situations. However, a warning has to be given even at this stage. This book does not offer criteria for legal interpretation as a list of rules enabling the judge to reach acceptable interpretations. The pursuit here is a search for ways to understand how legal texts can and do have legal meaning in the first place. If we understand how the meaning of a legal text is constructed, we can also say something about how legal decision-making can be just.

The inherent values of modern legal systems, at least in most Western countries, have to do with the idea of the rule of law. One aspect of this is that the judge should not be free to make arbitrary decisions but should follow the law that both restricts and protects the lives of people. Legal texts such as bills and precedents are there to guide the judge and limit their freedom to decide the case. But how can texts have this limiting function if meanings are always to some extent uncertain? This is the pressing question in theories of legal interpretation and connected to its crisis.

The open texture of language is often seen as a reason for asserting the impossibilities of interpretation (see Lyons 1999: 309). But why does uncertainty lead to impossibility? It can just as well be the other way around. Uncertainty leads to the possibility, if not even to the necessity, of interpretation. But the reason why the contrary has been claimed may be seen in the obscure way in which literal meaning or other similar arguments deriving from language have been considered as neutral arguments for choosing one interpretation over another. Faith in language as something from which guidance in interpreting legal texts can be found is, or at least has been, strong. But even though this faith is ungrounded, we cannot deny that semantics plays a role in meaning. The words of a legal text are of course important. Meaning is therefore, according to post-semantics, founded and unfounded on semantics.

Chapter 1

# The shared nature of language

The starting point in this book is the writings of Wittgenstein, especially his later philosophy. Wittgenstein has been widely studied in legal philosophy, especially in the Anglo-American tradition. He has been referred to by theorists who believe in the force of linguistic arguments but has also been an inspiration to those who claim that legal texts have no determinate meanings. But no matter how much he has been read, the later Wittgensteinian view of language is still fruitful and adds to our understanding in the field of legal interpretation. It serves well as a starting point also because it is compatible with other theories that are central to this study.

## Reading Wittgenstein

Wittgenstein is one of those philosophers whose thinking has given rise to many opposing interpretations. Rather big differences exist between supporters of the different schools of Wittgenstein research.[1] His way of writing is certainly one reason for this, as is also the complexity of the issues he examines. A witty exposition of what the reader should and should not expect when studying Wittgenstein is given by O.K. Bouwsma. He is commenting on Wittgenstein's *The Blue Book*, although the same precautions apply to all Wittgenstein's writings.

> [A]s for inventing any new apriori synthetic, a new drug to cure this or that, or any and all, sorts of incertitude, though he [Wittgenstein] seems at one time to have been interested in inventing a new type of airplane propeller and showed a keen interest in all sorts of gadgets, a milk bottle, for instance, from which, with the use of a spoon, one could pour off the cream – 'Now, there's America for you!' – this particular form of invention he seems not to have been

1 Jaakko Hintikka goes so far as to say that Wittgenstein has become an outlaw in philosophy because his thoughts are constantly interpreted arbitrarily and even falsely (Hintikka 2004). Alain Badiou is another writer who expresses a critical attitude towards the reception of Wittgenstein, his target being especially the *Philosophical Investigations* and the way it has become a central book of Anglo-American philosophy of language (see Badiou 2009: 10).

> interested in. He was more inclined to recommend a few old home remedies and common herbs, garden variety simples which he was insistent one should not confuse. And as for those readers in general who want answers to their questions and who, if they already have answers, want better reasons, the author gives neither better reasons for the old answers nor any answers, and those readers who keep their questions may be considered either fortunate or unfortunate as the case may be.
>
> (Bouwsma 1961: 145)

Wittgenstein does not invent new drugs to cure incertitude. It is certainly well advised to warn readers of Wittgenstein's work that it is not to be approached with the aim of finding answers easily.[2] We are left with considerable incertitude that derives partly from the object of study, the questions that we try to find answers to, and partly from the way we study them and the ways that *they can be studied.*

Lately two prominent schools of Wittgenstein research have emerged. One is the so-called 'resolute interpretation', which has been put forward above all by Cora Diamond and James Conant. The other has been called the 'ineffability interpretation', which can be seen as the more traditional reading put forward by, for instance, P.M.S. Hacker. Although it seems that at the heart of this dispute lies interpretation of Wittgenstein's early work, the *Tractatus*, the different readings also understand his later philosophy in slightly different ways. The interest in this book is to concentrate on Wittgenstein's later writings. I do not take sides in the quarrels between supporters of the resolute interpretation and supporters of the ineffability interpretation but, rather, take advantage of ideas put forward by both.

## Wittgenstein's way

Wittgenstein's way of philosophising causes many a problem for understanding his work, even more so because the way he philosophises is so important for the meaning of it. He is puzzled by philosophy, by how it can and should be done. The *how* is one of his central questions. It is so central that it partly dissolves the *what*, the content or object of philosophy. What is studied and how it is done are in philosophy essentially intertwined. Especially in his later philosophy, Wittgenstein avoided developing a theory or putting forward theses. The reason may be that by avoiding theories he can uphold a richer view of the things he is interested in than by building a coherent theoretical structure. In *Philosophical Investigations*, he writes that by presenting only a model, a measuring rod to which we can compare reality, we avoid the pitfalls of injustice and dogmatism into which, according to him, 'we fall so easily in doing philosophy' (Wittgenstein 1958: § 131).

2 Georg Henrik von Wright says that even though he has studied *Philosophical Investigations* daily for almost ten years, he can still only partly understand Wittgenstein's thoughts (von Wright 1957: 228).

His later work consists of different approaches to the same themes, each mapping the subject and explaining some elements of it but not painting a whole picture at once. He tries to construct models of how things might be, models which we can compare with reality and perhaps by the comparison see reality in new ways. Such models are, for instance, Wittgenstein's 'clear and simple language-games' (Wittgenstein 1958: § 130), which function as examples of how words can be used. The *Tractatus* can be mentioned as an example of the kind of dogmatism that Wittgenstein in his later work wishes to avoid. The *Tractatus* suffers from problems of emptiness and injustice in that it talks about what we must always do when we encounter philosophical problems. It claims that every possible proposition can be revealed to be a picture, or that the *essence* of every proposition is that it is a picture (Kuusela 2006: 310–311). Later, Wittgenstein's style is quite different.[3] He does not want to make claims about how things essentially are (see, also, Wittgenstein 1958: § 109).[4] According to him, we need to remove the logical glasses through which we look at reality, the glasses through which it seems that things must be like this or they must be like that (see Malcolm 1954: 546). Instead, we have to study the phenomena of language as they are in their different, sometimes even surprising, shapes and colours.

In *Philosophical Grammar*, Wittgenstein says that if we look at the actual use of a word we see something constantly fluctuating. In his own investigations he sets against this fluctuation something more fixed, just as one would paint a picture of a constantly changing landscape.

> When we study language we *envisage* it as a game with fixed rules. We compare it with, and measure it against, a game of that kind. If for our purposes we wish to regulate the use of a word by definite rules, then alongside its fluctuating use we set up a different use by codifying one of its characteristic aspects. Thus it could be said that the use of the word 'good' (in an ethical sense) is a combination of a very large number of interrelated games, each of them as it were a facet of the use. What makes a single concept here is precisely the connection, the relationship, between these facets.
>
> (Wittgenstein 1974: 77, § 36, emphasis in original)

3 According to Tommi Uschanov, the style in the *Tractatus* is 'cosmic', in contrast with the style dominant in Wittgenstein's later writings, which is 'quotidian' (see Uschanov 2006: 135, 140). Badiou, who does not appreciate the later work of Wittgenstein and underlines the fact that Wittgenstein himself was never satisfied with, for instance, the *Philosophical Investigations*, defines the difference in style between the *Tractatus* and later work thus: '*Je soutenais que, dans le Tractatus, l'équivoque est toujours sévèrement cadrée par la syntaxe. Le second Wittgenstein supprime le cadrage et s'installe dans une méthodologie du flottement.*' One could say that the methodology of the later Wittgenstein is a floating one (Badiou 2009: 107).

4 It is evident, however, that even if Wittgenstein does not like to make grand claims about the nature of things he nevertheless does so to some extent.

Here he explains that we can envisage language as a game with fixed rules and then compare it with this kind of game. In the comparison, it seems, we can discover interesting things about language without falling into dogmatism. Studying language in this way, we can see the fluctuations and get some kind of understanding of them. These investigations allow us to see the manifold ways in which words are used (see Wittgenstein 1958: § 130). Often, the use of words is a combination of a number of interrelated games, where the concept itself is the relationship between the different usages.

It must be noted that this way of looking at different language uses also applies, in Wittgenstein's view, to the way of studying concepts such as 'language' and 'meaning' (see Wittgenstein 1958: § 108). He is thus in no way blind to the self-referential nature of his method. He says that the word 'language' also has many uses. But what happens to the philosophy of language then?

> But if the general concept of language dissolves in this way, doesn't philosophy dissolve as well? No, for the task of philosophy is not to create a new, ideal language, but to clarify the use of our language, the existing language. Its aim is to remove particular misunderstandings; not to produce a real understanding for the first time.
>
> (Wittgenstein 1974: 115, § 72)

Philosophy is concerned with thoughts, sentences, and language. It does not have access to anything beyond what everybody else has access to. Philosophy cannot point to any real essence or truth, and it cannot define *the* meaning of something. It is concerned with language but not with a concept of language that would be the definition of language. This would require metaphilosophy; but for Wittgenstein there is no such thing (Wittgenstein 1974: 116, § 72; 1958: § 121).[5] Philosophy is also language, even when it studies language.

> In reflecting on language and meaning we can easily get into a position where we think that in philosophy we are not talking of words and sentences in a quite common-or-garden sense, but in a sublimated and abstract sense. – As if a particular proposition wasn't really the thing that some person utters, but an ideal entity [...].
>
> (Wittgenstein 1974: 121, § 77)

5 Compare this to the notion that philosophy is and should be the activity of bringing words back from metaphysical use to the language game that is their 'original home' (Wittgenstein 1958: § 116). This is, according to Henry Staten, a new language game invented by Wittgenstein. Bringing words home is not an everyday language game but one *specific to philosophers*. It can well be argued, as Staten does, that Wittgenstein himself did not stop with the return home (see Staten 2001: 44). In contrast, Stanley Cavell argues that philosophy is in Wittgenstein the quintessential activity that has no language games of its own (see Cavell 1995: 143).

Dogmatic claims about how things must be or what the essence of a thing is include the danger of injustice in that these claims are not able to appreciate the manifoldness of things, the different cases, exceptions and individual characteristics of the things studied. The emptiness that derives from such theorising consists in the level of abstraction needed for the theory to be able to say something general about how things must be (see Wittgenstein 1958: § 92). For instance, the idea of propositions as pictures is a generalisation: propositions are considered on an ideal level (Kuusela 2006: 312–313). The style of Wittgenstein's later philosophy is an interesting attempt to try to avoid the emptiness, injustice and dogmatism that haunt philosophical work (see Wittgenstein 1958: §§ 128, 131).

The notion of language games can also be seen as a model, as a certain kind of heuristic tool.

> Our clear and simple language-games are not preparatory studies for a future regularization of language – as it were first approximations, ignoring friction and air-resistance. The language-games are rather set up as *objects of comparison* which are meant to throw light on the facts of our language by way not only of similarities, but also of dissimilarities.
>
> (Wittgenstein 1958: § 130, emphasis in original)

Thus the point with language games is, first, that they are sets of rules that provide us with something concrete 'to be set against the manifoldness and blurredness of language use so as to bring order to linguistic relations and to make it possible to perceive them more clearly' (Kuusela 2006: 319). 'Language game' is a hypothesis, a thought experiment. In some cases language does function in ways that resemble games, in some cases it does not. By comparing language to a game we can grasp things about language that would otherwise be difficult to notice. But to understand language as a rule-governed game is only one possible way of describing it. When we see language according to such a model we see some, perhaps dominant, features of the phenomenon but not necessarily all (Kuusela 2006: 323–324).

For Wittgenstein, different language games are related to each other in different ways.

> Here we come up against the great question that lies behind all these considerations. – For someone might object against me: 'You take the easy way out! You talk of all sorts of language-games, but have nowhere said what the essence of a language-game, and hence of language, is [...]'. And this is true. – Instead of producing something common to all that we call language, I am saying that these phenomena have no one thing in common which makes us use the same word for all, – but that they are *related* to one another in many different ways.
>
> (Wittgenstein 1958: § 65, emphasis in original)

## The indeterminacy of meaning

We can now catch sight of the problems connected with Wittgenstein's thinking sketched above. By reference to what was said about his aims and style and his reluctance to build a theory or articulate theses, it becomes impossible for us to state that for Wittgenstein meaning is use, or anything else for that matter, in a definite manner. He is careful not to say too much.

> For a *large* class of cases – though not for all – in which we employ the word 'meaning' it can be defined thus: the meaning of a word is its use in the language. And the *meaning* of a name is sometimes explained by pointing to its *bearer*.
>
> (Wittgenstein 1958: § 43, emphasis in original)

In this famous quote he avoids saying anything general on meaning. He only states that in many cases the meaning of a word is the way it is used in a language. In *The Blue Book*, he says: 'But if we had to name anything which is the life of the sign, we should have to say that it was its *use*' (Wittgenstein 1969: 4, emphasis in original). He makes a model of how to understand meaning, and this model we can compare to different examples drawn from communication situations. In many cases meaning can be defined as use. But there can be situations where the word 'meaning' cannot be defined so that the meaning of a word is its use in language.

Wittgenstein considers language through the concept of family resemblance. Seen this way, there need not be one essential feature or necessary property through which we define language. Two neighbouring links in the chain are very similar to each other, whereas distant ones only belong to the same family (see Kuusela 2006: 333–334). Very different things fall under a concept, but they are united by family resemblance. There need not be one way of using a word. A number of kinships can exist between cases of language use that connect them as links in a chain.

That meaning exists is the self-evident starting point here. Language does include meanings that are sometimes even certain, in the sense that a person who knows a language knows how to use it and knows what the words in the language mean. The fact that words have meanings is something that we must take for granted (see Wittgenstein 1958: §§ 99, 100). Using words of a language that one knows is generally not very difficult and can certainly be done. It is also a fact that somebody starting to learn a language does not fully understand the meanings of the words, or can understand a word to mean something that it usually does not. So we can say that words have meanings and their meanings can be understood and misunderstood. The question is not if, but *how*.

Wittgenstein's thinking leads to the idea that there is no such thing as *the* meaning of a word. The fact that words do have meanings does not mean that we could draw limits to them, or that we could scientifically (mathematically or logically) determine what a word means and what it does not. This is caused by the rather trivial fact that words are used in different ways in different situations. Moreover, the meanings of words can change, as they frequently do. Meanings are slippery. Language bends, stretches, reflects and changes. It is like a labyrinth of paths. 'You approach from one side and know your way about; you approach the same place from another side and no longer know your way about' (Wittgenstein 1958: § 203).

There can be no strict limits to the meanings of words. In *Philosophical Grammar*, Wittgenstein discusses in an illuminating way the fact that we cannot draw clear boundaries for the use and the meaning of a word. It is only in special cases, not every time we use a word, that we draw boundaries between what falls under the word and what does not. Considering, for instance, the concept 'plant', we can distinguish between plants and what are not plants even though we do not draw clear boundaries. Wittgenstein points out that we commonly do not draw boundaries where we simply do not need them.

> We are able to use the word 'plant' in a way that gives rise to no misunderstanding, yet countless borderline cases can be constructed in which no one has yet decided whether something still falls under the concept 'plant'. Does this mean that the meaning of the word 'plant' in all other cases is infected by uncertainty, so that it might be said we use the word without understanding it? Would a definition which bounded this concept on several sides make the meaning of the word clearer to us in *all* sentences? Would we understand better all the sentences in which it occurs?
>
> (Wittgenstein 1974: 117, § 73, emphasis in original)[6]

Wittgenstein follows Gottlob Frege in that concepts have certain properties. There are certain necessary criteria that anything must fulfil in order for it to qualify as a plant (see, for example, Wittgenstein 1958: § 182). But these criteria are not given. In his later philosophy, Wittgenstein underlines that to know the criteria for something being a plant you have to look at the use of the concept. 'Meaning is use' implies that there may be some criteria, some rules, which are followed in communication. The problem is that when we concentrate on ordinary language, as Wittgenstein does, we notice that people may use different rules and have different criteria for something being a plant.

> You say: the point isn't the word, but its meaning, and you think of the meaning as a thing of the same kind as the word, though also different from the word.

6 See also: 'The use of the words "proposition", "language", etc. has the haziness of the normal use of concept-words in our language. To think this makes them unusable, or ill-adapted to their purpose, would be like wanting to say "the warmth this stove gives is no use, because you can't feel where it begins and where it ends"' (Wittgenstein 1974: 120, § 76).

> Here the word, there the meaning. The money, and the cow that you can buy with it. (But contrast: money, and its use.)
>
> (Wittgenstein 1974: 122, § 77; 1958: § 120)

This illustrating example shows how we tend to think of a word and its meaning as money and the cow that you can buy with it. This kind of thinking leads to innumerable philosophical problems that Wittgenstein tries to clear. He suggests that we should rather see the connection between words and their meaning as that of money and its use. This is one of his many examples or pictures that he draws, by which we can grasp different aspects of language. In *The Blue Book*, he says:

> The mistake we are liable to make could be expressed thus: We are looking for the use of a sign, but we look for it as though it were an object co-existing with the sign. (One of the reasons for this mistake is again that we are looking for a 'thing corresponding to a substantive.')
>
> (Wittgenstein 1969: 5)

Even if words do not have definite meanings in the sense that we could give a comprehensive and all-inclusive explanation of them, this is no flaw.

> One might say that the concept 'game' is a concept with blurred edges. – 'But is a blurred concept a concept at all?' – Is an indistinct photograph a picture of a person at all? Is it even always an advantage to replace an indistinct picture by a sharp one? Isn't the indistinct one often exactly what we need?
>
> (Wittgenstein 1958: § 71; see, also, §§ 68, 70)

Wittgenstein says that, first, concepts are more often than not blurred, in the way that a photograph can be indistinct. However, this does not mean that a concept would not be a concept or that it would not have any meaning at all. It does not follow from the fact that meaning is open-ended that no meaning exists. Second, he seems to think that it is an advantage, perhaps even a necessity for language to function, that concepts have blurred edges.

Georg Henrik von Wright points out that language games do not form a limited given group. New games spring up as others vanish, and they are unlimited in number. Thus the meanings of words also are unlimited (von Wright 1957: 236–238). Wittgenstein says in *The Blue Book* that we are unable to circumscribe concepts because they do not have any true or real definitions (Wittgenstein 1969: 25). Words do not have independent meanings somewhere, and the meaning of a word is not an essence, it is not something fallen from the sky. We cannot study what words *really* mean, they mean what we mean by them when we use them. In *Culture and Value*, he warns us against seeing meaning as something that the word drags with it.

> People say to us: 'You understand this expression don't you? Well, I too am using it with the meaning you are familiar with.' (Not: '… with *that* particular meaning – '.) This is to treat meaning as a halo that the word carries round with it and retains in any sort of application.
>
> (Wittgenstein 1980: 44; see, also, 1958: § 117, emphasis in original)

In addition to the impossibility of determining the definite meanings of words at a given time, meanings of words also change in accordance to changes in practice and communication. This makes it impossible to state what the proper meaning of a word is.

> Nothing is commoner than for the meaning of an expression to oscillate, for a phenomenon to be regarded sometimes as a symptom, sometimes as a criterion, of a state of affairs. And mostly in such a case the shift of meaning is not noted.
>
> (Wittgenstein 1967: § 438)

The idea of language games illustrates in many of Wittgenstein's examples the way signs, for instance words, function in connection with other signs. The system of signs, which consists of the many relations between them and the grammar that binds them together, is important. Words have functions in language, and the meanings of words can be studied by analysing the different ways in which the words are used.

> The appearance of the awkwardness of the sign in getting its meaning across, like a dumb person who uses all sorts of suggestive gestures – this disappears when we remember that the sign does its job only in a grammatical system.
>
> (Wittgenstein 1974: 133, § 86)

In *The Blue Book*, Wittgenstein says that the sign gets its significance from the system of signs, that is, from the language to which it belongs. He even says that, roughly, understanding a sentence means understanding a language (Wittgenstein 1969: 5).

## The community as the foundation of language

> Yes, meaning something is like going up to someone.
>
> (Wittgenstein 1974: 157, § 107; 1958: § 457)

There have been differing views in Wittgenstein scholarship on how to understand the importance of the community or the community consensus as the basis

for meaning.[7] The subject relates closely to Wittgenstein's views on meaning and rule-following as well as the problem of a private language, which has acquired much attention. What relevance does the community or a group of communicating people have for linguistic meaning? For words to have meaning, must more than one language user exist? According to some researchers, language is necessarily something that is shared by many, while others hold that it is sufficient that language is something that *could* be shared. The first-mentioned see the community as necessary for language. This view is held, among others, by Lars Hertzberg. Hertzberg does not, however, claim that social consensus determines linguistic meaning, as some other scholars do. Additionally, he does not see that the right way to use an utterance is determined in the practices of a certain group of language users (see Hertzberg 1994: 22).

Private language is a peculiar example of Wittgenstein's because he means a language that others *cannot* understand (see, for example, Hacker 1993; Schroeder 2001). If somebody keeps a private diary, then it is not written in a private language as long as it is possible for somebody who finds the diary to understand it. Even if the diary was written in a secret language, it is not a private language if it is possible to translate what has been written into an existing language. Wittgenstein nevertheless maintains that even when using a private language, the user must take some things for granted. They must already have something that is linguistic in order for a private language to be possible. For example, the act of naming, which the private speaker undertakes, presupposes many things that have to be ready in order for the naming to make any sense. If the speaker of a private language gives a name to their sensations, for instance pain, the grammar of the word 'pain', its place and role in language, have to already exist (Wittgenstein 1958: § 257). Otherwise it cannot be named. There would be no place for the new name if there were no grammar. A private language, in which the words refer to the speaker's private sensations, already requires a grammar. In this way, even a private language presupposes at least some linguistic structures. It requires a system in which words refer to something and an understanding of what kinds of concepts words like 'pain' are. It presupposes a language in which it is possible to speak about sensations and pains.

How does the speaker of a private language use his language? How does he decide which word refers to which particular sensation? According to Wittgenstein, the user of a private language has no criteria by which to distinguish between

7 Works that have been at the centre of the discussion are, for instance, Saul Kripke's (1982) *Wittgenstein on Rules and Private Language* and Cavell's (1979) *The Claim of Reason*. Community is still the central question in much of the literature on Wittgenstein (see e.g. Zerilli 2001). It can be argued that emphasis put on community has opened up the tradition of interpreting Wittgenstein to new directions not possible in the 'orthodox' readings by, for instance, G.P. Baker and Hacker (see e.g. Putnam 2001). These new directions include a way of seeing Wittgenstein's thinking as having interesting similarities, to some degree at least, with some continental theories.

correct and incorrect language use (Wittgenstein 1958: § 258). There is also no point in asking the question if the speaker of the private language has understood the meaning of a word correctly. A language which has only one user makes differences of opinion concerning meaning impossible. Nor can there be agreement on meaning. There is also no need or use for utterances that explain what different words mean in a private language (Hertzberg 1994: 25). Wittgenstein presents the following analogy:

> Why can't my right hand give my left hand money? – My right hand can put it into my left hand. My right hand can write a deed of gift and my left hand a receipt. – But the further practical consequences would not be those of a gift. When the left hand has taken the money from the right, etc., we shall ask: 'Well, and what of it?'
>
> (Wittgenstein 1958: § 268)

Defining meanings for private words is the same thing as donating money from one hand to the other: it makes no sense. It only makes us ask: So what? The act is empty.

Many interesting questions are connected with private language of which I here concentrate on only two. First, as mentioned above, a private language would presuppose many things that are not that private to begin with. A private language needs certain linguistic features, structures and functions, which have developed and belong in the use of language in a community, that is, in communication between more than one language user. Second, a private language is peculiar in the way that no agreement or disagreement in meaning can arise and that certain speech acts lose their meaning. These are the utterances mentioned above by which the meaning of a word is asked, defined or corrected. There is no place and no need for such utterances in a private language. From these short remarks on private language we can see some features of how Wittgenstein sees language as connected to its use.

It can be argued that a central feature of language is that there is somebody who listens. Hertzberg discusses the example of giving and following orders. These expressions, like those that have to do with punishing, asking questions and answering, have their primary use in relationships between people. Even if it were possible for somebody to give themselves an order and to follow it, the background of all these expressions is that they belong in the communication between at least two people. Without their interactive background, they lose their meaning. The possible meaning that giving oneself an order might have derives from the meaning that giving somebody else an order has (Hertzberg 2002: 254). Wittgenstein says explicitly that only of a person who can talk in the ordinary sense can we say that he talks to himself (Wittgenstein 1958: § 344). Talking is by nature something shared, something that is done together with other people.

To give an order or to follow it presupposes another person's reaction. In *Culture and Value*, Wittgenstein says that the origin and the primitive form of a language game is a reaction. Only from this can more complicated forms develop.

'Language – I want to say – is a refinement, "in the beginning was the deed"' (Wittgenstein 1980: 31).[8] Asking, commanding, answering and obeying are utterances that clearly tie persons to one another. The origin of all language use can be seen as a reaction, that is, a reaction to somebody.

Of course, some ways of using language do not clearly require a speaking partner. Hertzberg takes as an example telling a story. Stories are told to other people, but we can easily imagine somebody telling themselves a story, for instance writing it in a diary, just for amusement. To tell a story to oneself does not require language users other than the person telling the story. But also this way of using language has its roots in communication. If we disconnect the act of telling a story from human conversation, the person's utterances would not connect them to other people. Telling a story is an activity that can be shared and that can connect people. A story is something of which we can ask questions that the storyteller can answer and that can be discussed (Hertzberg 2002: 254–255). It is difficult to imagine storytelling that would lie outside communication and human interaction. Wittgenstein says that the concept of language is *contained* in the concept of communication.

> Where does language get its significance? Can we say 'Without language we couldn't communicate with one another'? No. It's not like 'without a telephone we couldn't speak from Europe to America'. We can indeed say 'without a mouth human beings couldn't communicate with each other'. But the concept of language *is contained in* the concept of communication.
>
> (Wittgenstein 1974: 193, § 140; see, also, 1958: § 491, emphasis in original)

Interaction and communication are part of the form of life of people, in which language has its home. Language is a form of communication. We could perhaps communicate with one another even without a language, so language is not the only way to communicate. But we cannot imagine language that would not be communication in some sense. Wittgenstein says a little earlier that language is characterised by linguistic activities (Wittgenstein 1974: 192, § 140). Linguistic activities are most importantly communication.

8 Wittgenstein refers here to Goethe's *Faust* (see, also, Wittgenstein 1967: § 545 where he says that our language is an auxiliary to and further expression of behaviour). See, also, Norman Malcolm's discussion of pain behaviour in his book *Nothing is Hidden*. Malcolm says that Wittgenstein's conception that much of our language replaces and extends primitive behaviour is a central thought in his later philosophy. Something that resembles the primitive reactions when language is learned pervades all use of language, even at sophisticated levels. A primitive reaction is, for instance, to treat the part that hurts when someone other than oneself is in pain, not only when oneself is in pain. This way of behaving is pre-linguistic. It is a natural reaction when we see that somebody is hurt. A language game is based on it, not the other way around. The way of acting and behaving is a way of thinking and not the result of thinking. Language does not emerge from reasoning but from natural forms of life (Malcolm 1986: 149–153).

Even if language and the language community go together in many ways, we cannot read Wittgenstein as saying that community consensus would define what the right way to use words is. Human agreement does not decide what is true and false, but in order to say anything about truth humans have to share a language. They have to agree in the language they use (Wittgenstein 1958: § 241). This is, however, not agreement in opinions, but agreement in a more profound sense. It is a background that is needed for meaning and debates on truth in the first place. In *Zettel*, Wittgenstein discusses the same question in connection to colour concepts. 'Does human agreement *decide* what is red? Is it decided by appeal to the majority? Were we taught to determine colour in *that* way?' (Wittgenstein 1967: § 431, emphasis in original). In *On Certainty*, he says that when we say that we are certain of something this does not simply mean that every individual is certain of something but that we belong to a community that shares a common upbringing and a common science (Wittgenstein 1975: § 298). In this passage, we see how a community is something that allows us to say that we are sure. We learn things in a community, and one of the things we learn is how to use language. The 'we' is important here. It refers to the common form of life that we learn and that we *share*.

## Rules and a background for language

Wittgenstein discusses rules and rule-following quite extensively in his later philosophy. By examining how people ordinarily and more or less automatically use language, we notice patterns and regularities in it. When somebody is learning a language we might want to teach them by stating some rules of the language, but language gives rise to these rules. Language is first. We can extract rules from it, but they do not define language use, language use defines them. Wittgenstein does not take rule-governedness to be a necessary condition of meaning. It is one aspect of language, but it would be misleading to claim that for Wittgenstein it is the essential one.[9]

Wittgenstein says that there cannot be a question of which rules are the correct ones for using a word. If we change the rules we change the meaning. He compares the situation with cookery rules. They are not arbitrary because the concept 'cookery' is defined by the end of cookery, whereas the concept 'language' is not. If you follow grammatical rules other than such and such it does not mean that you say something wrong but, rather, you are speaking of something else (Wittgenstein 1974: 184–185, § 133). In this sense, the rules of grammar are arbitrary; they

9 Wittgenstein does, in fact, give examples of expressions that cannot be explained by rule-governedness. One such example is the word 'boo'. The important thing about the word 'boo' for Wittgenstein is not its grammatical rules but its effect. 'Boo' is a word, Wittgenstein includes it as part of language, but it resembles an instrument that serves determined external purposes. The purpose of 'boo' is to frighten people. The role of this word is defined in terms of its effect (see Kuusela 2006: 326–330).

neither correspond to some reality nor are they constructed so as to fulfil an aim, unlike the rules of cookery. If you do not follow the rules of grammar you are not doing something wrong, you are doing something else.

It has been underlined in commentaries on Wittgenstein's later work that even if he discusses sense and non-sense, his idea is not that philosophy could determine how we should use language. Hertzberg writes that when we think of sense and non-sense, we often think that it has to do with the utterance being inside or outside the limits of language. If certain conditions are fulfilled, then the utterance belongs in the group of utterances that have sense. However, we should keep in mind that Wittgenstein studies utterances and their meanings in situations where they are used, in different language games. Here, sense and non-sense are understood differently. What is central in language is what the utterance is used for, what message is being communicated by it. The situation in which the utterance is used and the function of the utterance are what is at issue. But, again, it is not the task of the philosopher to be the language police and tell us how utterances can be used in different situations. Rather, the philosopher can study an utterance that seems odd or strange and assess why it cannot be used in this situation in the same way as in another one (see Hertzberg 2001: 100). Hertzberg refers to paragraph 117 of *Philosophical Investigations*, but paragraph 116 also fits well here.

> When philosophers use a word – 'knowledge', 'being', 'object', 'I', 'proposition', 'name' – and try to grasp the *essence* of the thing, one must always ask oneself: is the word ever actually used in this way in the language-game which is its original home?
>
> (Wittgenstein 1958: § 116, emphasis in original)

> You say to me: 'You understand this expression, don't you? Well then – I am using it in the sense you are familiar with.' – As if the sense were an atmosphere accompanying the word, which it carried with it into every kind of application. If, for example, someone says that the sentence 'This is here' (saying which he points to an object in front of him) makes sense to him, then he should ask himself in what special circumstances this sentence is actually used. There it does make sense.
>
> (Wittgenstein 1958: § 117)

If we accept the premise that the most important function of language is to partake in communication and that this is likely to make language a certain kind of thing rather than another, then the meaning, the sense and the non-sense of utterances cannot be studied irrespective of the situations in which they are used. We cannot draw borders for the sense and non-sense of words in advance.

According to Meredith Williams's interpretation of Wittgenstein, we cannot define the meaning of a word by reference to a rule, which means that rules do not determine the meanings of words. This is because rules are indeterminate in themselves unless they are connected with a method of application (see Williams 2001: 63–65). To define the correct meaning of a word by interpreting a rule for its use becomes impossible if nothing secures the fact that the interpretation of the rule is correct. Interpretation and application of a rule needs support. Something has to be given already; a context or some kind of background is needed. This background is that against which and by the help of which we interpret, and it is something that ultimately justifies our interpretations.

Even if a background or context is necessary for us to be able to understand and obey a rule, it is not always enough. Wittgenstein says in *Philosophical Investigations* that a rule is like a signpost. Does it show beyond doubt which way I should go? Where does it say how I should follow the sign, in the direction of the pointing hand in the sign or in the opposite direction? It is possible to interpret the sign in many ways. Without background information we cannot know which way the sign wants us to go. There is room for doubt in interpreting it. Or rather, Wittgenstein says, sometimes there is room for doubt and sometimes not. This, however, is not a philosophical sentence but an empirical one (Wittgenstein 1958: § 85). The signpost is fine if it fills its function in normal circumstances (Wittgenstein 1958: § 87). But taken alone without normal circumstances, the background of normal practices, the signpost could mean anything or nothing. Wittgenstein says of the signpost that every interpretation hangs in the air along with what is interpreted. Interpretations do not determine meanings (Wittgenstein 1958: § 198). The connection between the signpost and action is that we have been taught to follow the signpost in a certain way. A signpost can only be followed at all if it is connected with use that is stable, at least to some degree. To follow a rule, such as a signpost, is essentially a practice (Wittgenstein 1958: §§ 198, 199, 202).

The idea of a background that is needed for meaning gets support in many of Wittgenstein's writings. In *Philosophical Grammar*, the grammar of language forms the background. In *Philosophical Investigations* and *On Certainty*, the system and practices of language and the communicating community function as a kind of background. The idea of a community as a background for language leads us to the difficult notion of form of life, which Wittgenstein discusses especially in the *Philosophical Investigations*.

## Meanings are lived

Form of life is something that has caused much wonderment because Wittgenstein does not explain what he means by the notion.[10] He mentions form of life five times explicitly in the *Philosophical Investigations*, and the term appears in some

10 Disagreement has arisen for instance on the connection between form of life and language game, as some researchers have thought them interchangeable. Besides, the question of whether Wittgenstein means that many forms of life exist or only one has also aroused debate (see e.g. Newton Garver on these discussions in Garver 1994: chapter 4).

of his other writings as well. In the first passage of the *Philosophical Investigations* in which the notion appears, Wittgenstein says that to imagine a language is to imagine a form of life.

> It is easy to imagine a language consisting only of orders and reports in battle. – Or a language consisting only of questions and expressions for answering yes and no. And innumerable others. – And to imagine a language means to imagine a form of life.
>
> (Wittgenstein 1958: § 19, emphasis in original)

Later in the book, when he discusses language games, he says that the expression 'language game' is meant to show how speaking a language is part of an activity or a form of life.

> But how many kinds of sentence are there? Say assertion, question, command? – There are *countless* kinds: countless different kinds of use of what we call 'symbols', 'words', 'sentences'. And this multiplicity is not something fixed, given once for all; but new types of language, new language-games, as we may say, come into existence, and others become obsolete and get forgotten. (We can get a *rough picture* of this from the changes in mathematics.) Here the term 'language-*game*' is meant to bring into prominence the fact that the *speaking* of language is part of an activity, or of a form of life.
>
> (Wittgenstein 1958: § 23, emphasis in original)

He discusses form of life in the context of agreement.

> It is what human beings *say* that is true and false; and they agree in the *language* they use. That is not agreement in opinions but in form of life
>
> (Wittgenstein 1958: § 241)

Later on he says:

> Can only those hope who can talk? Only those who have mastered the use of a language. That is to say, the phenomena of hope are modes of this complicated form of life.
>
> (Wittgenstein 1958: 174)

He discusses agreement in another passage as well and again connects it with a form of life, although hesitantly. Reservation is written out in this passage, a 'one could say'.

> What has to be accepted, the given, is – so one could say – *forms of life*. Does it make sense to say that people generally agree in their judgments of colour? What would it be like for them not to? – One man would say a flower was red

> which another called blue, and so on. – But what right should we have to call these people's words 'red' and 'blue' *our* 'colour-words'?
>
> (Wittgenstein 1958: 226, emphasis in original)

We cannot really say that people agree in their judgments of colour. In order for any talk on colour and judgments of colour to occur, something has to be taken for granted. A form of life has to be accepted; it is the given on the basis of which talk of colours can occur in the first place.

What does all this mean? First, it means that for Wittgenstein something has to be taken for granted, that is, explanations come to an end somewhere (see, also, Wittgenstein 1958: §§ 326, 485). Second, the notion of form of life is a way of connecting language to an activity. Language is necessarily connected to acting, reacting and doing something. We live with language. Third, the idea of form of life illustrates the way that language is necessarily shared. This point is elaborated in the passages that concern agreement. We agree on a language and share a form of life (Wittgenstein 1958: § 242). This agreement is the common ground on which different language uses rest. The foundation of language is a shared way of living. A shared form of life means shared meanings. A shared form of life implies that people agree on language.

According to G.P. Baker and Hacker, agreement on form of life should not be understood as underpinning agreement on definitions and judgments. They are not separate. One could say that agreement on form of life *surrounds* agreement on definitions and judgments. It is the web of action and interaction, the context in which judgments and also language take place. Baker and Hacker warn us not to understand interpersonal agreement as a constitutive component of our rules for the use of expressions. The connection between agreement and rule is rather that if language is to be a means of communication we must agree on our rules of grammar and laws of logic. This agreement is a consensus in accepting a form of representation, a consensus in action, which manifests itself in our life and all our deeds (see Baker and Hacker 1988: 229–251; see, also, Malcolm 1954: 549–550).

Language and life are inseparable. When we learn a language we not only learn words and grammar but practices and the ways in which language is used. As Stanley Cavell puts it, learning a language means not only learning the pronunciation of sounds and grammatical rules but the forms of life that make those sounds the words they are. We learn what the words do and what can be done with them (Cavell 2000: 28).

Common form(s) of life make it possible for agreement to occur on meanings and definitions, that is, for people to be able to communicate. The question whether language works is not a question for Wittgenstein. It is evident that it does, even though it does not always work perfectly. It works because we share so much. We share ways of living, and because so much exists in common between us, we can also communicate with each other by using a sign system like that of language. Thus language is not primary because before language there has to be being together with other people and reacting to them. These ideas are developed further in the sections on hermeneutics and Levinas's view on language

'If a lion could talk, we could not understand him' (Wittgenstein 1958, part II xi: 223). Because language and meaning are anchored in life, it seems that even if an animal could talk, its form of life would most likely be so distant from ours that we could not understand it. It is interesting here that Wittgenstein mentions the lion as an example, not for instance the domestic cat, with which we actually do live.[11] It is most likely that the lion's life is so different from ours that even if it used a sign system, we could not understand what it meant with the signs it used.

It is argued in this book that whether or not form of life is something that there are many of or just one, it is nevertheless something that unites us. (Without going into the debate concerning relativism in more detail, it would be difficult to interpret Wittgenstein as being a cultural relativist. However, the scope of this book does not allow for a more detailed analysis of this issue.) What is argued here is simply that: (a) language presupposes something shared, that is, acting and living together; and (b) language is primarily communication with other people. The argument is that as language is something that we share in our forms of life, this means that there is something ethical in Wittgenstein's way of thinking about language.[12] Another important issue is the fundamental question of whether communication is ultimately built on consensus and friendship, or whether it can be based on disagreement and strife.[13] This topic cannot be thoroughly discussed with reference to Wittgenstein's theory alone, but we should notice that his ideas on language presupposing a shared background do not mean that agreement would always lie at the heart of it. People do not have to be altogether similar, and agreement is not a necessary requirement, in order for them to be able to understand each other. Some amount of similarity is needed for people to be able to communicate, but they do not have to agree. Communication can well be founded on disagreement and difficulties in understanding as long as certain willingness exists to engage in communication with the other person. Wittgenstein's theory only says that we have to agree *on* language before we agree or disagree *in* language. We agree on a language before we disagree in opinions.

11 I am not taking a stand here on the question of whether we can share form(s) of life with our domesticated animals. The question is intriguing but, sadly, goes way beyond the scope of this book. Also, the issue of animals lacking language is problematic, as Derrida also notes in 'The Animal That Therefore I Am (More to Follow)' (2002), but has to be left for discussion elsewhere (see, also, Wittgenstein [1958: § 25]: 'It is sometimes said that animals do not talk because they lack the mental capacity. And this means: "they do not think, and that is why they do not talk." But – they simply do not talk. Or to put it better: they do not use language – if we except the most primitive forms of language. – Commanding, questioning, recounting, chatting, are as much part of our natural history as walking, eating, drinking, playing').

12 See, also, Ben Tilghman on the ethical implications that can be seen to underlie Wittgenstein's discussions of agreement and human understanding in general (Tilghman 2001).

13 This opens up the very interesting questions of agreement, disagreement and democracy (see e.g. Chantal Mouffe's [2001, 2005] discussions on Wittgenstein in the context of political theory).

## The principle of charity

Donald Davidson has in his research on meaning and interpretation put forward an idea which has become quite well known. It is generally consistent with the later Wittgenstein and offers us a development of the question of how we (can) understand what a speaker says. Davidson argues that interdependence exists between belief and meaning. In interpretation of speech behaviour (and writing) two things are interdependent: the attribution of beliefs and the interpretation of sentences. A person's speech cannot be interpreted without knowing quite a lot about what they believe, intend and want. However, fine distinctions between different beliefs and attitudes are impossible without understanding speech. We find out exactly what a person wants and believes only by interpreting their speech (Davidson 1990: 317–318; 1973–1974: 17–18). The two, speech and beliefs, are interdependent, but what comes first? We must have a theory that takes both into account. Davidson discusses the example of two people looking at a ketch sailing by. One says: 'Look at that handsome yawl.' The other, convinced that the vessel is a ketch, is faced with a problem of interpretation. Maybe the speaker mistakes the ketch for a yawl and thus has a false belief. The other possibility is that he does not use the word 'yawl' quite in the same manner as the other person does (Davidson 1973–1974: 18). In this simple situation the question is about interpretation. The problem is that if we need to understand language to be able to understand and differentiate beliefs and if we need to be able to differentiate between beliefs to be able to understand language, then understanding seems impossible. Which it is not.

Davidson's solution to this is that what we do and what we have to do in order to interpret one another's utterances is to assume general agreement on beliefs. We have to assume a great deal about the speaker's beliefs in order for us to be able to interpret what they say. We can only assume them to believe more or less the same general things as we ourselves believe. This is the foundation for meaning and understanding. It can include certain sentences that are held true or general agreement on a theory of truth (Davidson 1973–1974: 19). The likeness of this theory with Wittgenstein's ideas on form of life becomes visible here.

The term 'principle of charity' describes this approach to meaning because what we actually do when interpreting others is to posit them having some general understanding of the world that we ourselves hold rational. Davidson says that charity is forced on us. If we want to understand each other, we have to count them right in most matters whether we like it or not (Davidson 1973–1974: 19).

> The possibility of understanding the speech or actions of an agent depends on the existence of a fundamentally rational pattern, a pattern that must, in general outline, be shared by all rational creatures. We have no choice, then, but to project our own logic on to the language and beliefs of another.
>
> (Davidson 1990: 320)

But logic only takes us so far. Davidson says that further interpretation requires further forms of agreement between the speaker and the interpreter (Davidson 1990: 320). This may mean that, for instance, specialised language or, say, a certain genre of literature, requires that the speaker and the interpreter share much more than just a general understanding of logic and truth. The interpreter has to be able to recognise certain attitudes, aims and beliefs of the speaker. These may also be normative attitudes, for instance their ethical or aesthetic commitments.

## Legal language games

Even if legal texts are similar to other texts in the sense that general difficulties of meaning haunt them, from a linguistic point of view we can also study their specific characteristics. According to Andrei Marmor, it is especially the pragmatic aspects that distinguish legal language from other forms of language use. Marmor's idea is to look at the various pragmatic aspects of language and see how these emerge in the legal field. His aim is to show how different pragmatic factors play a part in what is determined by legal expressions (Marmor 2008: 423–424).

In accordance with traditional linguistics, Marmor says that the pragmatic feature of language typically entails two things: the *context* and the *implication* of an act of communication.

According to Marmor, both of these are problematic in legal language. He draws a distinction between three different levels of content: first, what is *said* by the speaker, second, what is *asserted* by the speaker, and third, what is *implied* by the speech in the particular context. He admits that other ways of classification may be available and that these distinctions may not be very clear. Nevertheless, he uses this problematic classification to explain different levels of content (Marmor 2008: 425).

Legal language does not, according to Marmor, function in the way that ordinary language does. It is not often possible for speakers of legal language, here especially legislative, to assert something different from what they say. This is an interesting logic that Marmor draws his argumentation on. It is usually not possible for a legislator to assert something that they do not say. Why? Because the hearer does not have the contextual means of discerning between what the legislator has said and what they have asserted. This argument is intriguing, for the inability of the speaker to assert something is made dependent on the listener's abilities. Marmor says that usually:

> [...] the context is not rich enough to make it obvious and transparent that the legislature could not have meant/asserted what it said. It is just as likely that the legislature expressed some content that it took to be clear in some cases, and has not given much thought to others [...]
>
> (Marmor 2008: 429)

The problem here is that even if it were never possible to definitely show that the legislature did not mean what it said, it is still highly possible that the legislature did not mean what it said. Let us take a step back and consider what presuppositions the whole argumentation rests upon. It is haunted by the idea of literal meaning and the notion that it is something different from asserted meaning.

In the general picture that Marmor draws, the content as that which is said by the speaker is not sufficiently problematised. This is already evident in the way he draws distinctions between what is said and what is asserted. He does admit that the distinctions between saying, asserting and intending are not clear ones and neither are they unproblematic. It does seem, however, that the discussion on whether the legislature can assert what it does not say rests on them and the problems of the discussion are at least partly dependent on the multiple difficulties at the heart and at the boundaries of this classification.

Moving on, Marmor claims that the communication situation in the legal sphere is radically different from the 'ordinary' communication situation.

> An essential aspect of what enables parties to an ordinary conversation to express content that is not exactly what their expressions mean, consists in the fact that an ordinary conversation is, typically, a cooperative activity. In ordinary conversations we normally assume that an instance of speech purports to make a relevant contribution to the conversation, given the stage in which the conversation is, and the prior background knowledge of the relevant parties.
>
> (Marmor 2008: 429)

The fact that an ordinary communication situation is a co-operative activity makes it possible for the speaker to mean something other than what they say. Apart from what the speaker can mean and say, an interesting aspect would of course be how the listener can grasp that the speaker meant something other than what they said. The speaker can rely on the fact that the listener understands it because of the ordinary conversation situation they share and the prior background of the parties. This enables them to mean what they do not say.

According to Marmor, the legal communication situation is not a co-operative activity but strategic behaviour. It is this strategic nature of legal language that makes it unlikely that the prescribed content of an act of legislation differs from what it says (Marmor 2008: 429). The asserted content of a legal prescription is in most cases simply what the prescription says, that is, the literal meaning and syntax of the sentence. What is interesting to note is that according to Marmor, this is true only in the field of legal language, which is a sphere of strategic behaviour. In 'ordinary communication' one can mean something other than what one says. Here we see a firm belief in the possibility of distinguishing between what is said and what is asserted.

Problems concerning the speaker are, according to Marmor, well known in the field of law. He refers here especially to the identity of the speaker, which is not a simple thing. It is often difficult to say of a legal text who the speaker is.

What is overlooked by Marmor is that also in what he calls 'ordinary communication' it is often not possible to determine the identity of the speaker, especially if they express themselves in written form. The problem for Marmor is that if we do not have access to the speaker and their intentions, then content, and especially implied content, becomes very tricky (Marmor 2008: 434). Because legislation involves not one but many speakers, intent is a problem. Intent and implication here lie at the heart of meaning, and because they are difficult to determine in the field of law, we see that the content of the utterance is in trouble. As we will see in Derrida's discussion below, if this is trouble, then all language use is troubled.

'Context' is an equally difficult concept in the field of law. First, there are problems of insufficient information. As judges and litigants are not parties to the legislative conversation itself, they have to rely on secondary sources to gather information. The reliability of those sources varies. However, even if complete information is available, problems still remain. Uncertainty exists as to where the conversation begins and who the conversational parties are. This is in Marmor's view something distinctive of law. He says that in ordinary conversation situations the context is relatively closed by boundaries determined by the conversational situation. This is a difficult point in Marmor's argumentation. His view on communication seems to ignore how much conversation actually takes place in a variety of situations and also in written form, so that the parties to the conversation can be separated not only by distance but also by time. However, Marmor exclaims that the conversational situation of an act of legislation is much more open-ended than the ordinary situation (Marmor 2008: 435).

Marmor's analysis raises several questions. One problem is that he first seems to construct a general picture of legal language, where all incoherence and variations of real legal language are cleared away. The analysis ends in difficulties because it did not start off with real life. The Wittgensteinian way would be to bear in mind the manifoldness and incoherence of language and not try to fit it into an ideal theoretical picture, which then fails to do the explaining it should. Already the first distinction between saying, asserting and intending is in its simplicity at the same time deeply problematic. It may be problematic to such a degree that it makes the whole argumentation questionable. The most difficult thing to do is to differentiate between what is said, that is, literal meaning, and what is asserted and a theory that starts off by such a distinction faces severe challenges from the start. We can conclude at this point that an analysis of the pragmatics of legal language does not take us very far regarding the issue of legal interpretation.

An important question that was touched upon in Marmor's discussion is whether legal texts are decisively different from other texts. For sure, they cannot be seen simply as ordinary communication. They are normative texts, or strategic communication. This means that differences certainly exist between legal interpretation and other kinds of interpretation, which becomes evident especially towards the end of this book. Nevertheless, legal texts are texts expressed in language so that problems with interpreting any texts are also problems for law. This is why it is necessary to start off from considering language, meaning and interpretation in detail before we can turn to the specific character of legal texts.

## Shifting meanings and the tragedy of law

What about the linguistic arguments used to justify legal decisions? Can we, following Wittgenstein, admit that there is an ordinary usage of words that could function as a limit for interpretation? He certainly does not say that a word has a correct meaning, or that it 'has' any meaning at all. Words are used in language games and involve different meanings according to their different uses. Everybody uses words according to some rules or criteria, and in this sense meaning is not indeterminate. The problem is that we have no way of checking what criteria other people use, including the legislator. Perhaps the biggest problem with the argument of standard meaning from a Wittgensteinian point of view is that when we try to determine what the word 'vehicle' *really* means, we try to refer to somewhere outside any real language game. We try to construct a language game that is over and above existing ones, in which it would be possible to say authoritatively what the meaning of a word in 'ordinary language' is.

If we take Wittgenstein seriously in that meaning is use, then the way interpretations are justified by reference to the meaning of words seems to have the structure of a circular argument. In trying to find out what a legal text means we refer to the meaning of words, but the meaning of words is only the way they are used, these uses including the particular text that we are interpreting. The circularity is lessened if a privileged language use existed to which we could refer in order to find out the meaning of a word. This is something that Wittgenstein rejects. He does say that we return words to their homes and that we should study meanings in their own language games, but this is not to mean that there are privileged or correct uses of words, or that we could limit the way words should be used. His idea is that we should not consider the meaning of a word separately from the situations in which it is used and the way it functions in language games. A word can have several homes in different uses and language games. It is by studying these games that we see the different ways in which the word can have meaning.

The most important lessons drawn from Wittgenstein here are that even though the meanings of words are not definite and exactly calculable, this is not a flaw. It may become a problem in the kind of *theory* that expects language to work this way. The fact that language has a certain kind of open structure seldom causes difficulties in communication, but for a theory of legal interpretation it means that we cannot justify decisions through reference to the meaning of words. Another important thing to note in Wittgenstein's thinking is the importance that he places on shared practices, judgments and values. Without this shared background, language would not work. Form(s) of life explain the relative stability of meaning.

However, in law the situation is often such that the decision-maker has to decide between two or more competing interpretations which are both plausible in

the shared language game. In these situations we do not find much help from Wittgenstein's theory but have to turn our attention elsewhere.[14] A shared background is not definite enough to settle disagreements. It is understood here rather as that which enables us to even begin to disagree (or agree). Wittgenstein does not analyse situations that could be characterised as 'hard cases' of interpretation. In addition, his analyses are not directly applicable as such to the legal sphere, where justice and power lie at the heart of the matter. His discussions of language take place on the (relatively) neutral level of everyday communication.

There are those who connect the failures of law with a conceived failure of language. The general idea is that in order for law to be something else than mere arbitrary commands backed up by force, it has to have a general rule-like character which in turn has to be made possible by language. Language should thus safeguard us from impartiality, injustice and unfairness. That way, law, language and justice are conceptually linked together. Now that it seems that this link has been broken because of a pessimism concerning rules and definable correct meanings, it is often claimed that law turns into violence and irresponsibility. We can see this deduction as a version of nihilism.

In his book *Law's Task: The Tragic Circle of Law, Justice and Human Suffering*, Louis Wolcher examines the links between human suffering, law, and justice. He argues that law is scandalously indifferent to human tragedy and sets forth to study the tragic effects of law and justice and the reasons for them (Wolcher 2008: xi–xii, xxi). One central part of Wolcher's analysis of law concerns language, meaning and interpretation. There is a phenomenon that he calls 'reception', which characterises legal interpretation and application. Wolcher bases his discussion of meaning heavily on Wittgenstein and criticises what he calls the magical view of language, a view which, in short, understands every linguistic sign to stand in logical relation to a meaning. The magical view leads, according to Wolcher, to philosophical confusion and, more importantly, to ethical evasion (Wolcher 2008: 7–8). So, the argument in a nutshell is that we have a false view of language, which leads to evasion of ethical responsibility.

Wolcher's aim is to show that every legal decision-maker carries the ethical responsibility for the way that they apply norms. This is an important thought. Wolcher's idea concerning language and meaning is that from the way language works, certain consequences follow for legal interpretation. He sees that the difficulties involved in legal decision-making are at least partly caused by language. Linguistic signs, which express legal norms, can do nothing in and of themselves, but this means that nothing has been lost that we ever had the right to rely on in the first place. Meaning is not something that legal words 'have'. The

14 Some theorists with a Wittgenstein-inspired view on language still claim that semantic limits of the meaning of words can be upheld. For instance, Matthias Klatt argues that by reference to rules for the use of words we are able to hold on to the existence of semantic limits. He seeks to rehabilitate semantic interpretation in law (see Klatt 2008).

magical view of language treats words as if they were labels on bottles with particular contents (Wolcher 2008: 120–121). Wolcher supports his arguments by Wittgenstein's later philosophy.

The reason why the magical view has so many supporters is that any other conception of language is mentally linked with disaster, especially in the field of law. According to Wolcher, the motivation behind the idea that words are vessels full of meaning is to defeat scepticism. Saul Kripke has defined the sceptical argument (reading Wittgenstein in a controversial way) as follows: there can be no such thing as meaning anything by a word (Kripke 1982: 55). The problem in the legal field is that, according to Wolcher, instead of discarding the magical view altogether, most legal philosophers continue to frame the problem of meaning in terms of that view. 'It is as if the magical view were grounded in a metaphysical opposition that is ineluctably binding on all rational beings: either legal norms "have" meanings or they do not' (Wolcher 2008: 122). The result, according to him, is that absurd claims are advanced and a fierce kind of self-deception is cultivated. Examples of this are, for instance, according to Wolcher, Hart and Dworkin (see Wolcher 2008: 122–125, 137).

The result that academics should come to, according to Wolcher, is to acknowledge the limits of reason in legal interpretation. What ultimately happens in legal interpretation is *reception*. He says that when we judge, we look at the words and images and simply react. There is nothing else. The question of what a norm means can be asked by a judge, and they can keep on giving one interpretation after another if they want. But explanations of signs have to come to an end somewhere. There comes a point where the judge simply acts (Wolcher 2008: 157–158). According to Wolcher, this has some grave ethical consequences. He says: 'Catching sight of the phenomenon of reception in legal practice allows one to recognise, at long last, that historically contingent irrational violence and rationally grounded legal violence are not strangers to one another – that they are, in fact, opposite sides of the same coin' (Wolcher 2008: 167).

Thus, by opening our eyes to the real nature of language, Wolcher tries to prove how legal decision-making is in the end only reception. Legal decisions are not backed up by rules expressed in language. They are acts that are simply just done, and it is here that the tragedy of law resides. Law is grounded on human suffering, and violence is the way law manages and produces suffering (Wolcher 2008: 222). The whole argument is centred on language and the Wittgensteinian idea that explanations always come to an end somewhere.

A possible objection exists to this argument on the tragic nature of law, a very Wittgensteinian idea, according to which it is doubtful if Wolcher's argumentation ultimately succeeds. It is hard to understand how this theory relates to the fact that language, after all, does work. It might be difficult to explain how and why, but it usually does work. This is not emphasised by Wolcher, and therefore he reads Wittgenstein in a slightly different light than is done here. The interpretation I have put forward here is not pessimistic; it does not see language as a failure. It is intriguing to note, however, that Wittgenstein is one of the figures that keep

popping up when the discussion turns to the crisis or the tragedy of law. That he of all philosophers would be the name to drop at the beginning as the premise from which to start seems odd – he, whose own starting point is that language works and usually rather well.

We certainly have reason to repeat Wittgenstein's name and not only repeat it but also think of what he says. He can be helpful in our attempts to get over the trauma that the 'indeterminacy' of language has caused legal theory. The reason for the disappointment might be that we are still, after all the years when language was at the focal point of all theorising, expecting too much of language, or expecting the wrong things, and getting disappointed. Wittgenstein explicitly warns us not to search for a definition of meaning and not to think of language as a word referring mysteriously to an object. This is not the way we should start our studies of language and meaning. It is a false reflex in our thinking that we should try to get rid of.

This is a conclusion that Wolcher also draws, but he does nevertheless start off by discussing the magical view of language. The magical view is false. There is only reception, and thus law leads to suffering. One almost gets the impression that he too would be happy if language could guarantee interpretations, that is, if precise meanings were somewhere to be found. It would perhaps mean that law could be something other than a tragedy, something better. But is there no middle ground? What is needed is to find some leeway between the magic and the crisis. We should not accept that *either* legal interpretation is guaranteed by language *or* it is simple brute force causing suffering.

Let us stay a little longer with Wolcher and Wittgenstein. For Wittgenstein, there is always a limit to our reasoning, which means that explanations come to an end at some point. This is what Wolcher says as well. Interpretations end in reception, and then we simply act, without justification. For Wolcher, explanations come to an end in a kind of habitual emptiness. But Wittgenstein can be read differently. As has been argued above, we do not 'just act' arbitrarily. Language is necessarily connected with common ways of acting. We live with language. Another aspect that Wolcher does not pay attention to is the way language is necessarily shared. We do not live with language alone. We agree on a language and a form of life. This agreement is the common ground on which different language uses rests. Meanings are shared. Thus something exists that we can call the foundation of language if we wish to hold on to such a thing: a shared way of living. Common form(s) of life enable agreement on meanings and definitions, that is, for people to be able to communicate. They also enable disagreements. Meaning does not rest on emptiness.

## A tragedy or something else?

Why is it taken for granted that to obey the law literally, to follow exact rules, would be a guarantee of good law? For some writers, the fact that law cannot be followed to the letter but room is always available for competing interpretations is one reason why law can be *misused* for the purposes of power, greed, and violence. Does this imply that the law, in an ideal situation, would be rule-bound, strictly regulated and easily calculated, instead of interpreted? Is this the only way to be safe? Is this the only way to avoid power and violence? Interpretation lies at the heart of the tragedy. Let us turn the thought upside-down. Because of the way language flexes and bends, room always exists for choices. Every decision on meaning is a choice where force and violence are possible but also responsible action and justice. It is a simplification to say that law and legal interpretation always imply suffering and violence. Where there is room for violence there can equally be room for responsibility. It is indeed the flexibility and the vagueness of language that in a radical way give room for responsibility. This has far-reaching consequences for the way we understand the connections between law and suffering, power and violence.

As was claimed earlier, Wittgenstein disliked general descriptions and definitions of language. He thought that this kind of philosophy leads us astray. It creates knots in our mind that are acutely difficult to untangle. This also applies to general descriptions of the nature of law. They tend to be too simplified in order to be useful. But another, even more important reason, exists why we should refrain from making grand claims about law's violence and tragic character: these claims are too extreme. What they do is blur the distinctions between more and less bad, more and less just, more and less suffering. It is a discourse of all or nothing. If the system is fundamentally bad, then it seems that we can do nothing about it. It can also lead to absolution. If everybody is guilty, then nobody is guilty.[15] We have to be able to differentiate. To say that justice is impossible and that law always implies suffering is to give up.

In order to be able to say something new about interpretation that would provide at least some guidance on the question of how law and language are intertwined and how law's commands can be read from legal texts, a new approach is needed. This book searches for answers to the problem of meaning in ethics. The approach may not be as radical or novel as it seems. We can build on Wittgenstein's philosophy and locate the foundation of language in interpersonal relationships. There is an *ethical dimension* in the notion of being together that is somehow necessary for language. The question of law's failure is an important subplot here. It is a question that keeps coming up through the readings of the philosophers chosen for discussion. A reading of Wittgenstein such as that done here does not give us an answer to the difficult question of legal interpretation. Lifting up the background for language and the necessity for language being something that is shared does not give us any definite clues on what criteria could be found for good and bad interpretations. But it opens up a path and a possibility. The idea of the necessarily shared nature of language takes us from Wittgenstein to Derrida, Levinas and beyond. An echo of this idea can be heard in Jean-Luc Nancy's *Being Singular Plural*. The starting point of the essay is the same as the beginning of this book.

15 See Hannah Arendt's discussion on this kind of logic in *Responsibility and Judgment* (2003).

> It is often said today that we have lost meaning, that we lack it and, as a result, are in need of and waiting for it. The 'one' who speaks in this way forgets that the very propagation of this discourse is itself meaningful. Regretting the absence of meaning itself has meaning.
>
> (Nancy 2000: 1)

In saying that we have lost meaning we actually already affirm that there is a meaningful discourse in place. But meaning is not lost in the sense that we would not be able to communicate. In fact, we are meaning. Nancy continues:

> But we are meaning in the sense that we are the element in which signification can be produced and circulate. The least signification just as much as the most elevated (the meaning of 'nail' as well as the meaning of 'God') has no meaning in itself and, as a result, is what it is and does what it does only insofar as it is communicated, even when this communication takes place only between 'me' and 'myself.'
>
> (Nancy 2000: 2)

Words have no meaning in themselves but only in communication. Meaning is communication, and it is necessarily shared. Here we can discern the affinities between Wittgenstein and Levinas, as the thinking of both corresponds to what Nancy expresses beautifully. 'There is no meaning if meaning is not shared, and not because there would be an ultimate or first signification that all beings have in common, but because *meaning is itself the sharing of Being*' (Nancy 2000: 2, emphasis in original).

I now turn to examine the philosophy of Derrida because in a way he picks up where Wittgenstein's thinking ends. Of course, differences abound between the methods and topics of the two philosophers, but some of their ideas on language and meaning are not that far apart. Derrida develops further some thoughts that we can already discern in Wittgenstein's writings. But he raises many new questions as well.

Chapter 2

# Derrida on language and meaning

Derrida's most important philosophical influences were without doubt the works of Husserl and Heidegger. In a way, it is in this context that Derrida's thinking becomes understandable, but it also expands in other directions that take distance from these classics. He claims that he learnt from Husserl a methodological prudence and reserve and a rigorous technique (Derrida 1984: 109). The phenomenological reduction that Husserl developed, the *epoché*, is central to Derrida's philosophy. It is a way of interpreting in which the interpreter's own relation to their surroundings and to what they are interpreting is acknowledged. Derrida uses this method when he reads texts, in this way unveiling some hidden meanings and structures. But Derrida also develops the method further and in doing so applies it to Husserl's own texts as well. The phenomenological reduction in Derrida's hands is directed towards the phenomenological tradition itself, in which he functions as a critic but also takes part and continues the tradition. Derrida's deconstruction is thus not mere criticism in which Husserl would be proved to be wrong, but rather, a case of Derrida developing Husserl's method further by also showing its weaker points. The problems and contradictions that Derrida is able to show in Husserl's phenomenological reduction do not derive from the fact that Husserl simply missed something: they show in a significant way how it is generally impossible to reach a method of interpretation that would be infallible (see Kaarto 2008: 11–13).

Derrida's philosophy is also closely connected with Heidegger's critique of metaphysics. Important affinities exist between Derrida's and Heidegger's thinking, the most prominent perhaps being the notion of 'deconstruction' that Derrida develops from Heidegger's '*Destruktion*'. However, there are also many points on which Derrida's and Heidegger's thinking and method differ. Derrida claims an important difference between him and Heidegger in the way they see language. Derrida says that he writes in a different language from Heidegger, which does not mean only that he writes in French and Heidegger in German. He notes that the writers and poets that interest him (for instance Mallarmé and Blanchot) are completely different from those that interest Heidegger (Hölderlin and Rilke) (Derrida 1984: 110; see, also, Miller 2009). Derrida explains this difference in the following way:

> Now, what I called and what I practiced as 'deconstruction' was contextualized in a very different way; it had to do, initially, with the hegemony of structuralism, or with the logocentric models in linguisticism, itself the model for the human sciences in France at the time. In fact, the entire tradition of logocentrism was the target, and I thought I could find in Heidegger himself some logocentric assumptions. So, from that point of view, deconstruction was inherited from Heidegger and sometimes directed against Heidegger with different points of application. Since I was born, brought up, and trained in a context that was so different from Heidegger's, the texts I was reading and the issues I was addressing were quite different. From that perspective, despite the debt and proximity, what I have done is something else; mine is another idiom, another language.
>
> (Derrida 1999a: 82)

## Grammatology

In his seminal work *Of Grammatology* (1976), Derrida discusses language at length. Here the cornerstones of his ideas and also his method are laid. Published in French in 1967, it is one of his earliest works.[1] By reading and commenting on Ferdinand de Saussure and other linguists, he manages to show how language has been thought of in the Western tradition and what problems are internal to this way of thinking. Linguistics was to be the science of language. Derrida studies how language is understood in this science, how it is defined both by determining what is proper to language and what is secondary. A central thought in linguistics, which stems from Aristotle, is the way it determines language by claiming that its essence is the unity of sound and sense within a *phonie*. With regard to this unity, in which sound is essential, writing has been seen as derivative, secondary, and accidental. This is *the* presupposition that institutes general linguistics. It reduces writing to an instrument enslaved by spoken language. Saussure, whose theory has been highly influential, sees writing as having only a narrow and derivative function. Narrow, because it is only one modality among others, it does not represent the true or natural essence of language. According to Saussure, language has an oral tradition independent of writing. And writing is derivative because it is representative: it merely represents the voice, the immediate, natural and direct signification of the thing signified or the object referred to (Derrida 1976: 27–30). What Derrida points out here is that Saussure, as the tradition before him, sees speech as something that has direct access to meaning. It does not hide anything. Speech is the real essence of language because it is immediate, self-present and, in a way, uncomplicated. Writing, on the other hand, is secondary and much more complicated.

1 Derrida's first published work was the translation to French of Husserl's *Origin of Geometry* with a long introduction, which came out in 1962. Next he published a collection of essays called *L'écriture et la différence* in 1967 and then *La voix et le phénomène* also in 1967, which discusses Husserl's phenomenology. After these came *De la grammatologie*.

According to Derrida, Saussure continues the tradition started by Plato and Aristotle in which language is defined not only according to the model of speech, but also according to words. The idea that comes from a definition given by Aristotle is that spoken words are symbols of mental experience while written words are symbols of spoken words. This affects how Saussure understands the word. The word is a unity of sense and sound, concept and voice, signified and signifier (Derrida 1976: 30–31).

Although Saussure sees writing as unrelated to the inner system of language, he does not want to disregard it altogether. Writing is, according to him, continually used to represent language. It is useful, despite its shortcomings and dangers. Derrida points out that writing has been reduced to a tool. It is seen as an instrument that does not always work. The fact that it does not always function perfectly is experienced as fatal, but the problems are understood to concern only writing, not language itself. Writing, in fact, threatens language. Derrida argues that this way of thinking about language has very long roots:

> [...] writing, the letter, the sensible inscription, has always been considered by Western tradition as the body and matter external to the spirit, to breath, to speech, and to the logos. And the problem of soul and body is no doubt derived from the problem of writing from which it seems – conversely – to borrow its metaphors.
>
> (Derrida 1976: 35)

Derrida's critique of linguistics is a critique of its presuppositions and the definitions and restrictions by which it limits itself and its object of study. There seem to be inconsistencies and hidden meanings in the way that linguistics defines itself. Derrida asks:

> Why does a project of *general* linguistics, concerning the *internal system in general of language in general*, outline the limits of its field by excluding, as *exteriority in general*, a *particular* system of writing, however important it might be, even were it to be *in fact* universal?
>
> (Derrida 1976: 39, emphasis in original)

According to Derrida, writing is not secondary to language if the logic of first and second is not considered inside the system from which the aim is to exclude the second. Derrida points out that writing cannot be a sign of a sign except if one says it of all signs. Herein lies for Derrida an important message: if every sign refers to a sign, and if a sign of a sign refers to writing, then writing contains something that is inherent in all language (Derrida 1976: 43). Writing, in fact, can tell us important things about language in general.

Derrida sees the exclusion of writing in a larger context as part of the metaphysical tradition. This tradition is 'logocentric', which means that it ultimately determines sense as presence. The way language has been defined as speech, and

the way writing has been excluded to become something derivative corresponds to this logocentrism (Derrida 1976: 44). By reading Saussure and others, Derrida thus develops his own thinking, which consists of a further development of some elements presented by these thinkers but which at the same time criticises them and moves towards something else. One of his principal aims is to offer a deconstruction of metaphysics, which he does here by way of concentrating on linguistics. He says:

> [...] I obviously treat the Saussurian text at the moment only as a telling example within a given situation, without professing to use the concepts required by the functioning of which I have just spoken. My justification would be as follows: this and some other indices (in a general way the treatment of the concept of writing) already give us the assured means of broaching the deconstruction of *the greatest totality* – the concept of the *epistémè* and logocentric metaphysics – within which are produced, without ever posing the radical question of writing, all the Western methods of analysis, explication, reading, or interpretation.
>
> (Derrida 1976: 46, emphasis in original)

Derrida thus uses Saussure as an example to show that Western methods of analysis, explication, reading and interpretation are constructed so that they necessarily involve the exclusion of writing and cannot pose the radical question of writing. By looking at the way writing has been understood, Derrida can deconstruct the concept of *epistémè* and the logocentric metaphysics that are essential in Western thinking.

What is Derrida's own suggestion, then? He says that instead of seeing writing as secondary and exterior, we must try to think of it as simultaneously exterior and interior to speech. This means that writing is something other than speech, but that speech is in itself already writing. He introduces the concepts of *graphie*, which is a unit of a possible graphic system in contrast to the phonetic one, and *trace*, which is the possibility of signification that is common to all systems (Derrida 1976: 46). The trace is an important notion because it enables Derrida to construct an account of meaning that does not rely on self-presence and thus logocentrism. The trace is the way otherness announces itself. It is not fully present but presents itself in the dissimulation of itself. The structure of the trace is the structure that language as writing has. It is a structure of relationship with an other and the movement of temporalisation (Derrida 1976: 47). There is no transcendental signified that would be the reassuring end of the chain of reference from sign to sign. Already Charles S. Peirce, in fact, went so far as to almost deconstruct the transcendental signified. He saw the chain of reference as indefinite. This means that every sign refers to another sign that refers to another. The so-called thing itself, or the object that the sign refers to, is never fully present. It is always hidden behind the never-ending chain of signs. In Peirce's semiotics the thing only shows itself by giving rise to an *interpretant* that itself becomes a sign and so on, until infinity. The identity of the thing itself conceals itself and is always on the move (Derrida 1976: 49–50). There is no transcendental signified that would shine as the thing itself in its own self-presence. Logocentrism and the metaphysics of presence is precisely a desire for such a transcendental signified.

Thus Derrida wants to think of language differently from what has usually been done in linguistics. To him, language is a possibility founded on the general possibility of writing. Oral language already belongs to writing (Derrida 1976: 55). Herein lies a problem for him. He must *redefine* 'writing' in order to make clear what he means by it. It is not wrong to stay in the structure of language opposed to writing as long as one sees speech and writing in the traditional way. But this way of thinking includes contradictions. The challenge for Derrida is that his own attempt to tackle the problem cannot start from the same origins as the traditional one but has no other base to start from. He thus has to use some of the concepts of that tradition but use them in new ways and give new significations to them. This is one reason why Derrida's style of writing is at times very difficult to understand.

Language has always been what Derrida calls '*arche-writing*'. It is something that can never be reduced to presence. By using the concept of arche-writing it becomes clear that Derrida's aim is not simply to disrupt the tradition of the phoneme by replacing it with a theory centred on the *graphie* instead. Arche-writing is a notion on another level, so to speak. It is at work not only in the form and structure of graphic expression but in non-graphic as well. It constitutes the movement of the sign function. This movement Derrida calls '*différance*', his own neologism (he also uses the form '*differance*'). It means temporalisation and the relationship between non-presence and language. It is the condition of all linguistic systems (Derrida 1976: 60). Here some of the most important elements of Derrida's theory of language are presented and take form.

The trace is an important notion in Derrida's philosophy of language because it is closely connected to the way that writing relies on differences.

> Without a retention in the minimal unit of temporal experience, without a trace retaining the other as other in the same, no difference would do its work and no meaning would appear. It is not the question of a constituted difference here, but rather, before all determination of the content, of the *pure* movement which produces difference. *The (pure) trace is differance.*
>
> (Derrida 1976: 62, emphasis in original)

The trace as *différance* founds the opposition between signifier and signified (Derrida 1976: 63). Meaning is not something that is present to itself in the unity of the sign. It is not founded on unity but on differences.

Derrida later commented on these early thoughts in different interviews. He stressed that his aim was not to found a *graphocentrism* instead of the hitherto reigning phono- or logocentrism. Thus the work is not strictly speaking a defence of grammatology. Nor is its purpose to return to writing its rights or its dignity. There is an ethical and political sense in which writing has been excluded in the past, and acknowledging this makes us see that there cannot be a question of now restoring writing's supremacy over its old sovereign in turn. Such a reversal would be 'ridiculous' (Derrida 1981a: 13). *Of Grammatology* is thus meant to be a question:

> [...] about the necessity of a science of writing, about the conditions that would make it possible, about the critical work that would have to open its field and resolve the epistemological obstacles; but it is also a question about the limits of this science.
>
> (Derrida 1981a: 13)

Derrida says that meaning derives from différance. A sign can mean something only in a chain or system of differences. It must belong to some figuration in order to function. This way the idea of literal meaning becomes impossible in his theory too. No meaning can be fully present in itself at any time because meaning always implies a reference elsewhere, to other signs and meanings. This is the basic function of the sign. 'The literal [proper] meaning does not exist, its "appearance" is a necessary function – and must be analyzed as such – in the system of differences and metaphors' (Derrida 1976: 89). Literal meaning is some kind of fiction. It is the dream in which meaning is present to the logos within its voice, thus being fully present and heard. It is to hear oneself speak and understand absolutely (Derrida 1976: 89).

## Writing and supplementarity

If we pay attention to writing instead of speech, and study language, especially its history, from this point of view, we see that we find no simple origin or uncomplicated development. Derrida lists different aspects of this history that show the many important roles that writing has played. The written sign has contributed to many things: all clergies were constituted at the same time as writing and by using writing; strategy, diplomacy, agriculture, fiscality and penal law are linked to writing in both their history and their structure. The origin of writing has in many differing cultures been connected to the exercise of power. Political-administrative power has been practiced through scribes, whose function was irreducible. Ideological, religious, scientific and technical systems have been made possible and have relied upon writing. From all this we see that writing has been much more than a mere means of communication. Derrida also argues that in fact the very sense of power and effectiveness in general, that is, meaning and mastery, was always linked to writing. He says that there could be no law without the possibility of trace (Derrida 1976: 93). This is not meant to be an exposition of *the* origin of writing but a study of its different origins. The idea is that if we look at writing instead of speech, we get a picture of language, in which we cannot see one simple origin but many different ones connected to different contexts.

What is it that links writing to violence? What is there equivalent in violence and the operation of trace? According to Derrida, the structure of writing as the possibility of violence is complicated. He differentiates between a first violence that is naming. It is by its nature an originary violence of language, which consists in classifying. The gesture of arche-writing inscribes the unique within a system, which means that the *proper* in proper name is lost. The second violence is the way that this arche-writing has been forbidden, forgotten, hidden, and excluded from language. This second violence has been reparatory, an attempt to protect language and meaning by concealing the structure of writing and the originary violence. From this, a third violence may or may not appear, this violence being the empirical level of evil and war. This is the level of the common concept of violence and morality (Derrida 1976: 112). The third level of violence is complex because it refers to the other two levels. It may or may not take place, and whether it does at a certain time in a certain situation is an empirical question.

By reading Rousseau's texts, Derrida studies in further detail the connections of language and logocentrism. Rousseau, and in his company Claude Levi-Strauss (a 'Rousseauist'), represent for Derrida an exemplary position in the history of logocentrism between Plato and Hegel. Therefore, Rousseau seems to be someone through whom we can study the history of metaphysics as the history of being determined by presence, which merges with logocentrism and is produced by reduction of the trace (Derrida 1976: 97–99). Rousseau's theory of writing is a phase in the complicated structure, in which meaning as presence has been developed.

In context with Saussure, Derrida points out the ethnocentric ideology that privileges phonetic writing over others. It is an ethnocentrism that does not realise its ethnocentrism but makes claims of liberation. It wants to liberate linguistics from writing without questioning the legitimacy of this move. It wants to found a science of authentic language by asserting that human and fully signifying language does not need writing. It wants to say that nothing is missing from peoples who are nevertheless described as 'without writing'. By this definition, it is, however, already asserted that, in fact, something is missing. These ambiguities can also be found in Levi-Strauss's texts. He upholds the rigorous distinction between language and writing. This permits the classification of people as those who use writing and those who do not. According to Derrida, Levi-Strauss is not suspicious of these distinctions (Derrida 1976: 119–120). He does not question the ethnocentrism that is included in these classifications.

Rousseau's view of language is not the same as Levi-Strauss's because Rousseau is, in fact, mistrustful of speech. Derrida explains how Rousseau saw speech as something in which presence is promised but at the same time refused. Rousseau strains towards reconstitution of presence, and the threat to presence at the heart of speech is something that he wants to exorcise. He therefore comes to see writing not only as straightforwardly secondary but in a more nuanced manner. Writing here acquires a contradictory character, being something that opposes presence but at the same time saves it.

> [...] Rousseau considers writing as a dangerous means, a menacing aid, the critical response to a situation of distress. When Nature, as self-proximity, comes to be forbidden or interrupted, when speech fails to protect presence, writing becomes necessary.
>
> (Derrida 1976: 144)

Writing is the necessary evil without which speech unfortunately cannot manage. In Rousseau we also find the idea of writing being a supplement. The verb 'to supplant' or 'to compensate for' defines writing. Writing is the supplement *par excellence*, being the sign of a sign. It takes the place of speech, which already incorporates the structure of the sign. Thus speech is signs, and writing is signs of signs. Writing displaces the proper time and place of the sentence it pronounces. This is the way writing has a doubling structure (see Derrida 1976: 280–281). But, by reading Rousseau's texts closely, Derrida shows that this structure is complicated. Writing is not simply the supplement. What can also be seen in Rousseau is an inconsistency in that while writing is secondary, it is also something that affects speech. Or rather, all language carries elements of this supplementarity. These elements are intricate, as a supplement is something that takes and keeps the place of the other. It is never itself fully present here and now; it stands in place of something else. The movement of supplementarity is therefore foreign to classical logos, which draws on presence and the opposition between presence and absence (Derrida 1976: 313–316). We see that supplementarity is a difficult notion because it is neither something clearly present nor something clearly absent. Derrida claims that language and signification carry with themselves the structure of a sequence of supplements. In the following significant passage he describes the mirage of immediate presence. Sense is connected with an infinite chain of mediation and supplementarity.

> Through this sequence of supplements a necessity is announced: that of *an infinite chain, ineluctably multiplying the supplementary mediations that produce the sense of the very thing they defer*: the mirage of the thing itself, of immediate presence, of originary perception. Immediacy is derived.
>
> (Derrida 1976: 157; emphasis added)

## Différance

How does Derrida solve the problem of meaning? What is his answer to the difficult question of how expressions can mean something and be understood? One way to study this is by focusing on the term 'différance', introduced above. It is one of the most important concepts, or non-concepts,[2] that he uses. He has changed

2 Derrida says that it is neither a word nor a concept (see Derrida 1982: 7).

the French term '*différence*' to 'différance' by changing one 'e' to an 'a'. This can be seen in the written form of the word but is not heard when pronounced. What then is différance?[3] It is the playing movement that produces differences. It is not simply something that precedes differences. It is the structured and differentiating origin of differences. But the characterisation 'origin' suits it badly because différance is something that is not really present as any thing (Derrida 1982: 11). Différance produces and constitutes differences.

A sign has meaning only in a system of signs. To put it simply, it is the way the sign differs from other signs that gives it meaning. This is the thought behind meaning being based on differences. Différance does not have an identity, and *is* not any thing. It is the differing that can be seen in a system of signs, and it shows itself in what Derrida calls the 'play of differences' (see Enwald 2004: 82; Derrida 1982: 11). Language, be it written or spoken, requires differences for meaning to exist at all. Every sign refers to other signs that are not present at that moment but that leave traces. The play of differences is an endless play of reference. This play, in which meaning is contained in an endless chain, leads to the fact that all elements of language are in relation to others. All the elements in the endless chain leave traces, and a weft of these chains is a text. Nothing in this system is ever purely present or absent; there are only differences, traces, and traces of traces.

We can think of différance as the space where, or the movement through which, the different elements of language relate to one another:

> The activity or productivity connoted by the *a* of *différance* refers to the generative movement in the play of differences. The latter are neither fallen from the sky nor inscribed once and for all in a closed system, a static structure that a synchronic and taxonomic operation could exhaust. Differences are the effects of transformations, and from this vantage the theme of *différance* is incompatible with the static, synchronic, taxonomic, ahistoric motifs in the concept of *structure*.
>
> (Derrida 1981a: 27, emphasis in original)

The differences that constitute meanings in language are not static. They do not form a rigid structure or closed system, determined once and for all. A structure exists in language, and it is a kind of system, but différance is meant to refer to the way that language includes ever-changing connections, relations and differences.

Différance is spatial and temporal. The sign is put in the place of the thing itself. It represents the absent thing. It takes the place of the present. When we cannot show or grasp the present, we use the detour of the sign. According to Derrida, the sign is deferred presence. The sign gets its meaning by deferring forever the moment

3 According to Gasché there are 'different kinds of differences drawn synthetically together in the term *différance*: difference as temporalizing, difference as spacing, difference as the result of opening a polemical rift between conceptual poles, difference as diacritical differentiality, difference as ontico-ontological difference, and so on'.

in which we encounter the thing itself, make it ours, consume it or touch it. This is the structure of signification. The thing itself is not present in time or place; it is something different from the sign, and it is also deferred by the sign. Différance is the movement in which language is constituted historically as a weave of differences. The movement of signification includes temporal differing. Derrida says:

> It is because of *différance* that the movement of signification is possible only if each so-called 'present' element, each element appearing on the scene of presence, is related to something other than itself, thereby keeping within itself the mark of the past element, and already letting itself be vitilated by the mark of its relation to the future element, this trace being related no less to what is called the future than to what is called the past [...].
>
> (Derrida 1982: 13)

Différance is a movement in time, between the past and the future. An interval exists in the structure of presence, a temporal spacing. It is necessary for the present to be present; it constitutes presence by dividing it and spacing it between the past and the future. This spacing that constitutes the present Derrida refers to by different notions: différance, archi-writing and archi-trace. It is both spacing and temporisation and includes differing both in space and in time (Derrida 1982: 13).

Semiotics sees the sign as something that refers to something else, something that is absent. It can be, for instance, approaching dark clouds in the sky as the sign of rain, smoke puffing out of a window of a house indicating fire, a smile on the face of a passer-by suggesting joy, or a word. Anything can function as a sign. We can say that signs are a postponement, a roundabout way that keeps us from the things themselves. Derrida, however, questions the idea that the sign is something secondary or provisional, something that is less important than the thing itself, a mere copy of that which is original and self-present. He asks if the sign itself could not be important. He makes us think of signs in opposite ways from how we usually do by asking if that which we have usually seen as secondary really is secondary. He reveals the structures that are at play in the thinking of signs as present but still secondary.

The play of differences is what enables conceptuality and a system of concepts. Through this notion of play Derrida distances himself from classical semiological theories, such as Saussure's. Differences in language are in constant play, they do not form a rigid structure. Différance is playful. This is one central difference between Derrida and many semioticians: according to Derrida, differences make differences and leave traces, but they are also traces themselves. They are not given and definable once and for all but historical and changing. The ever-continuing play of differences leads to the fact that no words or concepts have stable or given meanings. Meaning is dynamic. It is a play whose time and place cannot be defined in any text or book. It spreads from text to text, and thus we should not see difference as a linear process but as a more complicated structure, as the term 'play' suggests.

Marika Enwald takes as an example the picture in Figure 2.1, from which we cannot say if it represents two faces or a vase:

Figure 2.1

Here différance takes place at the limits of the pictures, on the borders where the black and the white meet. It is precisely at the limit where we can distinguish the two different pictures. The difference that gives meaning to either the face or the vase is a play because it is not stable. By shifting our focus we shift from faces to vase and back to faces again. However, this is a crude example, because difference is here shown as a bipolar structure. We should not see meanings as something as simple and static as this (Enwald 2004: 88–89).

Wittgenstein discusses similar pictures in *Philosophical Investigations*. His example is the duck–rabbit in Figure 2.2. It is a picture that can be seen as portraying a duck or a rabbit (Wittgenstein 1958, part II xi: 194; see, also, for example, Mulhall 2001). In this picture, too, it is the limit that defines identity and meaning. A play is going on between the two animals, and the meaning of the picture is not stable.

What is important to notice is that différance is not totally random but produces changes and differences with some level of regularity. How is this possible? Derrida says that it is not astructural. It produces structural and regulated transformations (Derrida 1981a: 28). For Derrida, as for Wittgenstein, structures and regularity, a grammar, must exist; otherwise language would not function. But these structures are dynamic and flexible and in a way beyond our reach. We cannot fully explain the meaning of a sign because something is always absent. Meaning escapes our definitions.

Figure 2.2

A necessary feature of language is that it works in the absence of a speaker or a writer (Derrida 1988a: 48). After the expression has left the writer's pen or been uttered aloud, it begins to have a life of its own. The linguistic sign is not under the utterer's command. It can, and does, fulfil its function even in the absence of a sender. This idea leads Derrida to his famous conclusion about the death of the author. The meaning that the utterer intended can get new nuances and change altogether. It is in the nature of signs that they work even when the sender, the receiver and the context have changed or are unknown. Traditional linguistics has regarded writing as uncertain compared to speech, which has been seen as direct and pure communication, but Derrida argues that the features usually seen as features of writing are actually features of all signs and therefore all language. This way an amount of uncertainty affects all language use. The possibility of something going wrong, of misunderstanding, is actually in the nature of language and not just an exceptional situation. This way of seeing language is characteristic of Derrida: he pays attention to the possibility of failure that is one central element in language. However, Derrida does not think that language would not work; he is in no way a nihilist about meaning. His point is simply that the possibility of failure is a central characteristic of language.

We can perhaps exemplify the way that Derrida sees meaning by considering one of his examples: the signature. A person's signature is repeatable, but it is also never exactly the same. All the instances of the signature, for instance in letters, official forms and on receipts, are the same signature, but none of them is identical to the other. In a signature, sameness and uniqueness come together. Language works in the same way, it has an element of iterability, of sameness, but at the same time it is always unique (Derrida 1988a: 10–19, 29–34). (Another important feature of the signature is that it can be forged. Just like a letter can go wrong, a signature can be a fake, it can be a failure.) A word does not have one meaning, but meaning is like an abyss. It is bottomless. The word covers this abyss. The abysmal nature of meaning is born in the spatial and temporal repetitions of a sign (see Enwald 2004: 177). Thus the meaning of a sign is never exactly the same as before, in another context, time and place, even if the sign looked exactly the same.

Because of the instability of meaning, interpretation never stops. It is never complete and final. There is no way an interpretation can give us the correct meaning of a text because no such thing exists. This does not, however, mean that there could not be better and worse interpretations. But the virtues of an interpretation have to be measured by different standards than by reference to correct or literal meaning. This way, criteria for a good interpretation have to be formulated in other ways. This idea is highly important for the claims made in this book regarding legal interpretation and also a focal point in Derrida's philosophy of language.

## Textuality

One of Derrida's best known phrases is '*Il n'y a pas de hors-texte*' (Derrida 1976: 158), normally translated as 'there is nothing outside the text' or 'there is no outside to a text'. We could draw from this the conclusion that Derrida thinks nothing exists outside language, that we are somehow trapped in language. It is, however, not that simple. Derrida says in an interview:

> I never cease to be surprised by critics who see my work as a declaration that there is nothing beyond language, that we are imprisoned in language; it is, in fact, saying the exact opposite. The critique of logocentrism is above all else the search for the 'other' and the 'other of language' [...]. Certainly, deconstruction tries to show that the question of reference is much more complex and problematic than traditional theories supposed.
>
> (Derrida 1984: 123)

Derrida maintains that there is no easy distinction between the interior and the exterior of language or texts.

> In the extent to which what is called 'meaning' (to be 'expressed') is already, and thoroughly, constituted by a tissue of differences, in the extent to which there is already a *text*, a network of textual referrals to *other* texts, a textual transformation in which each allegedly 'simple term' is marked by the trace of another term, the presumed interiority of meaning is already worked upon by its own exteriority. It is always already carried outside itself.
>
> (Derrida 1981a: 33, emphasis in original)

This quotation makes the above cited '*Il n'y a pas de hors-texte*' understandable. Meanings are formed in the play of differences. Each sign refers to other signs that leave traces and the interiority of meaning has always traces of exteriority. There is strictly no inside and outside of text. A text is always related to other texts, and its meaning stems from inter-textuality.

The notion of textuality is connected with the play of differences. Sometimes Derrida even uses the terms 'text', 'writing' and 'play' to refer to more or less the same phenomenon. Let us take as an example of textuality Derrida's reading of Plato's *Phaedrus* (estimated to have been composed around 370 BC), which Derrida discusses in *Plato's Pharmacy*. This reading revolves around the term '*pharmakon*', which has multiple possible meanings. It can be a poison or a medicine, or something in between. The meaning of the dialogue shifts depending on how we understand this vague term. *Pharmakon* leads us away or astray. It is an example of how words are caught in chains of signification (see Derrida 1981b: 63–171; see, also, Enwald 2004: 121–122). The meaning of the term itself cannot be deduced from the text, or rather, the text offers possibilities for several meanings. In cases like this, we could imagine that something would exist outside the text that could help us define the meaning of the text and also the way we should interpret the term giving rise to problems. A context, for instance, would be such a thing outside the text on which we could base our interpretation. A context could give us the meaning of *pharmakon* and thus help us determine how the text itself should be read. However, Derrida sees that this is not possible. Even if we connected a text, its sign system, to anything whatsoever that lies outside the text and with the help of which the uncertain elements in the text could be sorted out, the text is still left incomplete. There is no definite interpretation of a text. Even if we created a new text, which would include the original text and an explanation or definition for it, the new text would still be incomplete. It would need interpretation and explanation. The meaning of a text is never fully present; something is always hidden.

What importance does a *context* have? A context consists of the time, space and presuppositions on the basis of which a text, be it only an utterance or an epic novel, is interpreted. Every time we interpret a text we do it in one context. But the context is never saturated, nor is the choice of it unambiguous (see Derrida 1988a; Kaarto 2008: 311). The context in which a text belongs or in which it should be read can never be fully and completely determined. A context refers to other contexts, and its borders cannot be clearly and unambiguously defined. This view has been criticised because it undermines the idea that the context is that which should guide interpretation towards the correct meaning of a text. If we cannot clearly define the context, how is it supposed to guide interpretation? However, it has to be noted that the fact that we cannot clearly define contexts does not mean that there are none, nor that they would not be of any use whatsoever in interpretation. Derrida says that his own effort has not been to belittle the importance of contexts but, on the contrary, to take the *limitless* context into account. He even says that the slogan 'there is nothing outside the text' means nothing else but that there is nothing outside context (Derrida 1988a: 136).

## Searle's and Derrida's differences in meaning

As a way of concluding the central ideas of Derrida's philosophy of language, I will discuss one of the numerous critiques directed against him. There is a famous debate between John Searle and Derrida, of which some of the essays have been collected in *Limited Inc* (1988a), where Derrida's fundamental ideas on language and meaning can be read. Derrida's essay and his reply to Searle illustrate the major differences but also many similarities between Derrida's philosophy and the so-called analytical theories of language, speech act theory in particular. Derrida reads John L. Austin as does Searle, and hence they have some common ground at least in this respect.

Whereas speech act theory tends to concentrate on common and unremarkable communication situations, Derrida pays attention to discrepancies and anomalies in language. Speech act theory sees language as a tool, a system that can be mastered by the speaker or writer. Meaning is a combination of the speaker's intention and conventions of the situation and context in which the speaker partakes (see Searle 1969). Derrida, on the other hand, seems to question all of this. However, it is important to notice that he does not reject speech act theory altogether. He does not say that it would be impossible for a speaker to say what they mean, or that the speaker's intention or the context would be irrelevant for meaning. But he does emphasise that things are not that simple; it is always possible that something may go wrong.

Derrida is sceptical about literal meaning. As has already been discussed above, literal meaning is a problematic idea and it has been questioned in the analytical tradition as well. Wittgenstein's views also correspond badly with a strong faith in literal meaning. However, literal meaning still seems to be something that many philosophers hold on to, even if they admit that it is problematic. Derrida's critical remarks are directed both towards the idea of literal meaning and towards the notion of context. He says that the absence of a sender and a receiver can be more clearly perceived in writing than in speech but that these are general features of language. It is in the nature of language that the sender and the receiver can be absent from one another's company, even worlds apart. This is how language works and how it has to work. It would be a much different language we had if it always required that the communicators were in each other's presence, in fact it would make language almost impossible. Iterability, that is, the possibility for words and sentences to be repeated and to travel in space and time, is what makes language possible. The sign has to be able to function in the absence of the sender. And the sign is understandable, at least to an extent, even if we did not know what the speaker or writer intended to say with it (Derrida 1988a: 5–12). This has to do with Derrida's view that language has a certain amount of authority. In speech act theory it seems that language is just an instrument, but for Derrida it has a life and certain ways of operating. It cannot be completely ruled by the speaker or the writer.

> The possibility of repeating and thus identifying the marks is implicit in every code, making it into a network [*une grille*] that is communicable, transmittable, decipherable, iterable for a third, and hence for every possible user in general. To be what it is, all writing must, therefore, be capable of functioning in the radical absence of every empirically determined receiver in general.
>
> (Derrida 1988a: 8)

These features that make language and meaning possible also include the possibility of failure. The iterability of the sign includes a kind of *citation*.

For Austin citations are not normal language use, they are exceptions. They are not utterances in which the speaker's intention directly contributes to the meaning. There is a disturbing presence of something other. For Derrida iterability implies citationality.[4] Now, if this is the general structure and possibility of language, then it seems that the speaker's intention is never enough to assert meaning (Derrida 1988a: 17–18). Meaning requires that the sign has a repeatable character and this

4 According to Gasché the term 'iterability' refers to repetition in general, to repeatability (Gasché 1986: 212).

repeatability is beyond the full control of the speaker. This way the speaker cannot say exactly what they mean.

> In the absence of the presumed author this function, which depends upon iterability, operates a fortiori within the hypothesis that I fully understand what the author meant to say, providing he [*sic*] said what he meant. But the function also operates independently of such an hypothesis and without in itself implying either that I *fully* understand what the other says, writes, meant to say or write, or even that he intended to say or write *in full* what remains to be read, or above all that any adequation need obtain between what he consciously intended, what he did, and what I do while 'reading'.
>
> (Derrida 1988a: 61, emphasis in original)

The structure of the sign, the way it stands for something that is absent and requires iterability as its possibility to function, leads to the non-presence of meaning. Literal meaning would be just this, a meaning fully present here and now, but there is always deferral at play, which makes literal meaning impossible. This conclusion derives from analysis of the functioning of signs.

The sign is a combination of two possibilities: first, the possibility of being repeated, and second, the possibility of being self-identical. Both of these are necessary requirements of the sign. Some level of self-identity is needed so that the sign can be recognised in its varying forms and functions. This is the idea of the signature again; it shows these two elements of the sign. Iterability means both identity and difference (Derrida 1988a: 53).

> In order for my 'written communication' to retain its function as writing, i.e., its readability, it must remain readable despite the absolute disappearance of any receiver, determined in general. My communication must be repeatable – iterable – in the absolute absence of the receiver or of any empirically determinable collectivity of receivers.
>
> (Derrida 1988a: 7)

In a way, Derrida here turns the picture painted by speech act theory on its head: what has been seen as a crisis for meaning and understanding is in fact a necessity that makes them possible.

Speech act theory, as its name implies, focuses to a large extent on what the speaker wants to say and do with their words. Derrida, on the other hand, shows that language works in ways that make the speaker's intentions less relevant. The speaker's authority to control meaning is put into question here. Derrida says that the speaker, the writer and the receiver are much in the same situation concerning the text: none of them has the authority to state what the meaning of the text is better than any of the others (Derrida 1988a: 8).

Signs have the power to break with their contexts in the way that there cannot be any 'real' context that the sign belongs to (Derrida 1988a: 9). Derrida does not say that signs function outside context but that actually contexts are not what they seem to be: they are not finite and definable but infinite and boundless.

> Every sign, linguistic or non-linguistic, spoken or written [...], in a small or large unit, can be *cited*, put between quotation marks; in so doing it can break with every given context, engendering an infinity of new contexts in a manner which is absolutely illimitable. This does not imply that the mark is valid outside of a context, but on the contrary that there are only contexts without any center or absolute anchoring.
>
> (Derrida 1988a: 12, emphasis in original)

This is one of the problems of speech act theory: it requires a context that can be defined. The circumstances and the situation in which speech or writing takes place contribute to meaning, and thus it must be possible to define the situation. However, even speech act theorists, especially Austin, acknowledge that this does not always work and that many communication situations do not follow this ideal picture. Austin excludes from his analysis non-ordinary instances of speech that he calls, for instance, parasitic or non-serious, thus basing his theory on an idealised version of language. In a rather Wittgensteinian vein Derrida questions this theoretical move as it does give us a purified and idealised picture of language. He asks what justifies the differentiation between certain kinds of speech in the manner that Austin can claim some versions to be normal and others not (Derrida 1988a: 16–18).

The main problem with context in the way it is seen in speech act theory, is, according to Derrida, that it is conceptually very closely linked to the speaker's intention, for instance when expressions such as 'I pose a question' or 'I challenge you to a duel' are concerned. Intention dictates the context in which the meaning of these utterances is to be understood. However, the problem is that because of the general iterability of the sign, intention can never be fully present to itself (Derrida 1988a: 18). The iterability of the mark exceeds the speaker's control and this in its turn prohibits the saturation of context, as the context in Austin's theory was dependent on the intention of the speaker.

Derrida's theory does not combine the meaning of an utterance with understanding the speaker's intention. Language as a sign system works both when we think we know what the speaker wants to say and when we do not. It also works in situations when the speaker themselves does not even (fully) know what they want to say. The structure of language is such that it works in all of these situations, but Derrida finds the first example to be an ideal, that is, the situation in which we understand what the speaker wants to say and they say what they mean. The ideal is untenable because iterability can always alter what the speaker wants to say so that it is always already something other than what they meant (Derrida 1988a: 62). Derrida does not, however, say that intentionality would be impossible in general. He only claims that it can never be fully present to itself. The intention of the author does not disappear but its power to govern the meaning of utterances is criticised (see Derrida 1988a: 105, 128–131).

No utterance can define its context and nor can the writer or speaker limit the text to only one context. The choice of context is a choice made by the interpreter in the interpretation situation. The interpreter carries responsibility for these choices. What Derrida's discussion on meaning in *Limited Inc* shows is, above all, that some leeway always exists for the interpreter inside which they can choose meanings. He calls this 'undecidability' and expressly denies that it would be indeterminacy. Undecidability is an oscillation between possibilities that are pragmatically determined.

> I say 'undecidability' rather than 'indeterminacy' because I am interested more in relations of force, in differences of force, in everything that allows, precisely, determinations in given situations to be stabilized through a decision of writing.
>
> (Derrida 1988a: 148)

Situations in which the meaning of an utterance is decided are real-life situations in which people act and make choices. What directs these choices are, above all, ethical, political and social considerations.

We should not understand communication as meaning passing from a sender to a receiver in a manner that some original meaning could be found. However, this does not and should not in Derrida's view lead to free and endless interpretive games. Language is open for many, even conflicting, interpretations, but this does not mean that all of those interpretations could be possible in an interpretation situation (see Norris 1986: 63). Texts cannot be made to mean just anything because texts exist and get meanings in social contexts.

## Derrida saying 'yes'

The situation in which a text is interpreted is not the only thing anchoring meaning. On a more fundamental level, Derrida observes that behind every speech act stands an affirmation. Every speech act implies that the speaker at the same time says 'yes' as an answer or response. As soon as we speak, we commit ourselves (Derrida 1995a: 383–384; see Attridge 1992: 254; Llewelyn 2002a: 209). Communication means that we decide to take part in language, to welcome the other speaker and to reply to them. We affirm this by every utterance, so every time we say or write anything, be it just a simple 'I', we also say 'yes' to language and the other person.

Derrida ponders the word 'yes' and its enigmatic grammatical and semantic status. The word does not seem to say anything very definite; 'yes' names nothing and describes nothing. The least that can be said of it is that it is always in the form of an answer. Here is the possibility of an allegory with language in general. To speak or to write is always to some extent an answer. Derrida says when discussing James Joyce's *Ulysses* (1922) that:

> It [the word 'yes'] is always in the form of an answer. It occurs after the other, to answer a request or a question, at least implicit, of the other, even if this is the other in me, the representation in me of another speech. *Yes* implies, as Bloom would say, an 'implicit believer' in some summons of the other.
>
> (Derrida 1992a: 265, emphasis in original)

The 'yes' of language is implied even if it is not expressed. To use language implies an affirmation to take part in something that is shared with others. Language needs a 'yes'. It is like saying 'Hello!', 'Here I am', 'Yes, we are speaking' (Derrida 1992a: 297). It precedes speech and cannot be erased from it.

> The minimal, primary *yes*, the telephonic 'hello' or the tap through a prison wall, marks, before meaning or signifying: 'I here', listen, answer, there is some mark, there is some other. Negatives may ensue, but even if they completely take over, this *yes* can no longer be erased.
>
> (Derrida 1992a: 298)

Derrida also conceptualises the idea of affirmation as a *promise* that is inherent in communication. All language use entails a promise, even language with which one lies or hurts other people. It is the fundamental structure of language.

> This general structure is such that one cannot imagine a language that is not in a certain way caught up in the space of the promise. Before I even decide what I am going to say, I promise to speak to you, I respond to the promise to speak, I respond. I respond to you as soon as I speak and consequently I commit or pledge myself.
>
> (Derrida 1995a: 384)

Even if we here see a distant affinity with Wittgenstein and a closer one with Levinas, who will be discussed later, the idea of language being ethical should not be exaggerated. Derrida is ambivalent on this point. On the one hand he sees a 'yes' standing in the background of communication, but on the other he is quick to reveal violence and power as well. This will become more apparent later on when deconstruction is discussed.

## Comparing Derrida and Wittgenstein

We have already seen that some similarities exist between Derrida's and Wittgenstein's views on language as well as their ways of doing philosophy (see, for example, Cavell 1995; see, also, Zerilli 2001). According to Henry Staten, who makes interesting comparisons between the two thinkers, Derrida's project is parallel to that of Wittgenstein's (Staten 1985: xiv). Of course, this cannot be said of everything in Derrida's oeuvre, his thinking spanning across such vast areas, but it is a reasonable description of his philosophy of language. Staten compares

Derrida's idea of différance with Wittgenstein's ideas of grammar (Staten 1985: 26). Both philosophers place importance on the structure and function of language. For Wittgenstein grammar is important. A system of language with a grammar is always already there when we use language. Likewise for Derrida, the structure of iterability and the play of differences are features of language that affect all language use. A sign can mean something only in a chain of references. To wonder about the meaning of a single word abstracted from its context and ways of use leads us astray as signs have meaning only in relation to other signs. Wittgenstein says this very clearly. Words get their meaning in grammar and in the ways in which they are used. We can recall, for instance, his discussion of the use of the word 'good'. It is a combination of several interrelated games, each of them a different aspect of the use. The concept is the relationship between these aspects. Derrida discusses language similarly following Saussure: signs function in connection with other signs.

Derrida stresses that meaning can never be fully present in itself and there cannot be such a thing as literal meaning. This is compatible with Wittgenstein's ideas. He says, for instance, that sometimes what we need might be a concept with blurred edges. Both philosophers argue that language is not a static or strict system in which every word would have a defined referent. Meaning is not like a halo that the word carries around with it, Wittgenstein says. The meanings of words can be studied by looking at the many different ways that they are used. Likewise, Derrida underlines the practical aspects of language.

For both philosophers the meaning of a word has no essence. It *is* nothing. Meaning is not a thing. It is not a mental representation of a sign, nor is there any language of the mind. A context can give meaning to an utterance, but contexts have no limits. Thus both philosophers agree that the sign does not belong to the one who utters it (see Staten 1985: 85, 122–125). On the reading put forward here they also share an understanding of the openness and flexibility of meaning. For a theory of interpretation this means that the ultimate goal of interpretation cannot be to find out the speaker's original intention or the original meaning of the text. There is no such thing as original meaning because meaning is always already fractured. And once something is said it lives on. Language directs us towards new meanings.

Wittgenstein and Derrida understand language not as neutral or detached from people but in close connection to our lives. However, Derrida focuses on choices of meaning and the element of force that can be involved in these in a way that is foreign to Wittgensteinian thinking (see, also, Kauppinen 2000: 39). Wittgenstein thinks that for language to have meaning people have to share a way of living and some fundamental values. This might be so, but for Derrida an even more important issue to consider is the way meanings are defined and chosen from several possible meanings. This topic is discussed in more detail in connection to deconstruction in the next chapter.

Another idea that Wittgenstein and Derrida share on this reading, although the topic is not developed very thoroughly in Derrida's work and certainly not in

Wittgenstein's, is the thought of language presupposing a kind of welcome or saying 'yes' to another person. Wittgenstein's remark on meaning as going up to someone implies this as well as his remarks about a shared life being a necessary background for language. This is close to Derrida's thoughts about language including an affirmation, a response to another person. The affirmation takes place by necessity whenever we use language because it is the starting point of communication. Likewise for Wittgenstein: we share language and form(s) of life and this ultimately makes meaning possible.

Chapter 3

# Reading the law – hermeneutics and deconstruction

A view on language is sketched in the above chapters but many difficult questions remain. How can we say that a legal judgment is based on a text? How do we decide what the text means and what it commands? With the insights into language drawn from Wittgenstein and Derrida we are now better equipped to tackle these questions. But these theories contain nothing that can anchor meaning for the purposes of a theory of legal interpretation. It is necessary to widen the scope of research from the philosophy of language to interpretation and understanding on a more general level. This way we may get a better grip on the difficult questions of legal interpretation. Therefore, after the rather narrow discussion of language and meaning, the question that now has to be addressed is that of interpretation. We can already see that it is unavoidable to study interpretation as an activity, not just language as a system, in order to be able to answer any questions concerning legal interpretation. When focusing on the activity of interpretation, the interconnectedness of meaning and the choices of living, people in different circumstances become more visible. Interpretation is always done by someone in a certain time and place. In this chapter, interpretation is studied in the hermeneutics of Hans-Georg Gadamer and the semiotics of Umberto Eco. After this we can turn to Derrida's deconstruction, which includes a critique of hermeneutics.

## A hermeneutic view on interpretation

Hermeneutics is one of the great philosophical schools of thought of the twentieth century. Philosophical hermeneutics has roots in Heidegger's philosophy, but the central work is Gadamer's *Truth and Method*, published in German in 1960. Gadamer is first and foremost interested in human understanding. He develops the hermeneutical circle described by Heidegger.[1] The idea in its simplicity is that in order for us to understand anything we already have to understand something. But if all understanding depends on previous understanding, we are trapped in a circle.

1 See, also, for example, Llewelyn (1985: 99) on the ways in which Gadamer's philosophy is inspired by Heidegger.

However, the circle is not a vicious one. It is what makes understanding possible. For instance, a person who wants to understand a text constructs for themselves the meaning of the whole text as soon as they are able to grasp any meaning in it. And they are able to understand any meaning in the text only because they have some presuppositions about what the text means. Understanding is a process, where new meanings are projected continuously (see Gadamer 1979: 236). A person is always inside a horizon consisting of his or her presuppositions.

In hermeneutics, understanding and interpretation are intertwined and their structure is circular or spiral. The interpretation of a text takes place in this circular movement. The interpreter's anticipation of the text as meaning something, saying something understandable, is the attitude they have at the beginning of the interpretation process. This anticipation of meaning involves stepping into the hermeneutic circle. The interpreter is only able to understand meaning in a text because they have some presuppositions about what the text means. But this anticipation is only the step into the circle. Once inside the process, the prejudices of the interpreter are replaced by new ones as the interpretation evolves. This view of interpretation stresses the relationship between the parts and the whole. We can understand the whole only through understanding its parts, but the whole also determines the meaning of the parts. The two-way movement from parts to whole to parts is a basic structure of interpretation, and the task of the interpreter is to create a meaning for the whole. The harmony of the parts and the whole is one criterion for successful understanding.

In hermeneutics, interpretation is seen as taking place within a tradition without it being possible to take the interpretation out of the tradition or the tradition out of the activity of interpretation. Since tradition and historicity are important aspects of any interpretation, hermeneutics strives for a contextual, even situational, understanding of a text. Tradition, the text's home, as well as the place and time of the interpretation, should be taken into account when we strive for an understanding of the text.

> It is not, then, at all a case of safeguarding ourselves against the tradition that speaks out of the text but, on the contrary, to keep everything away that could hinder us in understanding it in terms of the thing. It is the tyranny of hidden prejudices that makes us deaf to the language that speaks to us in tradition.
>
> (Gadamer 1979: 239)

A text can of course use language in a manner different from ours. According to Gadamer, we usually notice language use that is different from ours in that a text does not seem to convey any meaning or the meaning is not reconcilable with what we expected. It is not the case that the reader can hold any meaning as the meaning of a text. He or she has presuppositions about the meaning and at the same time waits for the text to mean something – he or she seldom waits for it to mean nothing or anything. We have the right to suppose that, except in some exceptional circumstances, a person who speaks the same language as we, speaks it in the same intelligible manner as we do (Gadamer 1979: 237–238).

## Being open to the text

Tradition and prejudices are necessary for interpretation, but they do not absolve our responsibility for it. Prejudices are replaced by new and more appropriate ones as the interpretation evolves. Moreover, the tradition to which the text is seen to belong does not determine interpretation; at most, it pushes it in some direction. When we interpret a text we have to be both prejudiced and open to its meaning. We have to assume that the text wants to tell us something but not decide too rigidly what that something is. Our presuppositions should not be static so that we hold on to an anticipated meaning even where the text wants to tell us something else. At the core of hermeneutics is the requirement of sensitivity to the text's *newness*. What is important is that the interpreter has a basic level of self-knowledge that enables them to understand and acknowledge their presuppositions so that the text can show its own truth against them (Gadamer 1979: 238). Thus hermeneutics searches for the text's truth, its own new and singular meaning.

According to Gadamer, all language, including interpretation of texts, should be seen as conversation or dialogue. It becomes evident that one crucial precondition of interpretation is to listen to the other (be it a written text or a person talking) and be open to what the other wants to say (Gadamer 1979: 238; see, also, Taylor 2002: 127–128). '[L]anguage is conversation. One must look for the word that can reach another person. And it is possible for one to find it [...]' (Gadamer 1989a: 106).

What is essential in language for Gadamer just like it is for Wittgenstein is that it is an activity of sharing and being with somebody. According to Gadamer, every time language occurs, whether a text, a word or a whisper, conversation also occurs (Gadamer 1989b: 95). Language should not be studied and described abstractly because this gives an unnatural picture of what it is. Gadamer remarks in *Truth and Method* that Wittgenstein's idea of language games seemed natural to him when he came across it (Gadamer 1979: 500, note 12).[2] Language always has some context. It involves a constantly changing common way of being in the world, a shared orientation and shared understandings. This way language and understanding possess a social and ethical character (see Palmer 2006: 2–3). Language is living speech and writing.

Being open to a text, which is a prerequisite for understanding, is like engaging in a conversation with it. Thus the only way for an interpreter to understand the text is to listen to it and try to grasp what it wants to say. This dialogical structure is for Gadamer what makes the hermeneutic experience universal. Language is conversation always and everywhere: 'The word is what one person speaks and another understands' (Gadamer 1989b: 95). This universality entails language, meaning and interpretation being grounded in dialogue and inter-human

2 Gadamer refers to Wittgenstein on several occasions. He also mentions language games, for instance in 'Classical and Philosophical Hermeneutics' (2006b: 46) (see, also, Llewelyn 1985: 103).

understanding, which establishes a foundation for hermeneutics at a profound level (see Gadamer 2006b: 35). Hermeneutics is a general basis for all understanding as well as a background against which a variety of scholarly disciplines can be built.

Gadamer seems to be fully aware of the risk involved in dialogue. The speaker may mean something but be interpreted as saying something else. Meaning is never simply something that is transported from one person to another.

> What is pushed aside or dislocated when my word reaches another person, and especially when a text reaches its reader, can never be fixed in a rigid identity. Where understanding takes place, there is not just an identity. Rather, to *understand* means that one is capable of stepping into the place of the other in order to say what one has there understood and what one has to say in response.
>
> (Gadamer 1989b: 96, emphasis in original)

To understand what the other says is to be able to *respond* to them. But it is never easy to understand, and what we understand is not exactly what the other person says. And what is more, one cannot say fully and exactly what one means.

> Of course there is a person who speaks, but not without being restricted by language, for it is not always the right word that comes to one. Hermeneutics helps us to realize that there is always much that remains unsaid when one says something.[3]
>
> (Gadamer 2006a: 91)

A successful interpretation happens through a fusion of the horizons of the interpreter and the text. In conversation, the horizons of the participants must merge in order for understanding to be possible (see Gadamer 1989c: 119). Likewise in interpretation, the horizon of the interpreter has to merge with that of the text in order for interpretation to succeed. The risk in this way of thinking is that interpretation turns into a totalising activity in which the horizon of the interpreter, their prejudices and their tradition, come to dominate the horizon of the text, losing the otherness of the text in the hegemony of the interpreter. This is a Levinasian critique of hermeneutics to which Gadamer responds by underlining openness to the meaning of the other as a prerequisite for understanding. 'One must seek to understand the other, and that means that one has to believe that one could be in the wrong' (Gadamer 1989c: 119). Thus the idea of horizons fusing is not to be understood as the idea that the text is absorbed in the horizon of the interpreter, which would indeed mean a form of violence done to the text. Neither does communication carry one person's opinion across to another's but transforms the viewpoints

3 Here some rather obvious similarities with Derrida's conception of language can be heard.

of both (Gadamer 2006c: 17). Gadamer seeks to understand the other, but not to own them. And he underlines the need for the interpreter to be aware at all times of their fallibility.

The idea of dialogue also concerns our relationship with tradition. We are always in a tradition, and tradition plays a role in interpretation. The dialogue that understanding is takes place within a tradition and in itself forms part of a tradition, but dialogue also occurs *with* the tradition. As stated above, the tradition and the prejudices and presuppositions we have on entering a dialogue with the text are replaced by new ones during interpretation of the text, that is, in conversation with it. We enter into a dialogue with the tradition as well: it is by no means a fixed entity, something predetermined, or a straightjacket restricting our interpretation, but should rather be seen as a flexible background in which and through which interpretation takes place. Tradition is neither something given nor something clearly distinguishable. In fact, it is not clear how to separate a text and its tradition. All texts belong to some tradition, and a tradition is nothing other than a collection of texts.

> When I speak there [in *Truth and Method*] of tradition and of conversation with tradition, I am in no way putting forward a collective subject. Rather, 'tradition' is simply the collective name for each individual text (text in the widest sense, which would include a picture, an architectural work, even a natural event).
>
> (Gadamer 1989a: 111)

A conversation always carries with it the risk of misunderstanding. This risk looms at every interpretation. It is inevitable. It stems from language, since meaning is always slightly open and slippery.

> Language is such that, whatever particular meaning a word may possess, words do not have a single unchanging meaning; rather, they possess a fluctuating range of meaning, and precisely this fluctuation constitutes the peculiar risk of speaking. Only in the process of speaking, as we speak further, as we build up the fabric of a linguistic context, do we come to fix the meanings in the moments of meaning of our speaking, only in this way do we mutually agree on what we mean.
>
> (Gadamer 2006c: 25)

There is no final meaning for a text, nor is there an ordinary meaning. Gadamer puts it beautifully: '[...] the conversation that we are is one that never ends. No word is the last word, just as there is no first word. Every word is itself always an answer and gives rise always to a new question' (Gadamer 1989b: 95). We see that hermeneutics can leave room for otherness and differences. For Gadamer, the essence of understanding is to be responsive to 'what aims at being said beyond all words sought after or found' (Gadamer 1989c: 118).

## On the ethics of hermeneutics

If prejudices are necessary for understanding a text, how do we draw the line between acceptable interpretation and unacceptable interpretation? What if the reader is bad? A bad reader is, according to Derrida, a fearful reader, a reader in a hurry, or one who does not like retracing their steps (Derrida 1987: 4; see, also, Lindroos-Hovinheimo 2009). We may even call him or her violent if they use power against the text, stubbornly reading it in their own way. Such a reader is, in short, disrespectful of the text. Is this a danger that looms behind the picture of a hermeneutic interpreter? Are they respectful enough? Can Gadamer's views be criticised on account of his not recognising the threat of the bad reader?

We should not think of prejudices simply as conditions of understanding that somehow determine the outcome of the interpretation process. Rather, Gadamer thinks that interpretation is always subject to revision when we encounter new evidence or information (see Grondin 2002: 44). We do have anticipations of the meaning of a text when we start reading and interpreting it, but they are, and should be, shattered in the process of interpreting the text. This may be exactly what 'retracing one's steps' means. Ultimately, what is necessary in understanding is openness to something new, something other, and a readiness to replace one's prejudices by new ones (see Gadamer 1979: 323–325). The interpretation process creates something that is unique every time (see Gadamer 1989c: 117). In Gadamer's view, the interpreter learns something every time they interpret the text, just as the participants in a conversation can never know in advance where the conversation is taking them, or control it, or direct it towards a predetermined meaning.

The hermeneutical method does not guarantee 'correct' interpretation. This would require that the understanding reached would fully correspond to the 'fundamental' or 'true' meaning of a text. Gadamer's theory gives no guarantees. This can be understood to mean that the ideal of objectivity is abandoned. But the hermeneutical circle is for Gadamer neither subjective nor objective. Hermeneutics is a way of thinking that dissolves traditional conceptions of objectivity and subjectivity. An interpreter is always necessarily inside some tradition, time and world. Although in Gadamer's view no definite meaning is contained in any text or work, the interpreter's preconditions structure the interpretation in the sense that it cannot result in arbitrary meanings. Still, no fixed or fundamental meaning exists because anything that means something means it for someone in some place and time (see Llewelyn 1985: 103–105).

Hence hermeneutics does not include a search for the original meaning of a text seen as an author's original intention. As was discussed already in connection to Derrida, the text, be it a spoken utterance or a written statement, takes on an independent life after it leaves the author. The text and its meaning are no longer dependent on the author's intentions, which is not to say that the author's intentions are wholly irrelevant. Gadamer considers the case of a work of art. A work of art, unlike an object or handicraft, is not made for a designated use. It is in a strange way suspended from use as well as from misuse. It stands for itself and exists for its own sake. The intention of the artist has somehow gone into the work of art and can no longer be determined separately from it, nor found behind it or before it. Works of art are detached from their origins and begin to speak independently. When it comes to poetry or literature, Gadamer thinks that no word or sentence refers directly back to the intention of the author. Things are rather the other way around: every reader is subjected to the command of the text. The work in itself has something to say to us (Gadamer 1989c: 123). Thus the work of art enjoys autonomy in leaving the sphere of influence of its author.

A work of art has something to say to us: it commands something of us; it demands a response. It is a kind of sovereign that can give us orders. We see this in Gadamer's insistence on our being open to the text and its unique meaning; it is a short leap, almost no step at all, to the requirement of responsible interpretation. Openness is not restricted to mere neutrality but demands a more active stance in the interpreter. The sovereign authority of the work of art is also a call for responsible answers and dialogue (see Derrida 2004: 6). The interpreter has a responsibility before the work, a responsibility that he cannot avoid.

What I suggest here is that we can read Gadamer's hermeneutics as including an ethical element. What lies at the core of his theory is a willingness to understand, to listen to what somebody wants to say. To understand what the other says is to be able to respond to them. Also, the idea about the tradition can be read as meaning that the interpreter is never alone; they always carry with themselves the tradition and hence, other people (see Llewelyn 1985: 101). Thus we can see Gadamer's ideas being perhaps closer to a Levinasian view than would seem to be the case at first sight. In hermeneutics, language is communication and being together, so that interpretation necessarily involves a welcoming.

How, then, does this way of thinking provide any means of limiting interpretation? After all, hermeneutics does not offer us a clear method of interpreting: it does not give us any rules or procedures for how to interpret and it does not deliver criteria by which to determine a good interpretation from a bad one. However, it is not even the aim of an ethical view of interpretation to be able to develop clear rules. This should not be seen as a lack. First, it would be unwise to suggest that the only way to draw up some boundaries or limits for interpretation would be by defining a method including rules, which the interpreter, for instance a judge, would be obliged to follow. How a rule is followed is not something self-evident and, as can be seen from Wittgenstein's various remarks on rule-following, the power of rules to draw clear limits for an activity is questionable. This approach is therefore not what an ethical view of interpretation is after. But an ethical view does still search for ways of limiting interpretation; it simply does not believe that these limits can be found in methodological rules.

## Hermeneutics and law

Many differences set legal interpretation apart from other forms of interpretation. Let us concentrate on Gadamer's discussion of the work of art in which he stresses its autonomy. A work of art has a history of interpretations or readings, but to understand it and for the work to be able to speak to us, we do not need to know all it has been through (see Gadamer 1989c: 123). Likewise, the legal text has a degree of independence, but is it more like some handicraft?

Regarding the autonomy of legal texts, we face severe difficulties in specifying the identity of the text, including where it begins and ends. This was also seen above in discussion on the pragmatics of legal language. A marked feature of legal texts is their intertextuality. They usually refer both explicitly and implicitly to other texts. Legal texts can seldom be seen as independent or complete works; rather, they are like pieces in a puzzle. But to some degree this is true of all texts. Furthermore, because of this intertextual nature as well as because of the purposes for and situations in which they are written and read, legal texts do not speak to us alone. In addition to referring to other texts, they also refer to previous interpretations of themselves and of other texts. We do not need to know all that the legal text has been through in order for us to be able to make a legal interpretation of it, but we have to know a lot. Still, one could argue that some common features link interpreting a legal text and interpreting a work of art. The legal text, like the work of art, has a life independent of its author. Legal interpretation has to stay open to the meaning of the text itself, not simply to what the author(s) perhaps wanted to say.

An important feature in hermeneutics is that here interpretation, understanding and application are mixed. They amount to more or less the same thing. Interpretation and application of law are intertwined activities in that we always interpret the normative content of law from the point of view of a certain (or hypothetical) case. Interpretation has a goal that is inherent in the need to find an answer to the situation at hand. Hermeneutics is sensitive to the particularities of different interpretation situations. Gadamer says in his discussion of legal hermeneutics that to understand an order is to apply it to the specific situation to which it is relevant. 'The criterion of understanding is clearly not in the actual words of the order, nor in the mind of the person giving the order, but solely in the understanding of the situation and the responsibleness of the person who obeys' (Gadamer 1979: 298). The situation has to be understood, for sure. But I want to highlight not the responsibility of the one who obeys but the one who interprets. The most important feature of legal interpretation is the challenge that doing justice places on it. It is the ultimate criterion by which legal interpretations are measured. A necessary pretension to justice is built into the work of all legal institutions, and this way a requirement for justice is inherent in legal interpretation (see, also, MacCormick 2007: 276). The demand for justice influences the interpretation of legal texts and hence shapes the meaning of law, that is, what we can say to be in accordance with the law or prohibited by it.

We have now studied some features of Gadamer's hermeneutics, from which a certain view on what interpretation is has started to develop. Some preliminary remarks on the ethical elements contained in understanding and the responsibility of the interpreter have been sketched. It is necessary to ponder these ideas more deeply in order for us to be able to see what this approach really entails and, more importantly, what this kind of approach could give us when we consider the particular demands of legal interpretation.

## Eco and the text's rights

To understand the interpreter as an active agent with responsibility instead of somebody who can hide behind the meanings of words is a central idea in this book. This suggests that we can assess and criticise interpretive choices that have been made. In this section the ideas of interpretation and over-interpretation developed by Eco are studied because he makes an attempt to solve some of the puzzles regarding the freedom of the interpreter and the correctness of interpretation. A text can be given many meanings but should not be given just any meaning. There has to be something that limits interpretation, at the same time as a text always allows for multiple meanings. Eco thinks that a text cannot perhaps have one correct interpretation but that not all interpretations are equally good. There are better and worse interpretations of a text. The problem is of course how we tell these apart.

Eco thinks that the *text itself* and its particular characteristics set the limits for a successful interpretation. However, it is hard to find an answer from him on what these characteristics are exactly and how they set the demarcation between an acceptable and an unacceptable interpretation. In *Interpretation and Overinterpretation*, he distinguishes between the text's rights and the interpreter's rights, remarking that in recent discussions the interpreter has been given too powerful a role (Eco 1992: 23). Eco seems to claim that in interpretation, which is influenced both by the object of interpretation, that is, the text, and by an actor, that is, the interpreter, the text should be given the central position that belongs to it. The interpreter is never totally free in their actions; the text delimits them. Eco distinguishes between: (a) the intention of the author of the text; (b) the intention of the text; and (c) the intention of the interpreter. The intention that should be in focus, Eco claims, is that of the text. A good interpretation concentrates on finding the intention of the text (Eco 1992: 24–25).

What, then, is the intention of the text, which Eco finds so crucial for distinguishing a good interpretation from a bad one? It cannot be found on the mere surface of the text. To grasp it, conscious and focused effort is needed. The intention of the text is to create a *model reader*, who can make assumptions about the meaning of the text. To find out a text's intention is to recognise a certain semiotic strategy, which can sometimes be deduced from some stylistic features of the text. For instance, if the text begins with 'once upon a time', we can assume that the model reader is a child (Eco 1992: 64–65).

Semiotics often emphasises the importance of finding the right frequency of interpretation, the right code. Relevant factors are, for instance, the historical situation and the interpreter's characteristics, such as education and upbringing. A lawyer is trained to interpret legal texts, finding different meanings in them than a layman. However, this kind of analysis of a model reader does not take us very far. To find out what class or type the text belongs to is no doubt important, but it is seldom the problem. A legal text is usually quite easy to recognise, but to decide what the text commands, what it stipulates or what it allows is another matter. The schooling of a lawyer does not determine the interpretation that he or she makes. All texts, including legal ones, involve some openness, and in a way the difficult task of the interpreter begins after the text has been decided to be a certain kind of text, for instance a legal text. There is always room for interpretation in a particular category of texts. Lawyers and literature researchers alike are seldom unanimous regarding the correct interpretation of a text, regardless of their education and training. We can agree with Gadamer here:

> It is certainly correct that a certain decoding process underlies all writing and reading of texts, but this represents merely a precondition for hermeneutic attention to what is said in the words.
>
> (Gadamer 1989a: 112)

However, the importance of the first step of interpretation, in which the text is identified as belonging to a certain group of texts, should not be underestimated either. The interpretation process in law is of a particular nature. In order for legal reasoning to be able to claim at least a certain degree of autonomy, it is important to trace how we can define legal interpretation as properly legal. Eco gives us clues to this with his idea of semiotic strategies. They can be seen to include the particular encyclopaedic knowledge that a member of the legal sphere has learnt to use when engaged in legal interpretation. With the help of semiotic strategy, we can recognise a legal text and decide on the different ways that it can be understood. Semiotic strategy does not, however, explain how and why one meaning should be chosen instead of others.

According to Eco, the way to examine what the intention of a text is entails studying the text as a coherent whole. The internal coherence of the text, its own structure, controls an otherwise uncontrollable reader (Eco 1992: 65). Interpretations of different parts of the text have to fit together. However, this still leaves much open. Surely examples exist of coherent interpretations of texts that we still could not consider good interpretations. A functioning interpretation rests on the features of the text on which a coherent whole can be built, but this means that some other features are considered secondary or irrelevant at the same time (see Eco 1992: 144–146). The interpreter thus has great power over the meaning of a text.

Although Eco focuses on the text and its intentions, he does pay attention to the interpreter as well. The interpreter has to be competent. He or she has to have sufficient knowledge of the encyclopaedia. Every interpreting situation is a difficult encounter in which the competence of the interpreter and the competence that the text requires stand face to face.

## Interpretation or use?

Eco distinguishes between interpretation and use of texts. A text can be *used* for many things: it can be parodied, used as inspiration or as a sleeping aid. *Interpretation* means that the text's cultural and linguistic background is respected (Eco 1992: 69). To use a text is to exploit it for personal, political or ideological reasons. Interpretation, on the other hand, respects the text itself. In a way, Eco pinpoints this respect on a respect for the semantic meaning of the utterances that the text consists of.[4] When a text is used, its semantic meanings are not respected and the interpreter is reading it as he or she wants. He seems to partially identify false interpretation with use. However, he admits that an element of use is always present in interpretation, and that these two ways of encountering texts cannot always be clearly separated (see Eco 1990: 57–58, 62). A reader often uses and interprets a text at the same reading.

Even if we cannot clearly say where interpretation stops and use begins, use is the type of reading that is freer in Eco's theory. Interpretation can be good or bad, and ultimately it is the community's opinion and other interpretations that determine whether it is good or bad, but use of a text is in a way revolutionary. By using texts we can break free from earlier and approved interpretations and come to a new understanding of the text (Eco 1990: 62). Using a text is thus a means for the interpreter to free themselves from the conformity of interpretation and cannot be seen simply as something negative directed against the intention of the text. In using texts, we do not first try to establish what the text wants to say and it is not the intention of the text that directs the reading. Using a text is imposing the reader's intentions on it, but it is not the case that an encounter with a text is always at best interpretation and at worst use.

Eco sees a good interpretation as one that the consensus of the community would accept. His argument is based on the Peircean notion of habit in that the convention of the community is something similar to an ultimate criterion for a successful interpretation. Interpretation thus gets an intersubjective character, which lends it a degree of objectivity (see Petrilli and Ponzio 2005: 336). Here, Eco sees a similarity between his own views and Gadamer's ideas on tradition (Eco 1992: 144). Eco leaves room for new and groundbreaking interpretations in saying that a good interpretation can be built on preceding ones accepted in the community and at the same time form a new way of interpreting. An interpretation may be new and different, but only time will tell whether it is a good one. The

4 See also Eco's discussion on the differences between the meaning of words and the understanding of utterances (and texts) (Eco 2000: 270–279).

question that arises then is what help we have from Eco's theory in the interpretation situation when we try to achieve a good or just interpretation.

Eco attaches much weight to the community and its approval. His version of Popper's falsification thesis is that even if we cannot prove that any interpretation is absolutely the right one, we can still reach an agreement that certain interpretations are not allowed for contextual reasons. An air of pragmatism permeates Eco's views, which is perhaps natural when considering the close connection between his thinking and Peirce's semiotics. A good interpretation is one that the community comes to accept, use and base new interpretations on. Eco says:

> In spite of the obvious differences in degrees of certainty and uncertainty, every picture of the world (be it a scientific law or a novel) is a book in its own right, open to further interpretation. But certain interpretations can be recognized as unsuccessful because they are like a mule, that is, they are unable to produce new interpretations or cannot be confronted with the traditions of the previous interpretations.
>
> (Eco 1992: 150)

Bad interpretations are like mules: they are disconnected from the history and the future of the practice and tainted by uselessness.

When we try to transfer Eco's thinking to the field of legal interpretation, we encounter some problems. Clearly, he does not have in mind an activity in which the text interpreted has a normative character as it has in legal interpretation. Legal interpretation usually includes both interpretation and use. It is never neutral. When legal texts are interpreted, they are often used at the same time because the activity of interpretation has highly practical aims in law. Could the ideal of interpreting rather than using texts be of value in law? To think of interpretation as a respectful activity in contrast with (ab)use has a nice ring to it and could be combined with Gadamerian ideas of openness to the text. It seems that when seeking the meaning of a text, we should perhaps approach it with the respect that Eco has in mind, not with an agenda of making the most of the text for our own purposes. Why? Because this may be the only way for us to be able to say what a text means, what it wants to say. And in legal interpretation we want to know what a text means. Not definitely and for all eternity but with relevance to *this* case and *this* practical situation.

Legal actors often bend the meaning of legal texts to their own advantage. However, disinterested interpretation is also needed, and we can by no means assume that interpretation in the legal field is only (ab)use. All understanding has to involve a neutral element, something that is not totally determined by the egoistic choices of the interpreter, otherwise it would be hard to see how sharing meanings, that is, communication, would be possible at all. In the legal field, in situations where law is read with the parties' own interests in sight, there is also a common ground, a common legal language and a tradition within which legal interpretation moves in order for it to succeed at all. The idea of respectful interpretation, where the text itself is respected, as distinguished from mere use, is an interesting way of solving the problem of how to decide on a good interpretation when different conflicting ones are available. It is here, in the distinction between interpretation and use, that Eco's theory can be helpful. The intention of the text should reign supreme over the intentions of the different readers of the text. The task of the trained legal interpreter, the judge, is to hear what the text itself commands.

But at the same time, law constitutes a peculiar sign system in that more often than not new and groundbreaking interpretations are especially fruitful. In addition to the fact that interpretation as use is accepted for several reasons and even considered required behaviour by many lawyers, these interpretations, which often represent a borderline between accepted and not accepted, are what develop law. This makes law a flexible system keeping up with the developments surrounding it. It also enables law to stretch so that it covers all sorts of situations, that is, the multitude of people's lives. Law should be able to evolve in the practice of interpretation. Room should be available for over- and under-interpretation in order for law to change and develop. Still, there should be some limits on interpretation as well, not least because of justice. Hence it seems that legal interpretation has to be both free and restricted.

Eco wants to stress the text itself against theories that focus on the interpreter. But it seems that his own way of thinking, in which safeguards from arbitrary choices made by interpreters come from focusing on the text itself and its intention, is not enough to achieve its aims. If the aim is to respect the rights of the text, this task naturally falls on the interpreter and the focus shifts to *their responsibility* towards the text. I refer here to Derrida's idea of the bad reader: the power and the responsibility of the interpreter become the focal point even when we emphasise the rights of the text. If we want to hold on to the distinctions between the three factors of interpretation as Eco does (that is, the producer of the text, the interpreter of the text, and the text itself), then respecting the text's intention actually amounts to the same thing as focusing on the interpreter and their responsibility. The text lies naturally at the core of any account that tries to define the responsibility of reading or the ethics of interpretation. But the text only gets the importance it deserves if we pay attention to the choices of the interpreter, who has to approach the text with openness and respect.

We have seen that a discussion on the conditions of the possibility of understanding leads to questions of openness, dialogue and responsibility, which imply that questions of meaning are simultaneously questions of ethical importance. The interpretation situation described both by Gadamer's hermeneutics and Eco's semiotics opens up a space where the choices and the power of the interpreter are highlighted, and both theories lead us to focus on the responsibility of interpretation.

## Deconstruction

It seems that the crisis of legal interpretation referred to earlier haunts us still. Even though hermeneutics and Eco's semiotics are attempts to account for what happens when texts are interpreted, it seems nevertheless that they do not provide answers to the problems of legal interpretation. They do not fully take into account the problems that language and undecideability bring with them. They are not able to give us criteria on which to decide the meanings of legal texts, which can lead to doubts about justice. But it becomes more and more doubtful after this discussion that any criteria could ever be found. A different approach is needed and I shall continue sketching it by looking at deconstruction as a way of reading.

Derrida has on many occasions commented upon the word 'deconstruction' and the fact that the word has become so common that it is used in a variety of purposes both in academic circles as well as in some popular writings. He describes deconstruction as an attempt to bring together Heidegger's *Destruktion* and Husserl's *Abbau*. *Destruktion* is not suitable for Derrida's means because it has a negative connotation linked to destroying, a Nietzschean crushing. Deconstruction is meant to refer to something else. It is interested in structures, and the way structuralism operates is a starting point, although it is a point beyond which deconstruction moves (Derrida 1988b). Deconstruction studies especially linguistic, cultural, political and philosophical structures by disrupting them. This is not only something negative as the aim is not to break and put in pieces but to take the pieces apart in order to see how they are held together.

Derrida developed deconstruction very early in his thinking: it is already discussed in *Of Grammatology*. His attitude towards it varied over the years. At times, he uses the term 'frequently', and at others he expresses doubts about its usability. He was critical of the term especially later in his work, where he proposed other terms instead, for instance 'inscription' or 'double writing'. In fact, the term became so widely used and certainly also misused that it is easy to see Derrida growing tired of it. Likewise, it is easy to understand his annoyance at the critical attacks that were directed towards his work, which usually drew on a misreading of his texts or, as he often suspected, no reading at all.[5]

The notion of deconstruction is certainly not simple, and difficulties in understanding it perhaps stem partly from the impossibility of giving it a comprehensive definition. It seems to be easier to say what it is not than to state what it is. It is not a method (see Derrida 1984: 124).[6] It cannot be limited because it turns against itself as soon as it is defined as something. It cannot be used as a foundation for a system and it does not have any structure, because it dissolves structures

5 See for example, Christopher Norris (1990) on (especially American) misunderstandings of Derrida's thinking. See also Critchley's rather outspoken account of the mistreatment Derrida received in the English-speaking world (Critchley 2008: 26–27).

6 Method means here a worked-out tool kit of some kind. Nevertheless, just as Wittgenstein claims that he is not working out a theory, if we understand theory in a wide sense it is clear that his writing is a kind of theorising. Also, Gadamer's hermeneutics is not a method, if we understand method in a narrow sense. However, deconstruction (like hermeneutics) can certainly be understood as a way of reading, even if not a strict method with rules of procedure.

and systems. It has no existence before the text. It is a happening of the text. It is something that happens in a reading. Critchley points out that Derrida always preferred to refer to deconstructions, in the plural. This emphasises that deconstruction is not a thing but a praxis (Critchley 2008: 21). Every reader and reading is historical and all texts are open to deconstruction. The text itself, its words and sentences, enable different meanings. This way one can say that the text in a way deconstructs itself. Deconstruction includes sensitivity towards different meanings, some hidden better than others. It analyses the structures as well as the contradictions and incoherencies of a text. It is a way of reading in which meticulous attention is paid to how meaning is produced in the text through différance and a complex play of signification (see Derrida 1984: 125).

Still, deconstruction is something other and more than mere analysis or critique of texts. Because it can always be the object of deconstruction itself, it is something that cannot be definitely explained. Derrida has to say that deconstruction is anything and nothing (Derrida 1988b). Here we hear echoes of the difficulties we face when studying language in a language, as faced by Wittgenstein as well. No neutral medium is available in which to study language. It has to be done in and through language. Derrida says that deconstruction is modest in the sense that it admits that it is only one textual interpretation among others and that it has no privileged meta-language. This leads to the difficult language that Derrida is forced to use in order to be able to say anything at all about deconstruction. He uses different concepts and neologisms to express his ideas. In addition to passages where he describes his central thoughts, the idea of deconstruction can perhaps be best grasped if we consider how Derrida himself reads.

Most of Derrida's writings are actually readings of texts. His method of philosophising and bringing forth his thoughts is that of commentary and deconstruction. A good example of what a deconstructive reading is like is Derrida's own reading of Rousseau and Saussure in *Of Grammatology*, by which he uncovers the preconditions and presuppositions at play in the texts. His deconstruction of logocentrism entails that he questions the possibility of meaning being present for itself and the way this has been taken for granted in many theories as well as what this way of thinking has led to. This exposition or even *excavation*, if you like, of underlying structures and preconditions is an excellent example of deconstruction at work.

In connection with the discussion of Rousseau's theory of language, Derrida explains his way of reading. I shall concentrate on this for a moment in order to study some central features of deconstruction. He considers, among other things, the freedom of the interpreter. How far is a deconstructive reading allowed to interpret the text of an author, how surprising connections and anomalies should it be allowed to reveal, connections that the author might be fully unaware of? Derrida says:

> [t]he writer writes *in* a language and *in* a logic whose proper system, laws, and life his [*sic*] discourse by definition cannot dominate absolutely. He uses them

> only by letting himself, after a fashion and up to a point, be governed by the system. And the reading must always aim at a certain relationship, unperceived by the writer, between what he commands and what he does not command of the patterns of the language that he uses. This relationship is not a certain quantitative distribution of shadow and light, of weakness or of force, but a signifying structure that critical reading should *produce*.
>
> (Derrida 1976: 158, emphasis in original)

The 'produce' here does not consist of a reproduction or respectful commentary, although this, too, is important. The reading that Derrida proposes and claims to do himself is not a mere doubling commentary. However, he does not propose that the reading should try to reach something outside the text either, some historical or psychological facts for instance. It should not search for signification outside of the text and outside of language. We should remember that for Derrida the referent or transcendental signifier is always absent: all we have is the text and language or writing in general. This is one way of understanding the above-discussed 'there is nothing outside the text'. Neither the life of the author nor their psychological factors can be of prime interest when we read their text. Even if they were, we would have no other way of accessing them than through writing. However, a more radical meaning can be given to the quote. This has to do with the way that Derrida sees writing as supplementary. What he tries to show in his reading of Rousseau is that beyond what one tries to circumscribe as Rousseau's text there has never been anything but writing. There have never been anything but supplements, substitutive significations in a chain of references (Derrida 1976: 158–159). There is no reality that could be reached behind or above this chain.[7] It can be read in the text itself that the absolute present has always already escaped.

What Derrida actually does is to ascribe the reader a freedom. It is highly important to make a respectful doubling commentary of a text, but the reading should not end there. It can be taken further, towards uncovering hidden and surprising meanings. In this uncovering there are no limits because there is no truth or right meaning that should or could be discovered. The interpreter is on their own with only their reading to guide him or her. Here, the responsibility of reading actually begins because there is no right or wrong or rules by which the reader can comply. He has to find his own way. We can contrast this with Eco's distinction between using and interpreting texts. Although it is difficult to make a clear separation between the two, the main idea is that interpretation respects the semantic meaning of a text whereas use exploits the text for, for instance, political reasons.

7 The theme of supplementarity that Derrida brings forward is only one among many possible themes. There are many other meanings that a reading or the text could uphold, and supplementarity is only one in a chain of many. But it happens that this theme describes the chain itself. It shows how a textual chain is a chain and how it has a structure of substitution. By concentrating on supplementarity Derrida shows in a text what a text is (see Derrida 1976: 163).

A Derridean approach questions this stance because even though a respectful commentary can and should be done, there is no correct semantic meaning that could draw the boundaries between interpretation and use of a particular text.

Derrida insists that even though deconstructive reading is not a mere commentary, it has to remain within the text.

> Although it is not commentary, our reading must be intrinsic and remain within the text. That is why, in spite of certain appearances, the locating of the word *supplement* is here not at all psychoanalytical, if by that we understand an interpretation that takes us outside of the writing toward a psychobiographical signified, or even toward a general psychological structure that could rightly be separated from the signifier.
>
> (Derrida 1976: 159)

What are the appearances that connect deconstructive reading to psychoanalytical reading? One perhaps obvious similarity is the way that both approaches intend to discover and reveal hidden meanings and structures and do this by paying attention to things that may at the outset seem small or insignificant. Much of interest can be found if we pay attention to details and also accidents, mishaps, slips of the pen. But, as Derrida points out, deconstruction aims at a reading that stays inside the text. It should be intrinsic, thus approaching the text from the inside.

Derrida does not claim that the impossibility of pure and self-present meaning makes it futile to try to find out what the writer wants to say. Attempts at rigorous commentary and exegesis can and should be made. However, it is important to acknowledge that the person who writes is always inscribed in a certain determined textual system. There are different ways of using signs. For example, philosophical texts have the aim of trying to reach behind the chain of references, to the signified content, which is impossible. Reading these texts, one should be aware of this aim (see Derrida 1976: 160). The concepts and structures that are used in a text are often loaded with historic-political significance and depend on certain prevailing habits of the time and place in which they were written. Additionally, modalities of power and force are at play here. In philosophy, for instance, certain ways of using language have been institutionalised and forcibly imposed as philosophical (see Derrida 1995a: 216–219). Deconstructive reading should take into account the textual system in which the text is written as well as the aims of the text.

A deconstructive reader is aware that the writer's intention is absent. There is no going back to an original meaning. This is something that Derrida himself has been forced to face as well when his own texts have been interpreted in various ways. The original is never present, and the text is more like a translation or copy; it is separated from its origins. Also, deconstruction does not shy away from anomalies in the text. It does not read texts as coherent wholes, and its aim is not to make inconsistencies disappear. Deconstruction is a means of making visible the inconsistencies in every text. It reveals traces of otherness.

Deconstruction seeks not only to break down textual constructions: its aim is to reveal and clarify. It shows how concepts and structures function and what presuppositions they take for granted. It involves separating and connecting different thoughts and elements, which means that it not only destroys but also constructs. It is, however, different from critique in that it does not want to take the position of an outside critic but, rather, aims to study structures from the inside and explain them from there. It moves therefore on two levels: on the one hand it is internal to the text's own structures; on the other, it dissolves these structures (see Enwald 2004: 58). Through deconstruction we can study all that happens in a text but also look at what has been left out of it and the limits that the text draws. In this way deconstruction happens also on the borders of the text.

## Deconstruction between commentary and phenomenological reduction

What has already become clear is that a tension seems to be present in Derrida's deconstruction between a respectful commentary and a reading without limits that uncovers hidden meanings and structures. This is the double structure of deconstruction, which can be called double reading. It is both a patient and rigorous reading of the text 'in its own language' and a sensitivity to the text's blind spots, where contradictions or ambiguities are uncovered (see Critchley 2008: 23). Tomi Kaarto describes deconstruction as a sort of phenomenological reduction. The aim is to uncover a layer of the text that is invisible or unthought on the surface. Deconstruction tries to reach the operative layer of the text. The way to do this is by bracketing. This means that the theme that is read as the foreground of the text is not taken for granted but put aside or bracketed in order to make visible the structure or constitution of this theme. Deconstruction does not therefore imply an ignorance of the theme, of what the text wants to say. On the contrary, the theme is studied thoroughly. Deconstruction tries to get inside the text and its logic. The theme, the wanting to say, is explored, but what is even more important, deconstruction explores that which governs or controls the theme (Kaarto 2008: 448–449). This means that the theme, the surface level, is not everything in the text, but rather the structures and presuppositions that the theme draws on contribute to the meanings of the text as well.

How does this idea of a theme fit Derrida's ideas of meaning? Does it imply that he still believes in a theme that can be simply read as *the meaning* of the text? The answer is no. Reading the theme of the text is already active interpretation. In a later text, Derrida comments on his method of reading Rousseau in *Of Grammatology*. Here, he underlines that a commentary of a text is already an interpretation in which semantic decisions have to be made. Moreover, this kind of interpretation work requires a lot: competence in reading, which includes, in this case, translating the French at the time of Rousseau, and understanding the different contexts that determine Rousseau's text, as well as knowing Rousseau's different texts as well as possible, and so on. These are all requirements that deconstructive reading shares with other forms of interpretation. Without these competences one could say just anything at all, and Derrida points out how he has never accepted saying just anything at all nor argued for indeterminacy as such (Derrida 1988a: 143–145). Interpreting the theme of the text is not an easy task in itself. But deconstruction adds yet another difficult task to those of the interpreter, that of unveiling different textual and linguistic elements that function in the text.

It is significant that deconstruction has its roots in Derrida's critique of Husserl's phenomenology. Husserl's texts show a belief in the possibility of reaching, through phenomenological reduction, a purified form of knowledge or method by which it is possible to see how things are. According to Kaarto, Derrida's reading of Husserl demonstrates:

> [...] that each philosophical, historical, social scientific interpretation as well as any reading and theory within literary studies has its own quasi-transcendental conditions which render the interpretation or reading finite, attaching it to certain traditions and to a historical context. Not even a phenomenologist can attain such a state of transparency in which he or she would have an entirely fulfilled intuition of the conditions of his or her own acts.
>
> (Kaarto 2008: 450)

Interpretation is always forced to happen within some tradition and to draw on some presuppositions, very much a Gadamerian idea.

Deconstruction of a text can be done again and again. There can never come a point when we would reach the things themselves. No meaning can be found that could not be revealed as being conditional and dependent on operational concepts. This goes, of course, for Derrida's own texts as well. They too are made possible by socio-historical concepts and cannot strive at universality. For this reason, deconstruction cannot define the theme of a text any more concretely than any other way of reading, nor can it show without doubt what the operational levels working in the text are. Deconstruction is not the search for truth. Deconstructive reading acknowledges that the outcomes of reading depend on the reader. Interpretation is always fallible.

We discussed Derrida's view on language earlier and saw that language includes elements that the writer can control but also elements that they cannot. On the one hand, they use language to communicate, but on the other, to be able to do so they must use signs that are iterable and, in a way, beyond their control. A text therefore includes both a meaning (or meanings) that the writer wants to express but also meanings that derive from the concepts and structures that they use in order to get their meaning across, like grammar and the metaphoricality and multidimensionality of language. Deconstruction tries to take into account all of these. In the operational levels of the text, it finds meanings that the text contains more or less unintentionally. These layers are important because they condition the text and make its theme possible in the first place. 'That which the writer does not govern renders possible that which he or she does govern' (Kaarto 2008: 453). Deconstruction interprets what the text wants to say as well as how, on what grounds, and which linguistic elements and structures it draws on to say what it says. It works not only on the operational level or the thematic level but on both, and more importantly, it studies the relations between these two levels.

The idea of studying the different layers of a text is a way for interpretation to concentrate on the text itself. Here, Derrida's deconstruction means a startlingly clear return to the text and its intention, which for instance Eco demands. Deconstruction pays much attention to the text and its different structures but less to the author's intention or to his or her biographical history. Deconstruction always happens through a text in the sense that it is the text itself that forms the starting point and the framework for it. It can be called 'parasitic' for it is dependent on the text that is being read. It lives on and from the text.

Deconstruction cannot be reduced to a method, but this does not mean that it could not nevertheless have some methodological content. The central idea of uncovering otherness requires, for example, that one is open to the singularity of the text and singularities within it, and does not hold on to any particular methodological rules. The reader should be aware of operational concepts and theoretical presuppositions and the way that these condition reading. They must be brought under examination to the extent this is possible. Sensitivity towards the otherness of the text requires awareness from the reader. According to Kaarto, the reader needs to be alert to the fact that notions such as, for instance, 'author', 'man' and 'animal' are not natural, self-evident units. Without this alertness, the interpreter cannot be open to radical meanings in the text and may end up not really reading the text but simply subsuming it under his or her own familiar ontology (Kaarto 2008: 483).

There are different ways in which a deconstructive reading can operate. It can unmask presuppositions of hegemonic and dominant interpretations of texts. It can demonstrate the contingency of these interpretations and give optional readings. It can unravel the meanings that the author tries to thematise in the text and the operational structures that make the meanings possible. Also, it can show that theories that strive at a hegemonic position are contingent. What is important in all these different strategies is openness towards the otherness of the text and a sensitive reading of the text itself. We have seen some of these deconstructive strategies at work in Derrida's reading of Rousseau. This way it can be argued that deconstruction is not just undecidability and hesitance. It includes methodological fragments.

Because no reading of a text is able to prove that it is the correct one or the only natural or true reading, and if every theory holds some unaccounted presuppositions in its foundations, then one may question what kind of ethical and political aspects those readings and theories include. A reading is never self-evident but is always based on a decision. One may always inquire for and against whom or what the decision has been made (Kaarto 2008: 484). This is close to a central idea here that interpretation always involves choices, which involves ethical and political elements. But it is important to keep in mind that the situation in which reading takes place should not be seen as completely free. The reader is not free to choose whichever meaning he or she wants. The text itself leads the reader in certain directions.

## Comparing deconstruction and hermeneutics

A famous encounter between Gadamer and Derrida took place in 1981 at a symposium on *Text and Interpretation*. It has later often been called a non-encounter.[8] A dialogue did take place in the sense that both parties presented papers and commented on each other's work. But it is debatable whether it really was a dialogue, especially when Derrida's response to Gadamer consists of a strange and seemingly misdirected text. In his paper Derrida does not even refer to Gadamer by name.

A comparison between Derrida's deconstruction and Gadamer's hermeneutics cannot be limited to the encounter that happened in Paris. Many other texts of the two writers can be fruitfully compared, and the differences between the thinkers can also be discussed on a more general level. Even though their opinions differ on many points, they are not completely opposed. The points on which the two thinkers disagree and especially the points on which they agree are of importance here as they are at the same time the main problems of interpretation. They indirectly concern legal interpretation as well. I will focus this comparison of Gadamer and Derrida on three main issues: meaning, coherence and intersubjectivity.

### *Meaning*

The most important question of debate between the two philosophers is usually seen to be the question of meaning (see, for example, Michelfelder and Palmer 1989; Dallmayr 1989). Neither Derrida nor Gadamer are meaning nihilists in the sense that they would doubt the possibility of the existence of meaning. The debate is therefore not whether there is meaning but concerns the structures that make meaning possible and also the nature of meaning. Both Gadamer and Derrida stress that interpretation always takes place in a field of uncertainty in the sense that there is no return to any original meaning, for instance the original intention of an author. Nevertheless, both say that a text has meaning. Every text can have meaning, or rather meanings. The problem is not that there is no meaning but rather that there is too much meaning in every text. On this point both writers again seem to agree to a considerable degree. Deconstruction has no end. Hermeneutics has no end. No meaning is the first or the last one, and interpretation can go on forever. Meaning in deconstruction is not that different from meaning in hermeneutics as both theories give up fantasies of a single correct or original meaning.

Both Derrida's and Gadamer's views on language are to a large extent compatible with a late Wittgensteinian view. They acknowledge the shared background of

8 For instance: Fred Dallmayr calls it 'somewhat disjointed and non-dialogical' (see Dallmayr 1989: 77); John Caputo calls it 'an ill-fated non-exchange' (Caputo 2002: 512); Derrida himself says later that it was an encounter but also a missed encounter (see Derrida 2004: 5). See Michelfelder and Palmer 1989 for an account of the symposium.

language and its necessarily inter-subjective nature. But where do the respective philosophers find the limits of interpretation or the criteria for good interpretations? For Gadamer the limits of interpretation consist of the prejudices of the interpreter and the tradition, for these structure and direct interpretation in certain directions. They thus prevent arbitrary readings of texts. But they do not determine meanings, nor are criteria for correct and false interpretations to be found. A requirement for good interpretation is respect for the text, which includes openness to different meanings, for instance when listening to another person in spoken communication. Hermeneutics tries to strike a balance between the boundaries for interpretation stemming from the hermeneutic circle and the openness that is required for respecting a text's newness. Gadamer's idea of fusion of horizons demonstrates how the tension between the horizon of the text and the horizon of the interpreter are dissolved in the process of understanding (see Gadamer 1989d: 41).

For deconstruction, the question of the limits of interpretation is as difficult as it is for hermeneutics, and the conclusions are also similar: there are no criteria for correct interpretation because there is no such thing as a correct interpretation. Derrida does, however, stress that language is not arbitrary and that different structures are always at play, some consciously chosen by the speaker, writer and reader and some unconsciously utilised. The reader always exercises a certain kind of force when interpreting a text as they have to make choices on how to read and which meanings to choose but he or she has responsibility for the meanings that he or she projects.

A way to highlight the differences between hermeneutics and deconstruction is to focus on the role that the idea of a benevolent attitude plays in them. Where Gadamer thinks that a certain amount of goodwill is always necessary for communication and interpretation, Derrida pays more attention to other factors. Even though he too finds a welcome or a promise, a certain kind of ethical residue in the background of language, he does not see goodwill as a necessary requirement of interpretation.[9] This would only be so if the aim were to find out the meaning of the text, which is the aim of hermeneutics. This is not the aim of deconstruction. Derrida criticises hermeneutics for logocentrism because it still involves a search for some unified meaning that can be found in every text. Hermeneutics has not broken the bonds of the logocentric tradition in which thinking is centred on a meaning present in itself. Where hermeneutics aims at uncovering or excavating meanings in texts, deconstruction claims not to have any unambiguous aim.

Gadamer says that we expect the text to say something. The preconditions and prejudices that we have when starting the interpretation process are of focal importance in hermeneutics as it is on them that the possibility of understanding

9 Derrida also pays attention to the way that stressing goodwill actually commits Gadamer to a certain kind of metaphysics, similar to Kant's, in which the dominant will is something essential (see Derrida 1989a: 52–54; see, also, for example, Risser 1989: 182–184).

rests. According to Derrida, deconstruction has a slightly different approach. In its focus on uncovering structures and hidden layers of the text it does not give the prejudices of the reader an equal importance. To put it simply: where a hermeneutic reader ideally approaches the text with prejudices that he or she is aware of and prepared to change and with an open mind for what the text wants to say, the deconstructive reader does not presuppose that the text wants to say anything and is always interested in anomalies and contradictions that do not seem to make any sense. Both readers approach the text with openness and respect for the text's uniqueness, but deconstruction is not convinced that the text says anything at all.

Compared to hermeneutics, deconstruction is also more suspicious of the tradition or the setting in which interpretation takes place. Deconstruction does not neatly fold itself in the layers of tradition but questions them and their background. We do not simply accept a tradition as our own. Every tradition is mediated and interpreted and this is in accordance with Derrida's idea of deconstructing the metaphysics of presence. The ways of receiving traditions can be questioned and challenged. This way, deconstruction does not simply function inside a tradition, it intervenes in it (see Naas 2003: xviii).

### *Coherence*

Hermeneutics and deconstruction differ in their approach to the question of coherence, and this issue is of paramount importance. It is clear that Gadamer stresses coherence and holistic understanding, whereas Derrida in all his thinking underlines differences and exceptions. One could say that Gadamer is on a general level interested in the usual and the regular, but for Derrida the unusual or the deviant is more intriguing. Deconstruction searches for anomalies and discrepancies, hermeneutics for a coherent whole. In hermeneutics the parts and the whole are intertwined, and both partake in the construction of meaning. In deconstruction the parts, or just one part, can be of importance or alternatively the whole, or sometimes both.

In the debate in 1981, Derrida discusses Heidegger's reading of Nietzsche and the underlying presuppositions of logocentrism that this reading seems to portray. He demonstrates that Heidegger's thinking, caught in old unifying and totalising patterns, tries to make Nietzsche into a coherent unity. Hermeneutic thinking runs along these paths as it always searches for sense. It creates sense by interpreting wholeness, totality and coherence. Derrida asks: 'Who is this Nietzsche, who has been gathered and presented as a certain kind of person in a certain time and representing certain kinds of thoughts?' Attempts to construct a writer called Nietzsche, who said this and that, show a tendency to fall back on essentialism.[10] The ambiguities of Nietzsche and his writing are reduced in Heidegger's hermeneutic strategy (see Derrida 1989b: 58–71; see, also, Caputo 1989: 261).

10 In this vein Gadamer has been labelled 'closet-essentialist', the essence that Gadamer believes in being meaning (see Caputo 1989: 258–264).

Derrida does not believe in coherent or unambiguous meaning in the first place. For him meaning is always in a state of flux. It is never present in itself, for it is the general structure of the sign that it always already refers somewhere else in an endless chain of signification. Every text includes numerous signs that lead the reader in different directions at the same time. To reduce the meanings of it and to choose some as important over others is what the interpreter does, but this does not mean that the result could be called the meaning of the text.

### *Intersubjectivity*

Even though both thinkers stress the intersubjective character of language and a certain ethicity as the necessary requirement for understanding, Gadamer takes the idea somewhat further than Derrida. For Gadamer goodwill is there, he sees it happening in interpretive situations. Derrida does not deny goodness and ethical encounters, but he questions their possibilities and prevalence in real life. Language also works when we want to hurt one another, and we often intentionally or unintentionally understand each other wrongly. There is much misunderstanding – also deliberate misunderstanding – that Gadamer does not seem to take into account. Gadamer's search for the conditions and possibilities for successful communication and understanding lead him to a one-sided view of human communication. Interpretation is not all ethical but includes power, politics and even violence as well.

After Gadamer's death, Derrida published an interesting short text in which he expresses his admiration for him. Derrida speaks about their friendship that gradually developed after their first encounter. Derrida mentions the word 'dialogue' in describing his relationship with Gadamer, but he quickly adds that the word will remain for a long time foreign to his lexicon. Something happened in 1981 that began to grow and develop in the minds of the two thinkers. It was something like an interior dialogue, in which both were influenced by each other's views. The encounter left traces that have proved more fruitful than a harmonious dialogue would have been. Derrida's questions to Gadamer in 1981 were an interruption of a dialogue but not necessarily to be understood as failure of the dialogue. Interruption can just as well be a condition of comprehension and understanding. Interruption is indecisive, it opens the situation up for the future exactly in the way it withholds closure and final words. Derrida finds respect for indecision also in Gadamer's work, whose thinking is not only directed at coherence or unity. Indecision means openness to a future not yet determined, to new uncertain possibilities. The situation in which something is left open is a fruitful situation. Derrida here stresses the way hermeneutics is described by Gadamer as an infinite process. Perfect agreement is never possible, and it is not the aim either (see Derrida 2004).

## What could deconstruction mean for legal interpretation?

Despite the amount of attention that Derrida's work has received in legal theory, there is not that much research on how his views on language and his ideas on deconstruction could be implied on legal *interpretation*. Legal research drawing on Derrida's writings or inspired by them has seldom precisely tackled these questions but has more often been concerned with other legal philosophical issues (see, for example, Goodrich *et al.* 2008a; Cornell *et al.* 1992). Some few scholars, however, have applied a Derridean approach on issues concerning legal interpretation, some of which I discuss below.

Can the idea of deconstruction as interpretation of texts be somehow transported to legal interpretation? Does it bring something new to the way we see legal interpretation, something by which the crisis could be overcome? The problem with applying deconstructive thinking in legal interpretation might be the fundamental difference in the aim of each exercise. Deconstruction can go on forever, but legal interpretation involves the assumption that whether or not a text has one meaning or many and whether or not the concepts and the different elements of the text contribute to making it a coherent whole, a judge deciding a case has to make a decision and has to justify it with an interpretation of what the law commands. Legal interpretation thus has an intensely concrete aim and purpose, which deconstruction does not. A judgment has to be made.

One of the writers who has tried to develop an alternative account of legal decision-making inspired by Derrida is Jacques de Ville. De Ville compares traditional constitutional theory with other theories of language, especially speech act theory. Constitutional theories describe the constitution as a written document that determines the way people govern themselves. The reason why constitutions are written is that writing is viewed as something that increases legal certainty. The constitution is seen as a record of the desires of a conscious, wilful, political community. The constitution is a text that is used as an instrument in which intentional meanings are expressed, these being the fundamental principles by which the State functions. This view of the constitution responds to the way speech act theory, and many other theories of language, understand language and meaning. Writing is an instrument that in itself has no effect on the content or meaning of the text. Speech, on the other hand, is self-present, a living act that belongs to the speaker. De Ville argues that this has to do with the attempt by traditional metaphysics to domesticate and overcome death understood as absence or something being lost. The living act of speech does not seem to imply a risk of death when the sign is given over to the world (see de Ville 2008: 92–93).[11]

As we have seen above, Derrida points out how signs continue to function (and have to continue in order to function as signs), even in the absence of the author

11 It has to be noted that de Ville has a tendency to read Derrida in connection to Freud in ways that are not shared here (see, for example, de Ville 2009b).

who signs the text and also in the event of his or her death. The sign has the force to continue living and break with every determined context. The presence of a speaking or writing subject cannot be what makes the functioning of the sign possible. This applies to a constitution as well. Language is other to the speaker, sender and the addressee. It cannot be possessed. It always remains to some extent foreign and out of control. Here the other should not be understood as another person but as the relation with death (de Ville 2008: 92–94). And death can be death but also other kinds of absence.

The implications of this for constitutional theory are important. The constitution should not be understood as a way of transporting a meaning that is present and that originates in the people. Moreover, the idea of preservation and even that of legal certainty is challenged. According to de Ville reading Derrida, when the constitution is enacted, something radically other intervenes that no longer belongs to the people (de Ville 2008: 96). The people no longer have full control over the constitution. This does not, of course, mean that they have no control, but that the meaning and significance of the constitution is not fully determined by them.

In fact, de Ville's Derrida claims that the transportation of meanings and intentions is not the primary character of a constitution: it is only a secondary effect. What a constitution is in reality is a text. A constitution, like any other writing, is conditioned by différance and iterability. The origin of the constitution is not the people but writing. The possibility of death is the possibility of betrayal in the sense that the constitution does not return to or answer to the interests of the people. It becomes in a way untouchable, and the text of the constitution becomes in a certain sense unreadable (de Ville 2008: 107).

In order for an institution to be able to function, it must cut itself off from the empirical individuals who founded it. Further, here we find that signatures are important. The signatures of the founders, the people, sign the constitution through their representatives. However, the people as a people is created with the same document. In the act of signature, the people as somebody who signs is born. In traditional speech act theory a signature guarantees legitimacy, authority and meaning. It does this by claiming continuing presence. But, as a signature can only function if it is iterable, there can be no pure and complete presence of a signature. Signatures are also conditioned by différance and the possibility of absence, that is, death. Thus the signature is always divided. It is same and different at the same time. This applies to the signatures on the declaration of independence as well. Signing affirms both life and death, both presence and absence. The text and the signature are inscribed in the same structure of the text; they operate according to the logic of writing. According to de Ville, signing constitutes a risk but also a chance. Here the responsibility of the signatory is visible. It is not simply the responsibility of constitution-making but is reinstituted each time the constitution is given effect (de Ville 2008: 109–110).

The question of how the meaning of the constitution should be decided, even temporarily, when it is 'given effect', is left open here. Neither is it the question that de Ville is interested in. What he does say is that:

> Constitutional democracy should no longer be viewed in terms of the circular turning of a wheel – the people giving themselves a foundational document in order to rule themselves, giving themselves reason and rights in sovereign fashion. The wheel is also a free wheel, a dissymmetrical contract that does not return to itself.
>
> (de Ville 2008: 114)

To acknowledge this is the way that constitutional theory can responsibly confront questions about interpretation and application of a constitution and its fundamental principles and values. The stability of meaning, application, principles, values, citizenship and human rights that are usually connected with a constitution are thus put into question. This calls for 'the hospitable exposure to the event, without the domination and neutralisation of performative mastery and sovereignty, without alibi' (de Ville 2008: 114). This does not take us very far yet but still somewhat further along the road on which our argument is moving. If we adopt a view of legal interpretation that is inspired by deconstruction, then questions of responsibility and hospitality are inevitable.

Deconstructive theory is not something that can easily be applied to legal interpretation. It is not an easy solution by which we can save legal interpretation from its crisis. It is a way of reading from which it is very difficult to draw methodological conclusions that would apply as such in the field of law. Perhaps it contributes more to the description of the problem, the crisis, than to its solution. It does not, and cannot, give us rules for how to interpret legal texts. However, this does not render deconstruction worthless: on the contrary. Its merits are, first of all, that it does give a point of view on problems connected to all interpretation and meaning-giving, problems that are especially pressing in legal interpretation, where we have to decide the meaning of a text and justify that decision. Second, the fact that deconstruction cannot solve the problem of meaning does not mean that deconstruction fails. It is quite possible that the *problem cannot be solved*, at least in the way that we would like. By this I mean that it seems plausible that we cannot achieve a theory of interpretation from which clear rules for how to interpret legal texts could be derived. What deconstruction shows (similarly to but from a slightly different angle than Wittgenstein and Gadamer) is that meaning is something that we can never completely take hold of.

Even if deconstruction does not solve our problems, it still contains many insights. The question of the connection between interpretation and ethics is something that is opened up by deconstruction, and it is argued here that this connection should also be taken into account in law. Now it is time to consider in detail what has been hinted at on several occasions: that deconstruction has some kind of link to ethics.

## Ethical elements of deconstruction

Let us start by some interesting comments that Derrida makes on truth. To be sure, he does not believe in truth as a self-present entity or unified concept. However, he says that he does not contest the value of truth. Within interpretive contexts it should be possible to invoke rules of competence, criteria of discussion and consensus, good faith, lucidity, rigour, criticism and pedagogy (Derrida 1988a: 146).

> I have never 'put such concepts as truth, reference, and the stability of interpretive contexts radically into question' if 'putting radically into question' means contesting that there *are* and that there *should be* truth, reference, and stable contexts of interpretation. I have – but this is something entirely different – posed questions that I hope are radical concerning the possibility of these things, of these values, of these norms, of this stability [...].
>
> (Derrida 1988a: 150, emphasis in original)

He does not contest that there are and that there should be truth, reference and stable contexts of interpretation but asks *how these are possible*. The questions that Derrida asks are connected to the social, ethical and political rules that govern different contexts. He questions the structures that make contexts of interpretation possible and the different strategies that uphold truths and stabilise contexts.

The *Limited Inc* collection of essays, in which Derrida's responses to Searle are collected, includes an afterword by Derrida that is entitled 'Toward an Ethic of Discussion'. In this text, he discusses how ethical factors are at play in language and reading. He claims that in his essay on speech act theory and his reply to Searle he tried to say something about the violence, politics and ethics of debate. What matters most to him in afterthought is not the theoretical or philosophical content of the texts but the polemical scene of the debate. Large questions are inscribed in the academic debate between the two philosophers. They are questions of right, morality and politics, and they do not contain themselves inside the academic field. The violence contained in all intellectual discussions must be acknowledged. Derrida admits that his response to Searle was, in a sense, aggressive. But according to him, Searle had read him in turn with a brutality that actually consisted of an avoidance of reading and trying to understand (Derrida 1988a: 112–113). We can see that Derrida, too, emphasises respect on the part of the reader: the reader should at least try to understand what the other wants to say.

Derrida points out that when speech act theorists, for instance Searle, claim that in literal and serious language the sentences are precisely the realisations of the intentions of the speaker, this is not merely a philosophically neutral statement. It implies the normative or prescriptive statement that only serious and literal language can fully realise an intention or that language *at its best* is and ought to be serious and literal. Speech act theorists do not bluntly give us moral lessons and tell us to avoid metaphors. But, Derrida claims, while they are analysing language they reproduce, under the guise of describing it in its ideal purity, a certain ethicity with given ethical conditions. By doing this they ignore other conditions that are no less ethical. According to Derrida, it is such conditions that interest him when he writes of iterability, for instance (Derrida 1988a: 122).

Writing, philosophising and reading are connected with ethical choices. This much is made very clear in this text of Derrida's. However, we cannot jump to straightforward conclusions from this. To simply connect deconstruction with ethics is difficult because deconstruction is not something stable that can be defined, but it continuously has to be able to, and does, deconstruct itself.

Some commentators on Derrida have thought that his thinking underwent an 'ethical turn' that can be seen especially in his later work (see, for example, Gehring 2008: 56).[12] The reading offered here does not support such a view. We can see from many texts that he was already occupied with ethical and political questions early on, although he addresses them perhaps more directly in his later work. To say that his own understanding of deconstruction changed so that he later started seeing it as something ethical is also problematic, as he does not admit this himself. It is safe to say that ethical and political questions were always relevant for him, but this does not imply that deconstruction would be something ethical in itself. Difficulties in studying the ethical elements of deconstruction are made visible in Critchley's analysis in *The Ethics of Deconstruction* (1999) and also in a response by Derrida to claims about the ethics of deconstruction, which is studied next.

## Critchley's clôtural reading

According to Critchley, deconstruction should be understood as an ethical demand. His claim is not that an ethical theory can be derived from deconstruction, but that deconstruction of texts has an ethical structure. This means that deconstruction takes place ethically or that a duty is inscribed in deconstruction. This ethics is, for Critchley, Levinasian ethics. He claims that many similarities exist between Derrida's and Levinas's thinking that allow deconstruction to be understood as ethical (Critchley 1999: 1–12).[13] Thus Critchley reads Derrida and Levinas together and tries to make visible the ethics that deconstruction involves.

According to Critchley, there is an ethical moment that motivates deconstruction. It consists in saying 'yes' to alterity and to the unnameable.

> The ethical moment that motivates deconstruction is this Yes-saying to the unnameable, a moment of unconditional affirmation that is addressed to an alterity that can neither be excluded from nor included within logocentric conceptuality.
>
> (Critchley 1999: 41)

12 Gehring voices the commonly held idea that Derrida's writings 'shifted around the middle of the 1980s at the latest. Deconstruction is increasingly fascinated by ethical, political, and social questions.' See, also, Rosenfeld 2008.

13 This is a widespread way of interpreting Derrida, as many commentators link Derrida closely with Levinas's ethics. We concentrate on Levinas's theory later.

The yes-saying that Derrida discusses is interpreted by Critchley as an ethical moment that resonates with Levinas's thinking. The affirmation is what produces deconstruction but is also produced through deconstructive reading. It entails a duty for the reader towards the rigorous labour of reading, which opens a dimension of alterity (Critchley 1999: 41).

Critchley defines the problem of closure as the double refusal both of remaining within the limits of a tradition and the possibility of transgressing that tradition. As we have seen, the problem of limits and freedom haunts hermeneutic theory as well, but Derrida concentrates on it and takes it further. Deconstructive reading is the interruption or disruption of the limit that divides the inside and outside of tradition. It tries to transgress traditions. Critchley develops his own version of deconstruction, which he calls 'clôtural reading'. It is a double reading that studies how a text both belongs to a logocentric conceptuality and at the same time breaks through that conceptuality (Critchley 1999: 20–30). So clôtural reading is not exactly the same thing as deconstruction but a development of it. Critchley's idea is that this version would be able to answer the demands of ethics, especially Levinasian ethics.

The difference between deconstructive reading and Critchley's clôtural reading is that even if in clôtural reading the text is also read doubly, it is specifically situated in relation to a logocentric epoch, whereas deconstruction wants to breach any such epoch allowing the movement of alterity. As clôtural reading does not try to breach the tradition, the epoch or the historicity of the text, it is able to take into account ethically significant elements. Whereas history tends to be the history of the victors, clôtural reading is history read from the standpoint of the victims of that history (Critchley 1999: 30). Critchley thinks that deconstruction cannot have such a standpoint, for it is double reading that aims at overcoming historical epochs. Clôtural reading allows the question of ethics to be raised within deconstruction. The problem with deconstruction is that, in being constantly in flux and avoiding any stability, any questions of ethics seem to slip through its flexible cracks.

Critchley's reading of Derrida provides us with a way of understanding deconstruction in which responsibility is an affirmation of alterity and a 'yes' to the stranger. This is ethics, the 'yes' in which alterity is maintained. The text is not reduced to a unified whole, and no singular self-same and self-present meaning is projected on the text. It is analysed in a rigorous way but so that alterities are upheld. Reading includes a 'yes', but this 'yes' does not take total hold of the text. The reading remains hesitant. What this exactly means and what it could mean in practice when applied to the interpretation of texts is unclear. The central problem is noticed by Critchley: deconstruction fails to thematise the question of politics as a place of contestation, antagonism, struggle and conflict. He writes: 'The rigorous undecidability of deconstructive reading fails to account for the activity of political judgment, political critique, and the political decision' (Critchley 1999: 190).

It can be argued, however, that Derrida's work does not necessarily lead to such conclusions. Derrida has himself on several occasions emphasised the political potential of deconstruction. Already in 1986 he writes that deconstructive readings are not simply analyses of discourse but effective and active interventions that transform contexts. Deconstructive practices are 'also and first of all political and institutional practices' (Derrida 1986: 168).

What is interesting is that Critchley's reading not only implies that a political decision is impossible but that all other decisions are impossible as well. How can the problem of decision be resolved? According to Critchley, deconstruction needs a political supplement. This supplement can be provided by the political as understood by Levinas. Levinas traverses the difficult abyss from ethics to politics and is able to build a bridge between them. Thus the problems that Derrida's deconstruction falls into can be resolved with the help of Levinas's thinking. Otherwise deconstruction cannot move from undecidability to decision or from ethics to politics. The political is understood here by Critchley as something practical or empirical; it is a place for decisions in a similar manner to law. It is needed to prevent deconstruction from becoming an empty formalism (Critchley 1999: 236–241).

How do the ethical elements of deconstruction appear in the interpretation of texts if ethics amounts to hesitance and undecidability? And what does this entail for the actual reading of texts? The idea seems to be that leaving things open is something ethical in nature, a way of respecting differences and not imposing power or violence on texts. It is important to ask why alterity or difference is seen as more ethical than sameness. Derrida does emphasise and even defend differences in contrast to unity and sameness, but this does not necessarily mean that in his view alterity would be something better in an ethical sense. The respect for otherness as explicitly something good is a central feature of Levinas's thinking. But transported from the sphere of human encounters to the field of reading and interpreting texts, the preference that is given alterity over unity is problematic. This question is very important when we consider the ethicality or unethicality of hermeneutics, as some differences between hermeneutics and deconstruction turn on this point. Hermeneutics does not see reading that searches for coherence and unity as something unethical. But, before moving on to a discussion of the ethics of otherness in the philosophy of Levinas, one important thing remains to be considered in the context of clôtural reading, that is, Derrida's own answer to the question about the ethics of deconstruction.

Derrida does not accept the idea of ethical deconstruction. He maintains that as deconstruction cannot be simply defined, it cannot be defined either as a form of morality or as a form of amorality. He writes in 'Passions: "An Oblique Offering"' that:

> Some minds believing themselves to have found in Deconstruction ['*La Deconstruction*'], as if there were only one, a modern form of immorality, of amorality or of irresponsibility [...], while others, more serious, in less of a hurry, better disposed towards so-called Deconstruction, today claim the opposite; they discern encouraging signs and in increasing numbers (at times,

> I must admit, in some of my texts) which would testify to a permanent, extreme, direct or oblique, in any event, increasingly intense attention, to those things which one could identify under the fine names of 'ethics', 'morality', 'responsibility', 'subject', etc. Before reverting to not-responding, I would like to declare in the most direct way that if I had the *sense* of duty and of responsibility, it would compel me to break with both these moralisms, with these two restorations of morality, including, therefore, the remoralization of deconstruction which naturally seem to me more attractive than that to which it is rightly opposed, but which at each moment risks reassuring itself in order to reassure the other and to promote the consensus of a new dogmatic slumber.
>
> (Derrida 1992b: 13–14, emphasis in original)

This passage that says quite a lot states, above all else, that defining deconstruction as ethical carries the risk of nailing it down to something definite, and the risk of dogmatic slumber. Even if Derrida admits that his texts include passages that concern ethical matters or parts where he seems to imply that deconstruction is connected with responsibility, it would be too easy to define deconstruction as either ethical or unethical. Deconstruction cannot be clearly, directly or permanently connected with ethics, or with anything else for that matter, for there is nothing that deconstruction is. He says that the ethicality of deconstruction remains open, a suspended question, because ethics, morality and responsibility are, and have to be what they are: unanswered questions. Questions such as 'What is ethics?' or 'What is responsibility?' cannot get a rule-governed response: they are undecidable. They can be responded to only by deciding something every time and without guiding rules, but no permanent responses can be given. Deconstruction does not offer us a good conscience. It calls into question again and again. It can have links to ethics, but these are not solid or permanent. Deconstruction and ethics are perhaps intertwined, but how this is cannot be given a final answer.

In his appendix to the second edition of *The Ethics of Deconstruction*, Critchley discusses these views of Derrida. He maintains that the debate hinges on what is meant by 'an ethical demand'. He underlines that his claim that deconstruction should be understood as an ethical demand presupposes that ethics is understood in the *particular sense* it is understood by Levinas. Critchley does not try to define deconstruction as ethical so that it would lead to a programme of action including rights and duties. Rather, he maintains that the ethical moment in deconstruction is precisely the undecidability, the suspension that Derrida himself underlines in his critical comment. The moment of responsibility arises out of the restlessness of the suspension of choice and hesitation (Critchley 1999: 248–264). Here the reference to politics is not made as clearly as in the original text. The ethical element of deconstruction is simply the hesitance, the suspension of choice and the undecidability that deconstruction entails.

It is a simplification to claim that deconstruction would be ethical or not ethical. But we can certainly see it as a step in the direction of acknowledging the responsibility as well as the ethical and political structures and preconditions that are always present in texts and their interpretations.

Chapter 4

# The ethics of language

The ethics of language has been a recurring topic in this study, and it is certainly one of its main themes. The question of legal interpretation, as posed at the beginning, brought us to the problem of what to base an interpretation on and further to the question of the interpreter's choice and responsibility. These issues have been discussed in connection to Wittgenstein's theory of language as well as hermeneutics and deconstruction. The idea of law's tragic failure and the crisis of legal interpretation can be distinguished in the background of these discussions.

When studying Wittgenstein's views on language, ethical features were already discerned. The ethical nature of interpretation was clearly seen in Gadamer's hermeneutics as well and in another form in Eco's idea of interpretation compared to use. Through the discussion of Derrida and deconstruction, the question of the ethical became problematic. Now that a picture of language and interpretation is starting to take shape, it is time to concentrate on ethics in order to understand more thoroughly what significance ethics can have for a theory of legal interpretation.

Levinas's work is important for the question at hand, for even though it is a theory in which ethics is the main subject, it contains interesting insights into language as well. His thinking has been influential, and of the theories already discussed both hermeneutics and deconstruction can be understood to engage in a conversation with him. Levinas is a phenomenologist and the roots of his thinking lie in Husserl and Heidegger. He is interested in being and especially in the being of man, with the main focus on ethics. He asks questions like: 'What makes ethics possible?' 'Is there something without which there would be no ethics?' and 'What makes us ethical?' Levinas's thinking contains a certainty that ethics is possible and occupies a fundamental role in our lives. This is what he tries to convince us of. Ethics is famously 'first philosophy': it precedes ontology as well as epistemology.

Language is a substantial issue for Levinas. His work can be interpreted as building alongside a theory of ethics, which is a kind of metaethics, also a theory of language and perhaps even a theory of meaning. Language and ethics go together and belong together. To study the way Levinas understands language can be fruitful, first of all, from the point of view of the philosophy of language because Levinas offers us an intriguing view of communication. Besides, language is such a central theme for him that by studying it we can understand his thinking better. Another reason for concentrating on language is that language and the question of justice are intertwined in Levinas's work, which is highly relevant for the issues discussed here.

## Central themes in Levinasian ethics: responsibility for the other

Levinas's thinking did not go through very radical changes after his breakthrough work *Totality and Infinity: An Essay on Exteriority* (1969). Here he presents his ethical theory. His other major work, *Otherwise than Being: Or Beyond Essence* (1998), continues to study the same topics but sheds some new light on them as well. In this book the question of language is discussed at length because it had become clear that his previous work included some problems concerning the limits of language and what can be said and talked about.

At the core of Levinas's theory stands the infinite responsibility for the other.[1] It is the other person that makes us ethical. Ethics arises from our meeting with the other because through this meeting ethics is awakened in us. We are given the responsibility for the other, whether we like it or not. Ethics is something completely foreign to our egoistic and totalising attempts to take control of everything around us, to reduce everything to the sphere of sameness, to take hold of it by conceptualising and understanding it. Thus it is ethical to let the other be other, not to try to control alterity, to own it or even to know it.

Levinas's idea is that I exist in a world surrounded by things that are alien to me and different from me. At a very primary level, I have experiences which lead me to distinguish between myself and other things. I learn to live with these things, to play with them, to control them, to use them. I can enjoy the things at my pleasure. According to Levinas, we have a strong inclination to treat other things as either extensions of ourselves or as alien objects that can be manipulated. This is a primordial egocentrism that we find in ourselves. However, this picture is not applicable to the way we experience other persons. Levinas explains this basic idea of his theory in *Totality and Infinity*.

> The absolutely other is the Other. He [*sic*] and I do not form a number. The collectivity in which I say 'you' or 'we' is not a plural of the 'I'. I, you – these are not individuals of a common concept. Neither possession nor the unity of number nor the unity of concepts link me to the Stranger.
>
> (Levinas 1969: 39)

1 'Other' of 'the other' (*autrui*) sometimes takes an initial capital (the Other) and sometimes not. Levinas uses both versions rather unsystematically. Commentators have used different ways of translating Levinas's vocabulary. For instance, Llewelyn usually translates Levinas's *Autrui* as Other, *les Autres* as Others, *autre* as other and *les autres* as others (see Llewelyn 2002a: xiii). The problem is that Levinas is not fully consistent in his own use of the terms.

The other person is not experienced as a thing or an object. When I meet the other for the first time, they are a stranger. I do not know them, I cannot be sure who he or she is or what he or she is like. They inhabit an alien world of their own. I can try to treat them as an object and to place them under my categories, but this means that I would reduce him or her (see Wild 1969). The other person resists the ways in which I take hold of the world. He or she 'escapes my grasp' (Levinas 1969: 39).

How, then, is a relation to the other person possible? According to Levinas, this relation is language. In language a relationship is possible between me and the other, in which the other can be other and is not reduced. In language, despite the relation to the same, the other stays transcendent to the same. This relation is enacted in conversation (Levinas 1969: 39). In conversation, the same and the other do not form a totality. Levinas describes it as a face-to-face relationship.

> A relation whose terms do not form a totality can hence be produced within the general economy of being only as proceeding from the I to the other, as a *face to face*, as delineating a distance in depth – that of conversation, of goodness, of Desire – irreducible to the distance the synthetic activity of understanding establishes between the diverse terms, other with respect to one another, that lend themselves to its synoptic operation.
>
> (Levinas 1969: 39, emphasis in original)

For Levinas, knowledge necessarily possesses a kind of controlling quality. The idea is that when we know something we take control over what we know, and thus the object is not allowed to stay other. The ethical attitude to somebody is neither intellectual nor intentional. An ethical relationship or an ethical way of approaching someone is by not trying to know and control them but to let them stay other. Conversation is the way for the self and the other to be face to face in such a way that the other is not egoistically reduced to sameness. Conversation maintains a distance between me and the other person. In it, the transcendence of the other is possible. Egoism does not vanish in conversation, but the very fact of being in conversation consists of recognising in the other a right over this egoism (Levinas 1969: 40). The idea is that when encountering the other person face to face in conversation we cannot fully know or control them.

Levinas defines ethics in his own way. An ethical approach is a non-totalising approach to the other. It is a relation between me and the other that calls me into question.

> A calling into question of the same – which cannot occur within the egoist spontaneity of the same – is brought about by the other. We name this calling into question of my spontaneity by the presence of the Other ethics. The strangeness of the Other, his [*sic*] irreducibility to the I, to my thoughts and my possessions, is precisely accomplished as a calling into question of my spontaneity, as ethics.
>
> (Levinas 1969: 43)

The other person is a disruption of my egoism: I cannot know them and I cannot possess them. Levinas continues:

> Metaphysics, transcendence, the welcoming of the other by the same, of the Other by me, is concretely produced as the calling into question of the same by the other, that is, as the ethics that accomplishes the critical essence of knowledge. And as critique precedes dogmatism, metaphysics precedes ontology.
>
> (Levinas 1969: 43)

This rich quotation includes some central ideas in *Totality and Infinity*. Metaphysics, the transcendence of the other, is a welcoming of the other by the same. This means that the other is not reduced to a sum, a unity, or a 'we'. This transcendence is concretely produced. It happens through the calling into question of the same by the other. This is an ethics that produces the critical essence of knowledge. And because critique precedes dogmatism, this metaphysics also precedes ontology. According to Levinas, ontology actually presupposes metaphysics. Before ontology, there is the ultimate relation in being, the saying to the other, which is a relation with an existent, a singular existing somebody (see Levinas 1969: 48). This way metaphysics not only precedes knowledge, it also precedes ontology.

Western philosophy has often been ontology in which the other plays a secondary role. This has included a suppression and possession of the other. Possession affirms the other but strips it of its independence. Levinas goes as far as to say that ontology as first philosophy is a philosophy of power (Levinas 1969: 46). This egoism of ontology Levinas recognises in Socratic philosophy as well as in Heidegger's thinking. Levinas defines his own position as an aim to sketch how a non-allergic relation with alterity can be found in discourse (Levinas 1969: 46–47). This relation with alterity, in which the other person's otherness stays intact, is located in the face-to-face relationship of two people.

We encounter the other person in an ethical way, in a way that is not totalising, when we encounter the face. The face is for Levinas something abstract and also something that cannot be described but at the same time something very concrete: another human being. The face represents what is most human in humans, it marks an aspect of the person that is significant. Understandably, Levinas's use of the expression 'the face' has inspired some debate as to what he really means. It is a difficult concept in many ways. He defines it mostly in negative terms: the face is not something we can see or touch, it has no plastic form, it has no adequate idea, etc. (see, for example, Waldenfels 2002: 67). The face reveals the human being to me. It is what resists my totalising attempts. Another human being can never be completely and fully known, something always stays a mystery. Thus the face, which is the basis for an ethical relationship, is something that cannot be completely understood, otherwise it would not be able to refute totalising sameness. The face does not belong to the sphere of ontology or epistemology but to something more profound.

> For the presence before a face, my orientation toward the Other, can lose the avidity proper to the gaze only by turning into generosity, incapable of approaching the other with empty hands. This relationship established over the things henceforth possibly common, that is, susceptible of being said, is the relationship of conversation. The way in which the other presents himself [*sic*], exceeding the idea of the other in me, we here name face.
>
> (Levinas 1969: 50)

The face should not be understood as a picture that we see. The face of the other overflows the plastic images it leaves. It does not manifest itself in this way but by expressing itself in conversation, that is, through language. And what does it say? The first content of expression is the expression itself. To approach the other in conversation is to welcome their expression. It means to receive something that is beyond the capacities of the I. This is the idea of infinity (Levinas 1969: 51). It is, contrary to totality, the way in which the other can transcend. Conversation is a non-allergic relation, which for Levinas means an ethical relation.

Levinas also explains the face like this: the face resists our cognitive power; it cannot be known but *felt*. Here he opposes Husserl, who discusses the idea of intentional consciousness as the primary way of a person to relate to other things. For Levinas an important level exists *before* intentionality. Intentional consciousness is conditioned by life. Life is sentience, enjoyment and nourishment (see Critchley 2002: 20–21). Before the level of the conscious and self-conscious subject there is the level of a living subject, the self of enjoyment. It is this self of enjoyment that is claimed ethically by the other. The ethical subject is a sensible subject, not a thinking subject. The ethical subject is a subject who *lives, eats, drinks, enjoys and needs*.

> Only a subject that eats can be for the other, or can signify. Signification, the-one-for-the-other, has meaning only among beings of flesh and blood. Sensibility can be a vulnerability, an exposedness to the other or a saying only because it is an enjoyment. The passivity of wounds, the 'hemorrhage' of the for-the-other, is the tearing away of the mouthful of bread from the mouth that tastes in full enjoyment.
>
> (Levinas 1998: 74)

Ethics derives from the moment when we discover the face of the other. We realise that the face says, 'you shall not commit murder'. This is the primordial expression, according to Levinas. It is an epiphany. The resistance of the other 'gleams in the face of the Other, in the total nudity of his [*sic*] defenceless eyes' (Levinas 1969: 199). The way the other resists murder is ethical, not real. It is a resistance of that which has no resistance (the defenceless other). It is not resistance by struggle. The relation between the same and the other can turn into a struggle, but the primary relationship is with a defenceless other. This way war presupposes peace (Levinas 1969: 199).

I have a responsibility towards the other, and there is no way out of this responsibility. I am the other's servant. In meeting the face of the other, I engage in a conversation with the actual human being in front of me, and my attitude is more that of sharing than grasping, of exchanging rather than taking hold of something.

> The other (*autrui*) is not an object of comprehension first and an interlocutor second. The two relations are intertwined. In other words, the comprehension of the other (*autrui*) is inseparable from his [*sic*] invocation. To comprehend a person is already to speak with him.
>
> (Levinas 1996a: 6)

The face is the way the other presents himself or herself to me. And the face manifests itself by expressing itself. Thus language is more fundamental than being and ontology, and also more fundamental than truth. According to Levinas, in order for there to be any truth, knowledge or being, there already has to be the expression of the other. The first content of expression is the expression itself.

## The ethical relation is asymmetrical

We cannot choose our ethical responsibility because it precedes our choices. We are responsible regardless of whether we want to be or not, even if we neither do anything to deserve it nor do anything wrong. This responsibility is fundamental; it is what makes us human. 'To be an I means then not to be able to escape responsibility, as though the whole edifice of creation rested on my shoulders [...]. The uniqueness of the I is the fact that no one can answer for me' (Levinas 1996a: 55). Levinas describes responsibility as the fundamental structure of subjectivity. It is not strictly speaking responsibility on the level of norms and commands, that is, on the level of good and bad; it is a responsibility that precedes commands and rules.

It is important to notice that the ethical relationship is asymmetrical. The same owes more to the other than to itself; it must respect the other even more than itself. Responsibility for the other person is not reciprocal. According to Levinas, I am responsible for the other but their responsibility for me is their affair. The ethical relation is by definition the face-to-face relationship with the other wherein I am responsible for the other. This may be one of the most original features in Levinas's theory, but it also makes that theory quite challenging. The practical consequences of it are difficult, and attempts to import Levinasian thinking into the philosophy of law also face many problems, as we see below.

Levinas's ethics is situated on two different levels. Deep down is the face-to-face relationship that is ethical and that forms the foundation for everything. But there is also another level, the level of morals and our everyday ethical choices, the level of normativity. We are responsible for the other regardless of our actions and intentions. But how we carry out this responsibility is a complicated matter. This is the level of the good and the bad: it is the moral, political and juridical level. It is the level of the actual choices we make, but ethics is something else. It cannot itself legislate for society or produce rules on how people should act (see Levinas 1984: 65). So Levinas does require of us to take infinite responsibility for the other, but at the ethical level this is no request because we already have this responsibility even if we did not want to take it. Nevertheless, his theory is also a normative statement on how we should act: we should respect the life of the other even more than our own. 'To be for the Other is to be good' (Levinas 1969: 261). The ethical and the normative come together at the moment when the face asks us not to hurt it. The face asks, demands, or begs us not to kill. Language stands at the centre of *chiasmus* of the two levels; one can also say that language combines the two levels: the ethical-metaphysical and the normative.

## The saying and the said

As we see, ethics and language are very much intertwined in Levinas's thinking. The conversation with the other *is* the ethical relation. However, the way ethics and language come together is not simple. I will now turn to discussing language in more detail.

As noted above, for Levinas the ethical calling into question of the same comes first. It preceded everything, even intentionality and conceptualisation. But how can language be the happening of the ethical relation, when the ethical relation is something that happens before, or on a deeper level, than our conceptual way of taking hold of the world? What kind of language or conversation is Levinas thinking of when he says that the face-to-face relationship is conversation? He says that the profound essence of language is the irreversibility of the relation between me and the other in which the other is exterior and master. The other is an interlocutor and remains beyond the system of language. They are not on the same plane as I. Language can be spoken only if the interlocutor is the commencement of their discourse. Thus the communication of ideas and the reciprocity of dialogue, that is, what we normally understand as language and discourse, have their roots in the asymmetrical relation between the same and the other (Levinas 1969: 101, 195). The idea is that the face-to-face relationship takes place in a language that is a special kind of conversation. In it, the infinity and the alterity of the other are maintained. This conversation is the commencement of ordinary reciprocal language as dialogue. Levinas says that discourse founds signification.

> Language thus conditions the functioning of rational thought: it gives it a commencement in being, a primary identity of signification in the face of him [*sic*] who speaks, that is, who presents himself by ceaselessly undoing the equivocation of his own image, his verbal signs. Language conditions thought – not language in its physical materiality, but language as an attitude of the same

> with regard to the Other irreducible to the representation of the Other, irreducible to an intention of thought [...].
>
> (Levinas 1969: 204)

The language of the other is not ordinary language. It is the signification of the face of the one who speaks and something other than their verbal signs. But the language of the other also founds signification, that is, ordinary language. Meaning is founded in the primordial language of the other. 'Meaning is the face of the Other, and all recourse to words takes place already within the primordial face to face of language' (Levinas 1969: 206).

One of the most important critiques of Levinas's thinking was put forward by Derrida in his essay 'Violence and Metaphysics – An Essay on the Thought of Emmanuel Levinas', which is included in *Writing and Difference*. Here Derrida makes some very interesting remarks about language. First, he points out that there are problems in Levinas's method. He tries to study and explain something that is not ontology, something that is outside ontology as we usually understand it, but the only language he can do this with is the language of Western philosophy, which is thoroughly infiltrated by ontology. For instance, the critique that Levinas directs at Heidegger does not fully work, because Levinas operates within the same language and uses the same concepts as Heidegger. Levinas is not able to philosophise otherwise, because he is confined to the language he uses and all the tradition that this language brings with it (see Derrida 1978: 145–153). Levinas's thinking succumbs to the same totalising ways of conceptualising as Heidegger's does. To this kind of criticism Levinas says that:

> We have no option but to employ the language and the concepts of Greek philosophy even in our attempts to go beyond them. We cannot obviate the language of metaphysics and yet we cannot, ethically speaking, be satisfied with it: it is necessary but not enough. I disagree, however, with Derrida's interpretation of this paradox. Whereas he tends to see the deconstruction of the Western metaphysics of presence as an irreducible crisis, I see it as a golden opportunity for Western philosophy to open itself to the dimension of otherness and transcendence beyond Being.
>
> (Levinas 1984: 64)[2]

Thus Levinas agrees that there is a paradox in trying to overcome the very language one uses and the very tradition that one is in. But he sees it as an opportunity.

Another theme of Derrida's criticism concerns the face-to-face relationship and the role language plays in it. According to Derrida, there seems to be no way of conceptualising the encounter of the face.

2 See also Levinas' short text *Jacques Derrida: Wholly Otherwise* where he discusses Derrida's critique explicity (Levinas 1996b: 55– 62).

> The infinitely-other cannot be bound by a concept, cannot be thought on the basis of a horizon; for a horizon is always a horizon of the same, the elementary unity within which eruptions and surprises are always welcomed by understanding and recognized. Thus we are obliged to think in opposition to the truisms which we believed – which we still cannot not believe – to be the very ether of our thought and language.
>
> (Derrida 1978: 95, 147–148)

The face escapes all ways of categorising. The other has to be beyond or before language, otherwise it would not have the sort of irreducible alterity that Levinas means. How, then, is it possible for ethics to reside in language? And how is it possible for us, and for Levinas, to talk about the other, or to describe the face using language? Is it so that the face speaks but cannot actually say anything, cannot use words, because this would mean a shift from the pure non-totalising relation to something else? Levinas seems to propose a language without phrase. Derrida thus asks if this non-violent language, this silent intention, is language at all. It seems that the non-violent, non-totalising, non-conceptualising language can only exist as a silent language, and it exists only on the level of the face to face and thus before Being (see Critchley 1999).

Levinas tries to solve some of these difficulties in his later work *Otherwise than Being or Beyond Essence* (1998) by separating *the saying* and *the said*. Saying means the fact that somebody speaks, it is the happening of speech. What somebody says and means when they speak is the said. There are thus two important and meaningful features to language: that something is said and the content of what is said (Levinas 1998: 46).[3] It is in the realm of saying that the face appears to the same. The ethical relation is characterised by saying, that is speaking, conversation. The face is expressed in the saying, and what is important here is not what the face says but the fact *that it speaks*. The content of saying itself cannot be expressed in language, for the meaning of the speaking face is in that it speaks. The said, on the other hand, is more or less what we usually call language: utterances consisting of words that usually have some content. This is something other than saying, which is the purely ethical aspect of language. The origin of all meaning and signification is saying, that is, the fact that something is said.

Levinas presents the distinction between saying and the said in the first chapter of *Otherwise than Being*, entitled 'The Argument'. Here, he says that saying precedes language like a foreword.

3 Levinas's idea of the separation of the saying and the said resembles to some extent the way Giorgio Agamben discusses the Voice in *Language and Death*. The Voice is the pure indication that language is taking place. It is the ground for language, something that is not yet meaning and that disappears when meaning takes place. The Voice discloses the place of language; it shows that language takes place by showing the instance of discourse. It cannot be spoken in the discourse of which it shows the originary taking place (see Agamben 1991: 34–35, 84).

> Saying is not a game. Antecedent to the verbal signs it conjugates, to the linguistic systems and the semantic glimmerings, a foreword preceding languages, it is the proximity of one to the other, the commitment of an approach, the one for the other, the very signifyingness of signification.
>
> (Levinas 1998: 5)

Saying is the proximity of the one to the other. It is a commitment that gives rise to signification itself. But the commitment does turn into language. The foreword and what is said are connected. The saying and the said are correlative to one another (Levinas 1998: 6).

Saying has different aspects. It founds signification and sign systems, but according to Levinas, it is also understanding and listening. In a difficult passage he says: 'A word is a nomination, as much as a denomination, a consecrating of the "this as this" or "this as that" by a saying which is also *understanding* and *listening*, absorbed in the said' (Levinas 1998: 36, emphasis in original). Saying, in being the signifyingness of signification, includes understanding and listening. In the face-to-face relationship, saying that is the foundation of language consists not only of saying but listening and understanding too. But how does saying appear? The signification of this saying must be distinguished from the way the said, that is, language as signs, signifies. The signification of saying occurs in proximity. Thus it signifies otherwise than the said. Whereas the said is meaning through naming and through words, the meaning of saying is responsible proximity.

Levinas argues that to engage in a conversation with another person is to approach them. What happens here is not exhausted in what is said. Saying, the fact that one says something to somebody, has meaning that is irrelative of the particular signs used. There is something else or something more to mere communication of signs from one person to the other and a deciphering of these signs by the receiver. What precedes is an exposure of the ego to another, a non-indifference to the other person. This non-indifference is not mere intentionality to address a message, he says; it is proximity, exposure, vulnerability (Levinas 1998: 48). Language always includes that the egoism of the I is compromised in proximity to the other person.

What is interesting here is that saying does not operate through signs such as words, but it is nevertheless meaningful. Saying means a radical vulnerability.

> The one is exposed to the other as a skin is exposed to what wounds it, as a cheek is offered to the smiter. On the hither side of the ambiguity of being and entities, prior to the said, saying uncovers the one that speaks, not as an object disclosed by theory, but in the sense that one discloses oneself by neglecting one's defenses, leaving a shelter, exposing oneself to outrage, to insults and wounding.
>
> (Levinas 1998: 49)

This can be read as a radical openness to the other (see Levinas 1998: 119), an openness that means exposure to that which is unknown, a stranger, something unpredictable. Here we encounter also the idea of the risks included in communication that was emphasised by Gadamer as well. Communication is not safe as one makes oneself vulnerable to the other person by engaging in a dialogue with her. Saying uncovers the one who speaks and leaves him defenceless. Here the theme of the needy and vulnerable human being appears again.

What is the relationship between the saying and the said? This is one of the difficult points in Levinas's thinking. He explains the relationship so that the saying and the said correspond. It is necessary that the saying and the said go together. The one could not exist without the other. The two components of language, the saying and the said, together form what language is. Nevertheless, Levinas argues that saying is primary: it is more important than what is said. Language is born in the face-to-face relationship through the welcoming of the other, and the ethical approach to the other is manifested exactly in that we expose ourselves to the other in communication. This involves uncertainty, a risk, even a sacrifice (Levinas 1998: 120). The human encounter comes first, and only this encounter founds language. And because the human encounter and the welcoming of the other is the seed of all language, it means that language always has at least some ethical quality to it, even if at the same time it is also totalising. Levinas says in *Totality and Infinity* that the essence of language is goodness, friendship and hospitality (Levinas 1969: 305). This way his theory can be read as holding on to the ethical in language no matter what is said and how. Saying can never be fully betrayed by the said.

According to Critchley, ethics is possible on the level of the said as a just said, that is, a said that contains a trace of saying. He reads the argument in *Otherwise than Being* in the following way: the first moment of the argument is an exposition on the level of the said, of entities and their essence and the domination of totality. The second moment is the move from the said to the saying. In the third moment the exposition moves back from the saying to the said in order to discuss questions of justice, politics, community, ontology and philosophy, which belong to the sphere of entities. The question then is whether this third moment is necessarily caught in the logic of totality and the said. Critchley argues that the said of the third moment is different from the said of the first moment, or rather, it is the same said but the said in the third moment includes a trace of saying in it. In the third moment ethics radiates to the levels of politics, justice and ontology. The said in the third moment is a justified said. 'The originality of *Otherwise than Being* perhaps consists in its recognition of the need for an account of the justified Said – that is, of a political language of philosophical questioning that does not reduce ethical transcendence' (Critchley 1999: 229).

Critchley's interpretation is very reasonable. It draws on Levinas's discussion of justice in connection with the problem of the third party, which we return to later. For now, it is important to note that Levinas's theory does not lead to the fact that ethics were impossible on the level of language, intentionality and action. He is not proclaiming the impossibility of moral action, nor is he drawing a distinction between an ethical way of communication, which would be mute, and communication in everyday language, which would necessarily be something outside the ethical sphere. His aim is, rather, to explain the advent of ethics. He wants to describe the ultimate foundation for ethics. This foundation coincides with the foundation for language. Levinas says:

> The pre-original, anarchic saying is proximity, contact, duty without end, a saying still indifferent to the said and saying itself without giving the said, the one-for-the-other, a substitution. It requires the signification of the thematizable, states the idealized said, weighs and judges in justice. Judgments and propositions are born in justice [...].
>
> (Levinas 1998: 161)

An interesting question that springs from the connection between language and ethics is how we can talk about ethics. How is our language equipped to talk (about) ethics? Do we have a specific language game for it? Does Levinas agree with Wittgenstein, who in his lecture on ethics says that when we try to talk about ethics we go beyond meaningful language (see Wittgenstein 1965: 11–12; see, also, Critchley 1999: 264)? For Wittgenstein, ethics is silent. It is situated outside proper language. This idea is something that Levinas's theory includes as well. The problem that both philosophers encounter is that speaking about ethics – in a way that is really ethical – becomes impossible (see Llewelyn 2002a: 170–171, 176–178). But the problem is not as pressing for Levinas as it is for Wittgenstein, however, because Levinas thinks that there is a chance that ethics can leave traces and show itself in the said. Joan Greisch argues that we can also find similarities between the two philosophers by comparing Levinas's the saying and the said, and Wittgenstein's showing and saying (Greisch 1991: 77; see, also, Overgaard 2007). The thought is that there are two sides to language which both carry different kinds of meaning is illustrated in this reading.

According to Greisch, in later Wittgenstein the big question that he is studying is what the essence of language is, and this question gets its answer, or one could argue, is *dissolved* in the diversity of language games. Levinas's philosophy amounts to an attempt to identify *the* language game, which could be called transcendental, which contains in itself the condition for the possibility of all other language games. But this language game, which is signifyingness anterior to signification (the Levinasian version of the meaning of meaning), is located both inside language and prior to it (Greisch 1991: 70).

It is interesting to compare Levinas and Wittgenstein because there are some similarities also in their views on the content of ethics. Levinas does not offer us a thorough theory on how to be ethical or on what is good and bad in particular situations. He focuses on the condition of the possibility of ethics.[4] Through the

4 Levinas claims that he is only interested in meta-ethics, or in the meaning of ethics: '*Ma tâche ne consiste pas à construire l'éthique; j'essaie seulement d'en chercher le sens*' (Levinas 1982: 85).

notion of saying, the ethical becomes something that is *in* language, but which we cannot talk about. Wittgenstein also thinks that the content of ethics is beyond the reach of language. This idea, which is developed in the *Tractatus*, can be seen to influence his later thinking as well. We can see form of life as something at least partly ethical of which we cannot really talk because it is the horizon of language. Wittgenstein was preoccupied with ethical and religious questions and what it means to be good during his whole life (see, for example, Malcolm 1993). In a way he, through excluding ethics from language, leaves it as it is, as a question of every person's subjective choice, which is similar to Levinas's approach. However, one could disagree with Greisch who argues that neither of the philosophers found a morality (see Greisch 1991: 72–74). Levinas's theory does strive at having consequences because he offers at least a sketch of what ethics is and what it is to be responsible.

Whatever the similarities between Levinas and Wittgenstein are, it cannot, of course, be stressed enough that major differences between the two also exist. One can say that Wittgenstein, especially in his later work, is primarily interested in language, whereas Levinas's main concern is ethics and the ethical nature of being human. Their projects are rather different. However, on a rough scale, Levinas and the later Wittgenstein seem to agree that the foundation of language is some kind of intersubjectivity or a 'being with'. Wittgenstein only takes us so far, to the common shared life underlying language; he does not say that language has an ethical foundation. The background for language consists of shared judgments and agreement, but we should be careful not to read too much ethics into this. Nevertheless, we can recall here, for instance, Wittgenstein's fascinating remark that meaning is like going up to someone. Wittgenstein has also been read as a transcendental thinker. Sami Pihlström writes:

> This emphasis on 'the background' is an emphasis on our common life with other language-users (i.e., our potential listeners) as a transcendental condition for the possibility of our ever making meaningful utterances or producing meaningful bits of writing.
>
> (Pihlström 2006: 191–192)

According to Pihlström, the social nature of language and the possibility of a listener are presuppositionally necessary for the kind of meaningfulness we take to be actual in our language-use. However, the background of shared language as a necessary condition of meaningfulness cannot be identified independently of the very language use whose meaningfulness it conditions (Pihlström 2006: 193–197). The conditions of language are in that language itself. This is similar to Levinas's view. In the last sentence of *Otherwise than Being*, Levinas speaks of 'unpronounceable inscription'. This notion is related to what Derrida calls '*arche-writing*', that is something that is presupposed by writing and speaking (Llewelyn 2002b: 128–129). It does not enter into any present and cannot really be named, but it is something that affects all naming. Thus it is unpronounceable. Saying cannot be expressed; it is something that lies beneath all writing and speaking. Saying is another kind of language, a communication otherwise that is still communication. Levinas challenges us to think about limits, about the other and the otherwise. It is the task of philosophy to reflect on that which cannot be spoken about. Thus both views on language contain the idea that language is founded on something that transcends it, but that is still shown in language itself.

## The third

What is the meaning of the ethical face-to-face encounter on the social level of day-to-day life? As the relationship between ethics and politics (or law) was left rather open in Levinas's work, later research has searched for different ways of seeing the problematic issue. Law and the legal sphere are a problem because it seems that law is fundamentally unethical (see Derrida 1999b: 20). Levinas's legal philosophical question is: How can there be justice? (Levinas 1982: 84). Is law necessarily a totalising activity, something that is completely other than the ethical relationship between two people? There are many inconsistencies, even contradictions, which follow from trying to expand Levinas's first philosophy to a more substantial theory.

According to Levinas, the question of justice is awakened when the I encounters the face of the other and realises that there are numerous others. These people are third parties, any one of whom can be other. The I and the other are not alone in the world. Who am I responsible for if there are an infinite number of others? My responsibility cannot be an infinite responsibility for all of them, because I can only be infinitely responsible for the other. Then how about the third? We are forced into a situation which is much more complicated than a straightforward face-to-face relationship in which I have responsibility for the other.[5] Because of the third, I have to compare people, to make calculations, to obtain information and knowledge, to compare something that cannot be compared (Levinas 2000: 230). The question of justice and with it questions of equality, fairness and the like spring from our encounter with the third.

The vast field of problems that are opened by the third are legal and political. It is here that we move into the level of social organisation and complex social relationships. If there were only two people in the world, we would in Levinas's view

5 Desmond Manderson offers an alternative interpretation of Levinas's idea of infinite responsibility. He claims that Levinas is often misunderstood on this point. 'When Levinas speaks of responsibility as infinite, he does not mean that it extends equally over everything it encounters, like some monstrous sump of duty. It is infinitely deep, not infinitely wide' (see Manderson 2007: 153). Manderson thinks that responsibility should not here be thought of as a responsibility towards an infinite amount of others. On this reading many problems of combining Levinas and law disappear, as Manderson notes. However, it can be argued that on this reading the whole discussion of the third that Levinas engages in becomes odd as the scope of responsibility is already limited from the beginning. In the essay 'Response', Manderson agrees that his understanding of infinite responsibility is slightly different from Levinas's (Manderson 2009b: 213).

not need law or courts of justice; there would only be the other of whom the I would be asymmetrically and infinitely responsible (see Levinas 1984: 58). It is important to note that the shift from the ethical relationship to the sphere of the third is not a temporal dislocation. The third is encountered in encountering the other. Levinas says: 'The third party isn't there by accident. In a certain sense, all the others [*autres*] are present in the face of the other [*autrui*]' (Levinas 2000: 106; see, also, Manderson 2006: 153). It can therefore be seen as a question of a double discourse (Critchley 1999: 227–229). A double structure is present here: the place of the ethical meeting of the same and the other is also the anonymous kingdom of innumerable thirds.

Levinas does not see the State as evil but acknowledges the importance of it. However, he does question the possibility of a political and totalising way of thinking to give answers to all social and political questions. According to Levinas, society and the political structure are dependent on the ethical relationship (Critchley 2002: 24). And vice versa: ethics also needs a just society. '[C]harity is impossible without justice, and [...] justice is warped without charity' (Levinas 2000: 121). Even if the law restricts the infinite responsibility for the other, a legal system is necessary. It is a sphere of responsibility where we are responsible for one another, similarly as in the face-to-face relationship. With the third, justice begins. Moreover, in law, responsibility is based on and awoken by the face of the other. The third can here too be encountered as an other (Levinas 2000: 229).

However, fundamental differences exist between ethics on the one hand and politics or law on the other. Ethics cannot in Levinas's theory dictate rules for how to act in different situations. When we move from the level of the face-to-face to the level of the thirds, the relationship between people changes from the ethical to morality, politics and law. In this transportation ethics hardens its skin (Levinas 1984: 65). How, then, does ethics play a role in politics or law, and can it really play any role? According to Levinas, the face-to-face relationship should *inspire* morality, politics and law (Levinas 1984: 65–66). Thus, even if law has a hard skin, it is still based on the face-to-face relationship between the I and the other. The foundation for different institutions of law is the relationship between people, and institutions can be controlled, criticised and changed, if need be, on that basis (Levinas 1982: 76).

## The difficulty of law

Law is above all else a collection of norms which include generalisations and universalisation. One challenge for law in a Levinasian way of thinking is to combine respect for the singularity of every person and every separate case with the general nature of the law. Responsible and just law remembers the uniqueness of each particular person, his special case and situation. It does not reduce persons to a faceless crowd but takes care of everyone in his or her otherness. How can this be achieved in law? In order to be responsible and just, law has to have room for individuals and it has to stay open to exceptions, to difference and to otherness.

This is a real and serious problem for law, but on the reading of Levinas put forward here, it is not impossible.

It is important to consider whether the fact that law operates with rules and exceptions necessarily means that law is confined to a totalising or generalising activity. The way legal norms appear in language can also be seen as a way to make room for difference and otherness, for exceptional situations, for strangeness, surprises and changing circumstances. Thus it is not necessary to think that law is only a field of totalisation. Law can be open to otherness and individuality. It is also possible in the field of law to remember the persons in a crowd. The shift from the sphere of the other and the same to the sphere of the third does not have to bring with it a complete forgetting of the ethical attitude (Levinas 1995: 176–178).[6]

We can think of a Levinas-inspired legal theory as one in which justice is not connected with coherence or stability. Pluralism and polycentrism are welcome because they allow for more flexibility and room for difference and otherness. Strict formalism and the ideal of a non-contradictory system of norms might be too unyielding for a situational respect for individuality and otherness. Fragmentation of the law can be welcomed from this point of view, if it means that the aims and values of law are kept as broad as possible (see, for example, Eriksson *et al.* 1998)[7]. Ethics needs space. The idea is that too tight a system, too rigid an organisation, does not allow for differing voices and otherness (Levinas 1995: 149–153; see, also, Heller 1992: 354–360).

It can be argued that law also brings people together on a very practical level. Legal practice, the trial for instance, brings them to the same room. Here parties come together and face each other on a forum provided by law. Law is also the medium in which people can make arrangements, enter contracts and marry, divorce, adopt, and so on. It is not necessary to see law as only something that dissociates us from relationships with each other, because it also brings parties to face each other and encourages them to take responsibility. In the sphere of legislation, this can also be seen when different means are taken to care for common tasks. Law therefore does not necessarily stand in contradiction with ethics. Ethics, when understood as responsibility taken for other people, is important in law as well.

Justice, for Levinas, implies also that the other is allowed to stay other. If this is justice, and if a call for justice is inherent in law, then respect for otherness should feature at the centre of law. The reception of Levinas's thinking in legal theory, which has mostly been confined to so-called critical legal scholars, has largely concentrated on this idea (see, for example, Douzinas and Warrington 1991: 117–124;

6 As Manderson points out, Levinas's own view of law is rather narrow. He does not say very much about it, but what he says points in the direction of law being positivistic, codified and rule-bound (Manderson 2006: 9–10; see, also, Manderson 2007).

7 See, also, Wilhelmsson on the fragmentation of law; for example, *Senmodern ansvarsrätt* (2001).

Diamantides 2000; Wolcher 2003: 109–116; Diamantides 2007).[8] Justification for the legal system comes from the way it respects and carries responsibility for the other. In Levinasian terms, an intrusion into the lives of people by force can be justified only in relation to faces, people. There are limits to the powers of a State. Levinas's view is opposite to a Hobbesian way of thinking in which the State is born from the need to restrict and limit the use of violence. In this view, there is, according to Levinas, no way of restricting the State's power if the State is necessary in keeping violent people reined in (Levinas 2000: 105). Levinas's thinking has quite different presuppositions. Here, there is not war but peace where people come together. Justice, the State and law are born in peaceful encounters. The justification of the legal system is assessed from this point of view, in which it is important to limit the State's use of power and coercive force.

As noted above, Levinas thinks that law as a system with institutions is necessary because we are more than just two people. Even a certain amount of violence is acceptable. Thus Levinas's ethics is radical, but it does not lead to anarchism: '[I]f one speaks of justice, it is necessary to allow judges, it is necessary to allow institutions and the State; to live in a world of citizens, and not only in the order of the Face to Face' (Levinas 2000: 105). But, Levinas continues, only through the relationship between the other and myself is the State and the legal system justified. A State that does not respect otherness and carry responsibility for the vulnerable is a totalitarian State (Levinas 2000: 100, 105, 120).

Responsibility in the field of law is not only a responsibility that the system or the sovereign carries; it includes a responsibility of everybody towards others. The relationship between two people and the relationship between thirds go hand in hand. A responsible attitude towards a fellow human is responsibility towards the whole of humanity (see Critchley 1999: 223). Ethical face-to-face responsibility always takes place in a society, in a time and a place. Ethics, justice and law are in the same place. The face is the face of the other but also the face of everybody else. The question of justice that is the challenge of law is an ethical as well as a legal challenge.

The ethical relationship is not a relationship of equality. The other always comes first. The radicalism of Levinas's thinking is the asymmetrical nature of my responsibility for the other person. The ethical relationship is not a relationship between two equal subjects because the central role is held by the other, whose hostage I am. And my responsibility is given to me regardless of my acts and intentions. I am always responsible already. How can this line of thinking be incorporated into the legal field? Levinas demands that law should mimic ethics, but how? The question of the subject who has been taken hostage is a point where the thinking of Levinas is perhaps most strongly at odds with that of a lawyer. It is very difficult to imagine a legal system in which responsibility would not follow

8 Many legal theoretical attempts to solve the Levinasian problem of justice have taken inspiration from Derrida's writings as well.

from actions and negligence. And a legal system should also be fair and treat people as equals. However, Levinasian legal theory is not utopian in that it would require inequality or moving away from the concept of the legal subject. The idea is simply that *qua* being human, a person is already given a responsibility for their actions and has no way of escaping this responsibility. Their egoism has limits. It is with the help of their responsibility as a human being that we can assess the acceptability of their actions.

Desmond Manderson has argued in a similar vein that justice and law proceed from the ethical relation between people. It is the face-to-face encounter, our proximity with other people, which compels us to think about justice and politics (Manderson 2006: 19–20). He understands the law of negligence as the soul and the foundation of law. The questions that this field of law has to solve are very Levinasian: Why should we care for others? And how much? (Manderson 2007: 145). Levinas acknowledges that it is necessary to weigh and balance, to compare and calculate. But the law can nevertheless be understood through proximity, and Manderson claims that, for instance, the High Court of Australia has done so in a number of cases.[9] The notion of 'proximity' was a radical jurisprudential development in that it allowed the Court to remain responsive to the unpredictable complexity of circumstances as it took proximity as an experience and not as a rule. In addition, through analysing cases with the help of the idea of proximity, the Court did not have to found responsibility on the conscious choices and information of the parties but could develop the idea of responsibility as a predicament instead of a choice. This was, in Manderson's view, a responsibility that comes close to Levinas's asymmetrical, non-consensual, infinite responsibility (Manderson 2007: 145–146).

According to Manderson, the question for the law of torts is a question that brings us down to the level of you and I, our responsibility towards each other. Tortious obligation, particularly the duty of care, can be understood in Levinasian terms as our initial indebtedness to the other instead of an artificial limitation on our freedom (Manderson 2009a: 115). Moreover, the law of negligence always introduces the particular, even though political and social issues might be attached. Here Manderson seems to recognise the soul of law, which is an ethical one (Manderson 2006: 186). However, one can disagree with this and argue that no legal decision-making whatever the legal field can be detached from the level of you and I. This is true for criminal law, family law as well as all other fields of law. The particular always comes into legal decision-making because legal decisions have to take responsibility for what is done to the parties in the case and other persons indirectly affected. The issue that Levinas's theory especially helps

9 Manderson connects this tendency of the court to the influential judgments of Justice William Deane, who was appointed in 1982. He retired from the Court in 1995 to become Governor General of Australia, after which the notion of proximity became decreasingly important in the rulings of the Court, finally disappearing by 1998 (Manderson 2007: 146–147).

us to see is the agonising fact that there are always more parties than one. Very often law has to choose between interests that are not easily reconciled and thus law always risks being violent. From the point of view of the judge in a civil law dispute, for instance, both parties are 'others' and should be respected.

What is interesting in Manderson's analysis is that Levinasian responsibility is something that cannot be codified or fixed, but it can nevertheless be applied. He claims that we need to insist on the value of such an approach in law that is not reducible to a rule. Law can be reconciled with the idea that responsibility happens to us whether we choose it or not. It comes to us through proximity, through us being close to other people, living and interacting with them. Responsibility 'is not a product of our intentions but of the vulnerability of the other' (Manderson 2007: 150). This can be understood as the basis of a legal duty of care. We are responsible simply because we are there, near the other person, who is vulnerable.

Levinasian ethics is intriguing in that, on the one hand, it makes ethics very abstract, something of which we cannot know anything, but, on the other, he stresses that ethics is here and now, in the everyday actions of people, in their lives from day to day. Ethics is something that is necessarily very personal (see, for example, Llewelyn 2002a: 85–93). It is not a theory, not a system of norms, not something hard to understand we have to study. It touches real people, it concerns everybody. Justice should be similar. It should be close to people and close to life. It should take its starting point in the uniqueness of real persons. This way we carry our ethical responsibility every day in the legal field as well. Ethics is not a spectator sport: nor is law (Critchley 2002: 22; see, also, Critchley 1999: 225). The unique personal experience of every human being should lie at the focus of attention.

A fundamental element in the reading of Levinas put forward here is the close connection between law and justice. It is taken for granted that justice is something internal to law, something that we have to demand of law, an ideal without which law cannot exist. Justice is a kind of gateway between ethics and law. It belongs in the ethical face-to-face relationship from which it is born, but it is also something internal to law. It brings ethics and law together as it opens law up for the ethical challenge but also contributes to making ethics something substantial, anchoring it in real life. However, ethics and law are still kept separate. They are not dissolved into each other. The positivity of modern law is not threatened, as law is a system of its own. Justice can be seen as a border or a limit that unites the two fields.[10] A Levinasian legal theory does not mean natural law theory; it does not force upon us some universal timeless values or rights that have to be upheld. On the contrary, it is open to different values. What it does impose on us is a limitless responsibility that can be carried in many different ways.

10 Levinas uses the term 'justice' in ways that make it difficult to know when he talks about justice as justness and when he refers to the legal system (see Derrida 1999b: 33: 'When Levinas says "justice," we are also authorized to hear "law," it seems to me.').

Levinas's theory opens up the problem of the compatibility of justice as responsibility and law as totalising force. It develops into a general problem about the possibility of justice, which has received many sceptical answers. Is it ever really possible for law to be just? Levinas's answer is that law is not, and cannot be, totally autonomous or independent. Because law is born as the face is encountered, it is born at the beginning, as the human being is born. The question of justice stems from the simple fact that we are humans. There is no way of escaping it. And the only justification that can be given law and its exercise of power is that ethics needs it. Ethics and law are like twins.

Critchley makes an interesting point on the Levinasian distinction between ethics and law. He wonders whether we could understand the practice of law as an ambivalence between the ethical saying and the language of the said. The saying can only show itself in the said by contesting and interrupting it. Nevertheless, even when disrupting the said it can only manifest itself in the language of the said. Thus a spiral of disruption occurs. The movement is between 'the unavoidable language of the Said and the attempt to unsay that Said in order to locate the Saying within it' (Critchley 2009: 210). If law is understood as the continuous oscillation between the saying and the said, this would mean an ongoing oscillation between anarchic proximity and codified black letter law. Law would be the enigmatic relationship between ethical responsibility, which is anarchic, and codified rules that form a totalising system (Critchley 2009: 209–211).

Ethics requires law and vice versa. But what precisely is required, what the exact content of law is, is not dictated by ethics. It does not follow logically or in other ways directly from ethics.[11] This way a strange kind of silence prevails between law and ethics (see Derrida 1999b: 115–118; see, also, Critchley 2007b: 98). This can be seen as a lack, even a crisis similar to that crisis of legal interpretation described above. Even if we could imagine law inspired by ethics, what would a jurisprudence of alterity look like? What kind of substantive commitments would it entail?[12] These are the questions of the reader who is frustrated by Levinasians' lack of answers.

Levinas does indeed leave many questions unanswered. Much of the research has striven to find in Levinas ways for criticising law. To criticise Levinas with the help of law has been much less popular. Critchley argues that an explosion of interest in Levinas's thinking has occurred in recent years (not only in legal theory), but much of the work has been commentaries, exegeses, comparisons with other thinkers and even homage. He urges scholars to also study Levinas critically and argues that politics is the critical point of Levinas's work (see

11 'In short, for a Levinasian, every particular norm is contestable but the *moment* of normativity – that the other makes a claim on me to which I cannot be entirely indifferent – is incontestable' (Perpich 2009: 34, emphasis in original).

12 See on these issues, for example, Smith (2009: 64–65).

Critchley 2007b). Arguably not only politics, but law as well. We shall return to Levinasian ideas on law and justice later on.

## A Levinasian theory of interpretation?

When it was suggested in an interview that the ethical relation is 'entirely utopian and unrealistic', Levinas answered:

> This is the great objection to my thought. 'Where did you ever see the ethical relation practised?', people say to me. I reply that its being utopian does not prevent it from investing our everyday actions of generosity or goodwill towards the other: even the smallest and most commonplace gestures, such as saying 'after you' as we sit at the dinner table or walk through a door, bear witness to the ethical. This concern for the other remains utopian in the sense that it is always 'out of place' (*u-topos*) in this world, always other than the 'ways of the world'; but there are many examples of it in the world.
>
> (Levinas 1984: 68)

It is interesting that here one example that indicates ethicality is an expression, an utterance of 'after you'. However, in this citation we sense yet again the tension between the ethical level and the level of morality, which is the level of this world. This tension is reflected in language, where language is on the one hand the place where the ethical relation is enabled and on the other a betrayal of the ethical where the other is reduced to the sphere of the same.

Language, understanding and knowledge belong to the sphere of thirds, not the face-to-face relationship with the other. However, it is important to remember that the sphere of the third begins in the ethical relationship. Language is something that resides in both spheres. It is both saying and the said, both hospitality and propositional speech. From here it follows that interpretation can be seen as both ethical and moral/political/social. Understood this way, interpretation is not *either* ethical *or* political: it is both. On this reading, some of the theoretical problems created by a sharp distinction of ethics on the one hand and morality, politics and law on the other can be evaded.

Can interpretation be considered as an ethical act in the Levinasian sense? Is it an act in which the other is reduced to the same, or does the possibility exist of preserving the otherness of the other? The starting point for a Levinasian theory of interpretation could be that we are conscious of the fact that the text in its otherness can never be totally understood or mastered (Tuohimaa (Enwald) 1999: 180–186). Interpretation should not strive at authentic or ordinary meaning, but accept that some meanings always stay hidden. It is through the other who resists our totalising endeavours that the same is questioned. Likewise, the resistance of the other also opens up the need for interpretation. The need for both ethics and interpretation appears when our normal understanding is prevented (Tuohimaa (Enwald) 1999: 189). But the problem of a Levinasian view on interpretation is that it cannot really explain how interpretation does not end up in totalising activity. How can we *not* transform otherness to the same when interpreting an utterance?

The problem of understanding and interpretation is that they carry with them hospitality and welcoming, but they also imply taking otherness into possession (see, also, Wyschogrod 2002: 199–202). It is around this paradox that a Levinasian theory of interpretation has to evolve. A central idea for such a theory could be that in interpretation the sender and the receiver meet in friendship. This means that the receiver is benevolent towards the text in a similar way as hermeneutic theory presupposes. Interpretation is preceded by a welcoming of the other, a tending towards the other, a 'yes' to the other. But a Levinasian view of interpretation takes the idea of benevolence further. Interpretation has to break free from totalising thinking. To acknowledge the fluidity of meaning is a step in this direction. Levinasian interpretation would resemble deconstruction more than hermeneutics in that it does not search for unity and coherence but allows for otherness and difference, anomalies and obscurities, to stay as they are.

Levinas's theory has inspired some (critical) legal theorists, but those who have studied him have more often concentrated on the above-discussed problem of law being fundamentally unethical. Much less attention has been given to a Levinas-inspired theory of legal interpretation. However, as we have already concluded that ethical elements are always present in interpretation, his ethics combined with his thoughts on language can clearly be relevant here. To bring back the idea of the crisis of legal interpretation, what Levinasian thinking proposes is that we should not see indeterminacy in meaning as opposed to responsible or good interpretation (see Levinas 1984: 58). An interpretation cannot be anchored to anything other than a respect for the otherness of the text and an acknowledgement that the interpreter has a responsibility of his or her interpretation whether they want to or not. This is not to deny that when interpreting we are necessarily dealing with politics as well. Meanings are found and made, interpretations are done. They are activities that include choices by people.

What we can conclude so far is that no meaning is the first, the last or the correct one. Legal interpretation is a process without end. It is a labyrinth in which we move with no guarantees that we have chosen the right path. It is essential that we acknowledge that it is always *somebody* who interprets. To arrest the play of signification is to make an arrest, it is an *act* that is done and that has to be done. As the word 'arrest' hints, it is an interruption.

I argue that the gap between a text and meaning is also a question of ethics. Language is always also ethical. This is a view inspired by hermeneutics as well as Levinasian ethics. What could an ethics of legal interpretation more specifically entail? An ethics of reading law could perhaps be a call to respect the otherness of the text; to respect its shifting meanings and endless references. We could say in a Levinas-inspired way that the interpreter should not try to possess the text, to own it or completely take hold of it. This requires a certain kind of humility on the part of the interpreter. They should listen to what the text wants to say and stay open to the uniqueness of the text. However, in the field of law this kind of approach is not fully appropriate. Law and legal decision-making are very different from other speaking and interpreting situations. The particular situation in which the legal decision-maker finds himself or herself has to be taken into account. They are often in a difficult position where much more is at stake than constructing a good interpretation of a legal text. The pressure of the situation, which is not void of ideological and political content, has already been hinted at. Now, in order to be able to focus on the unique character of legal interpretation, we have to deepen the analysis of the interpreter and their responsibility.

How to think about responsibility in connection with *legal* interpretation is the question. In the following, Miller's ideas on the ethics of reading are discussed. These ideas can complement the above-discussed picture of interpretation drawn from hermeneutics and deconstruction along with the strong ethical content that Levinas's theory introduces to the debate. Inspired by Miller's thoughts, we can divide the responsibility of the legal interpreter into two different but interlinked aspects.

## Miller and the ethics of reading

Miller, in his work entitled *The Ethics of Reading* (1987), offers a sketch of what ethics there is in reading. The book begins by asking just this question. What does the 'of' in the ethics of reading signify? Does it mean ethical action generated by reading, or does it mean an ethics intrinsic to meaning? In what sense can reading be ethical or have an ethical import? After all, is reading not something cognitive, striving at knowledge, something to do with understanding? According to Miller, a necessary ethical moment occurs in the act of reading as such. This moment is neither cognitive nor political, nor social, nor interpersonal, but ethical (Miller 1987: 1). The 'of' in ethical reading is a double genitive. It goes both ways at once. It signifies an ethics intrinsic to the act of reading but also an ethics of the act that reflects outside the text. Reading has ethical implications for our moral, social, and political lives.

Miller uses examples, and a large part of the book consists of him reading literary texts as well as him reading authors reading themselves. He claims that shifting ground from the common, almost universal, topic of literary studies, which investigates political, historical, and social connections of literature to ethics, means shifting focus to something less speculative and vague.

> To speak of the ethics of reading rather than, for example, of the 'politics of interpretation' returns from an area of investigation which is likely to be vague and speculative, often unhelpfully polemical, to something that has at least a chance to be concrete, namely the real situation of a man or woman reading a book, teaching a class, writing a critical essay. No doubt that 'situation' spreads out to involve institutional, historical, economic, and political 'contexts', but it begins with and returns to the man or woman face to face with the words on the page. My question is whether ethical decision or responsibility is in any way

> necessarily involved in that situation and act of reading, and if so, how and of what kind, responsibility to whom or to what, decision to do what?
>
> (Miller 1987: 4)

Here we see the same emphasis on the concrete, the singular and the unique that is important in Levinas's work. For Miller, the ethical moment in reading faces two directions. On the one hand, he explains, it means a response to something, responsible to it, responsive of it and respectful of it. Any ethical moment involves an imperative 'I must', so too in reading and interpretation. If the response is not grounded in some 'must', if it is a freedom to, for example, make a text mean whatever one likes, then it is not ethical. On the other hand, the ethical moment in reading is also an act. Therefore it enters into the social, political and also legal realms. Miller admits that the ethical and the political are undoubtedly always in some way intertwined, but there is also a difference between the two. An ethical act that is fully determined by political considerations is no longer ethical. The ethical moment in reading must be something individual and particular, itself a source of political and other kinds of acts, not subordinate to them. Input must flow from reading, from literature, towards the political and the social. An influx of performative power must flow from the linguistic transactions involved in the act of reading into the realms of knowledge or politics. In studies that focus on the political, social and ideological aspects of literature, the work is often seen as entirely accounted for and accountable to forces and powers coming from outside itself. Literature does not make history but is made by it. Thus the study of literature is actually a study of something else in which the work is only a symptom or structure of something else more important. Thus literature in these approaches is a by-product of history, not something that in any way makes history (Miller 1987: 5–8). It is these approaches that Miller especially wants to contest. He wants to return the focus to the work itself and the act of reading the work. The work's autonomy as well as its power to really say something is what a theory of interpretation should be interested in.

Thus Miller stresses the text, not the context. Interpretation has to begin with, and return to, the text and reading itself. He claims that hermeneutical theories of meaning, be they Marxist, Gadamerian or psychoanalytic, measure and ascertain the meaning of a text by something non-textual outside that text, for instance God, society, history or the psychology of the author.[13] These models of reading involve in Miller's view vagueness and unfounded speculation. The vagueness begins already where the relation between the text and the context is defined.

13 In light of the way Gadamer is read in this book it is unclear why Miller counts Gadamerian hermeneutics as one of these theories. Also, Gadamer's theory can well be understood as one that focuses on the text itself.

> All of these models belong to the problematic of inside outside polarities, open to a variety of crossings, displacements, and substitutions, as inside becomes outside, outside inside, or as features on either side cross over the wall, membrane, or partition dividing the sides.
>
> (Miller 1987: 7)

How do the text and its context actually relate to each other, and how does each of these take part in the meaning of the text? The problem of context is central in interpretation, but according to Miller, even when the relation of the text to its context has been determined, the work of interpretation has only just begun. The difficult task of interpreting the text still lies ahead. The problem remains of how the context inheres in the fine grain of the text and its language. The difficult work of actually reading the text still has to be done. It is therefore not the context, or the psychology of the author, or any other non-textual element that should be in focus in interpretation. It is simply the text itself that should lead the reader to its meaning. Each of the models – Marxist, psychoanalytic and so on – still requires a vigilant and sophisticated analysis of the text itself. Interpretation, even if the focus were on the historical or social relations of the text, always remains within the study of language (Miller 1987: 5–8).

Miller explains:

> [T]here is a claim made on the author writing the work, on the narrator telling the story within the fiction of the novel, on the characters within the story at decisive moments of their lives, and on the reader, teacher, or critic responding to the work. This ethical 'I must' cannot, I propose to show, be accounted for by the social and historical forces that impinge upon it. In fact the ethical moment contests these forces or is subversive of them.
>
> (Miller 1987: 8)

The ethical moment has these four dimensions, or rather, four ethical moments are connected with a text: that of the author, the narrator, the characters and the reader. Here, we see clearly that Miller mostly has in mind the literary novel; however, he also uses other texts as examples, for instance philosophical works. The ethical claim on the reader means that each reading is ethical.

> Far from being 'indeterminate' or 'nihilistic', however, or a matter of wanton free play or arbitrary choice, each reading is, strictly speaking, ethical, in the sense that it *has* to take place, by an implacable necessity, as the response to a categorical demand, and in the sense that the reader *must* take responsibility for it and for its consequences in the personal, social, and political worlds.
>
> (Miller 1987: 59, emphasis in original)

The ethics of reading has a twofold character: first, an 'I must' is inscribed in every act of reading, which means a necessary response to the text. Second, every act of reading takes place in a time and a situation, and the reader has to take responsibility for its consequences. This second element is a freedom the reader has, a freedom that involves a responsibility for the choices he or she makes in his or her reading and interpretation, choices in the social, political or legal context (Miller 1987: 43). The situation in which the reader finds themselves is one where an irresistible demand is placed on them to respond, but in which they are still free to choose their response. There is thus an ethical moment in the reading itself, but the reading is also an act that has ethical consequences in a broader context. Reading is not, therefore, seen as first, a cognitive, linguistic activity which then acquires implications, including ethical ones. The ethics of reading and interpretation is argued for in this study in a way that underlines an ethical element in using and understanding language itself, an ethical element right at the heart of meaning. It is a necessary element, even if not a sufficient one, for any meaning to exist at all.

Miller's reading of de Man gives us more information on how Miller sees ethics being inscribed in reading. He says that his choice in taking de Man as an example is motivated by the fact that in his view de Man's work has been widely misunderstood, partly because it includes difficult passages and is not easy to read. De Man is often seen as an example of the worst kind of deconstructive theory, which undermines the value of humanistic study and 'reduces the work of interpretation to the free play of arbitrary imposition of meaning, finds in each text only what it went there to look for, and so on' (Miller 1987: 42). This picture of deconstruction and other theories close to it, with which Miller's own work has also been associated, is far from correct, and it might be argued that this characterisation fits the critics of deconstructionists better than the deconstructionists themselves.

In de Man's work, ethicity is a reference to something extra-linguistic by way of the linguistic. It is somewhere in the midst of an intricate sequence in which language is interwoven with, for instance, referential, allegorical, ethical and political dimensions (Miller 1987: 44).

There can be no final reading of a text. Miller points out that the ethical moment occurs here. Ethicity is failure to read. Ethical judgment is a necessary feature of human language. Ethics does not derive from some transcendent law or imperative, but it is something that belongs to language. Thus de Man's theory, in contrast to Kantian theories of ethics, is a linguistic theory in a slightly similar vein to Levinas's. Ethicity intervenes when the act of reading bars access to an understanding of the act of reading. We cannot understand what it is that we are doing when we read. This failure involves making ethical judgments and demands (Miller 1987: 45–48). Exact and defined meaning always escapes and the failure has an allegorical structure: one thing is said and another thing meant, and what is meant is always out of reach. To acknowledge this is to acknowledge in a certain sense the impossibility of reading. Ethics, or ethicity, is present in the impossibility of reading.

Ethics is a kind of linguistic confusion. We are always confused when we try to make language referential. We go on in communication as if the allegory was not there. However, Miller thinks that we must strive for meaning and truth even though it is impossible to achieve them. It is necessary that we make ethical judgments, give commands and make promises and go on as if meaning could be transmitted so that we can mean exactly what we say. This is the form that law takes as well. Even though the intention of the lawmaker always escapes, we have to go on interpreting legal texts and the commands that they give. A careful interpreter of a text sees that they cannot get their interpretation right. Every legal text is fundamentally unreadable in the sense that no reading can find out the *truth* about the text. Still, every interpretation tries to make referential judgments of the text. This includes making ethical judgments (see Miller 1987: 53–54).

Interpretations of texts lack ground. In a similar way, ethical judgments also lack a foundation. Ethics cannot refer to something outside itself. There are no universal transcendent ethical imperatives, and thus ethics is fundamentally unjustified. Through this idea of the unjustified and ungrounded nature of ethics, we see how Miller's thinking leads to an affirmation of responsibility that is not grounded in any rules or determinable meanings. Responsibility does not become meaningless, that is, it is not annulled because of the fact that there is no foundation for meaning. It cannot be guaranteed by rules but has to find its way otherwise.

Critchley raises a number of objections to Miller's ideas. According to Critchley, Miller understands ethics very traditionally as a region of philosophical inquiry and not in a more radical Levinasian sense. Miller's conception of ethics is also explicitly and narrowly textual. The ethical moment arises as a response to a text, and the paradigmatic ethical situation is that of a man or a woman reading a book in a literature class. In contrast, for Critchley the ethical moment is that of being addressed by the other person in a way that challenges and requires responsibility (Critchley 1999: 47–48). Critchley also criticises Miller for leaving the passage from ethics to politics insufficiently elaborated. The precise nature of the political context and political actions is not explained by Miller. Additionally, for Critchley, Miller's ethics is too abstract. It may lead to an empty formal universalism. Ethics is simply a universal command to respect, an 'I must', or a moment of sublimity derived from a text and then somehow translated into political action (Critchley 1999: 47–48). How this happens and what actually happens in this 'I must' is not explained by Miller.

It is certainly true that Miller's exposition of the ethics of reading leaves many things open. It nevertheless invites a way of thinking that can be fruitful, even though it needs further elaboration. Critchley admits the merits of Miller but sees it necessary to complement his theory with that of Levinas and especially Derrida in order to construct an ethics of deconstruction. This way Critchley's project is in many ways close to the one in this study. However, it must also be remembered that both Critchley's and Miller's work is partly affected by their aim to defend deconstruction against charges of immorality, which is not my objective here.

Even though some things are left open, I nevertheless agree with Miller that an ethical responsibility arises not only in our everyday actions but also in the way we read and write.[14] Reading and writing are not something outside the ethical sphere. An element of ethics is necessary for meaning and understanding. It implies a foundational willingness to understand. But the ethics of reading has another dimension as well. The twofold character of the ethics of reading that spreads to the social and political spheres is an especially important idea in the legal field.

The legal interpreter has a twofold task when interpreting the legal text. Their ethical responsibility is double. They have a responsibility towards the text they are interpreting but also a broader responsibility for the situation in which the interpretation is done. They have to respond to the demand of the text and simultaneously to the ethical demand of the interpretive act with its consequences. The second dimension is the situational and practical level in which the meaning of the text becomes a meaning with regard to the reader, their identity and the application of the text in a situation.

## Returning to semantics

Even though a certain kind of foundation or provenance of meaning is located in the ethical field, this does not mean that language itself would be forgotten. Semantics is important, but it is important in a new way. The conception of interpretation put forward here is built upon the premise that the wording of a legal text takes part in producing the meaning of the text, but it cannot do this alone. Therefore, the argument does not deny that words have meanings, or that in many cases consensus exists on some common ways in which to use words in different discourses.

We interpret words on pages or spoken aloud, that is, different kinds of texts. They are and should be the starting point for legal interpretation. But their being what we interpret, they cannot at the same time be an answer to *how* we interpret. We interpret in order to get an understanding of and decide upon what a text and the words in it mean. They cannot explain themselves. This means that words and semantics are important after all. Words and the way they are used in the text, along with other features that the text contains, are extremely important. This is the whole idea of respecting the text. The text with its special and unique features is what should be focused on.

The crisis of legal interpretation includes the loss of criteria for good and bad interpretations. These criteria have sometimes been sought in language, but it has become clear that they are not to be found there. The idea was that by pinpointing correctness of the meaning of words we would have an objective and neutral standard by which to measure judges' interpretations. But this hope has been false for two reasons. First, it is clear that language does not have the structure that would allow it to function as grounds for correct interpretations of legal texts.

14 See, also, Derrida's discussion of Miller in "Justices" (Derrida 2005). This text highlights some similarities, or at least sympathies, between deconstruction as justice and the ethics of reading.

Second, the idea of criteria being something objective and neutral can be misleading. We should not aim at a theory of legal interpretation that gives us a complete and rigorous methodology. Such a theory would lead to dogmatism and perhaps even give us a false sense of clear conscience.

We end up with a *post-semantic* theory of interpretation which does not deny authority to interpretation that concentrates on linguistic meaning, but reaffirms this authority in a new way. The text itself is important. It is the text in which the meanings and the commands of the law are expressed. The text and its wording have to be respected. Words are not irrelevant in the sense that we could ignore them or take them lightly. In a way the legal theorists of the past were absolutely right: interpretation has to begin with the words of the text.

But semantics, even though it is important, is not enough for a theory of legal interpretation. This is a practice whose peculiar characteristics distinguish it from any other activity in which texts are interpreted. Legal interpretation is, above all, interpretation of legal texts for the purpose of deciding legal cases. This means direct consequences for many people and indirect for even more. The responsibility of the interpreter is not only directed towards text's otherness but has a much wider scope.

## The twofold ethics of legal interpretation: textual and situational

So, according to the kind of theory that has been pursued here, the ethics of interpretation implies a double structure that commands legal interpretation. First, interpretation includes a simple 'I must' that is directed towards the text and what the text wants to say. It is here that a willingness to understand, a welcome to the meaning of the text is essential. We can call this *textual responsibility*, the idea being that the reader is face to face with the text. However, even though the responsibility of reading cannot be accounted for by the social and historical forces that impinge upon it, interpretation moves beyond this level of the 'I must'. It extends to the moral, political and legal sphere because, as interpretation begins, the interpreter is not only face to face with the otherness of the text but also, at the same time, in the sphere of thirds. So the act of interpretation moves away from a simple bilateral ethical relationship. This second element of the ethics of reading can be called *situational responsibility*. In law, interpreting the text cannot be distinguished sharply from applying it. The interpretive act is always an act in a time and a place and usually inside the horizon of a legal case that has to be decided.

The two dimensions of interpretation, in which the interpreter carries their responsibility towards the text on the one hand and the situation on the other, take place simultaneously. No temporal or any other sharp distinction should be drawn between them. They are two features of the meaning-giving process, and a way for us to conceptualise the jump or gap between text and meaning. They structure the meaning-giving process. They are similar to Levinas's idea of the other and the third. When we encounter the face of the other we there and then also realise that there are numerous others. We always encounter the third with the other. The ethical face-to-face relationship is not hermetically sealed but spreads into the moral, the political and the legal. On the other hand, the two dimensions of ethicity echo the way Levinas divides language into the saying and the said. As we recall, saying also includes listening and understanding. It is the underlying welcome behind speech and writing similar to Derrida's 'yes'. This welcome is shared by all: the speakers and the listeners. It is the simple ethical welcome that makes any and all communication possible. The second level of interpretation is concerned with the said and its many manifestations and occurrences in different situations and contexts. Here the intentions and aims as well as the time and place of the interpretation become important.

An 'I must' is inscribed in the act of reading itself. This 'I must' can be defined as the requirement that the interpreter stays open to the meaning of the text, listens to what the text wants to say and respects the intentions of the text. Respecting a legal text requires that we let the text speak for itself and let the text dictate the means of its interpretation. If we approached it with a set of predetermined rules or a strict method of interpretation, we would not be attentive to what the law wants to say. Thus the 'I must' turns into a principle according to which no interpretation can be correct, proper or right if it is not also respectful and ethical at the same time.

## Interpretation doing justice

As the face-to-face relationship between two people always happens in a society with other people present, likewise the man or woman face to face with a text always has surroundings. Every act of reading takes place in a time and a situation, and the reader has to take responsibility for its consequences. The twofold responsibility of the legal interpreter means that they have a responsibility towards the text they are interpreting but also regarding the particular case that they are deciding. However, these two elements of responsibility cannot be distinguished completely because they come together in the interpretation situation. In the field of law, interpretation is penetrated by the *demand for justice* and the two ethical elements of reading law are aspects of the call for every interpretation decision to be just. Ethics as a welcome is the condition for meaning, and the responsibility of the interpreter is also a condition of justice.

The second element of the ethics of interpretation, interpretation connected to a time and a place, is in a way the hermeneutical circle turned ethical. The way an interpretation is always rooted in life is connected to the way the interpreter reads every text starting from his or her own presuppositions. An interpreter is always already somewhere, in a situation and a tradition that overlaps a potentially infinite period of times and places. The ethical elements of interpretation can already be seen in Gadamer's theory in the way he underlines the importance of the dialogical structure of interpretation, where it is essential to be open to the meaning of the text. It can also be seen in Eco's theory, when he emphasises the rights of the text. But the situational element of interpretation underlined here is more attentive to the consequences of interpretation than either of these. It requires sensitivity from the interpreter towards their own presuppositions, the tradition in which they are in as well as an understanding of the consequences of their interpretation. It involves an acknowledgement that interpretation is never neutral.

To sum up the arguments so far, if it is true that every interpretation is a choice that has to be made by somebody somewhere at some point in time, then with this choice comes responsibility. Ultimately, we choose meanings, and these choices are acts that can be good or bad in an ethical sense. This way the correctness and incorrectness of interpretation boils down to goodness and badness, to ethical criteria. Thus, to give a good interpretation means that the interpretation is well-grounded, thorough, and meticulous, but these criteria have at the same time ethical underpinnings. They include respect for the text and what the text wants to say, a willingness to understand and a willingness to make a good and just interpretation. It means that we do have something by which we can assess and limit legal interpretation on the one hand and perhaps justify our interpretive choices on the other. Underlining the ethics of interpretation does not mean that we allow random or arbitrary interpretations of legal texts; on the contrary, it also gives us a means of criticising interpretations.

The second aspect of the ethics of interpretation, the situational anchoring of the interpretive act, which includes moral, political, social and legal responsibility, is what makes an ethics of interpretation able to answer the question of what to do when a text is bad. An ethics of legal interpretation is not naïve in the sense that it would commit the interpretation to mere fidelity towards the text or to an uncritical respect for what the text wants to say. In being bound to a time, place and legal situation, and in these bonds being also committed to the demands of justice, the ethics of legal interpretation acknowledges the possibility of resistance towards a bad text. Thus the ethics of interpretation does not simply cry out for good interpretations irrespective of the goodness of the text interpreted. But herein lies a great difficulty. Fidelity to the text and responsibility for interpretation as a situational concept can easily collide, and potential tension exists between these two in every act of legal interpretation. Responsibility towards the text is part of the judge's responsibility to the legal system and their duty to uphold for instance legal certainty or foreseeability. Responsibility for the interpretive act, considering the situation and the consequences of the interpretation, widens the scope of responsibility and requires the judge to take into account the particular singular persons whose lives are decided upon. This is justice in the Levinasian sense, justice as responsibility for the other person in their uniqueness. Both these aspects of the ethics of legal interpretation can be seen as components of justice.

Chapter 5

# Uncertain justice

The main argument of the book is now taking shape. It implies that there are always ethical elements in legal meaning. The idea is that in the absence of linguistic criteria, the space for choices of meaning is always there, and this opens up legal interpretation to responsibility. We can also express this thought in another way: the search for linguistic criteria on which to found legal interpretations takes us eventually to ethics.

Language is essentially communication and requires a will to understand, to enter the hermeneutic circle and to welcome the other speaker, be that person present in the space and time of the listener or absent. The meanings that language is full of are shared in our life as (legal) speakers, writers, listeners and interpreters. Therefore, something exists to base our legal meanings on, but it is not something certain, calculable or easily defined. Ethics as the foundation of meaning is a very peculiar kind of ethics. From it follow neither rules nor other clear methods for legal interpretation. Nevertheless, ethics is significant in interpretation in a concrete way. Deciding on particular interpretations and choosing which interpretations are better than others are *political* as well as ethical matters.

To say that ethical elements always stand behind meaning is not to say very much. That an inbuilt responsibility is always at play whenever language is used and a text interpreted is not a sufficient place for a theory of legal interpretation to stop. Moreover, the idea of legal interpretation having to do with ethics probably does not strike the reader as very novel. Many have argued that law and ethics, or law and morality, are essentially combined. Is there then something new in the way the ethics of legal meaning is argued here? Costas Douzinas and Adam Gearey write in *Critical Jurisprudence*, that '[a]gainst the positivist lack of interest in ethics, the interpretative scholars assert that the law is all morality and that judicial interpretation implies or leads to an ethics of legal reading' (Douzinas and Gearey 2005: 8). What else is done in this book than just what these writers claimed in 2005 that the 'interpretative scholars', namely Dworkin, James Boyd White and others, have already done? The problem with these scholars' view, according to Douzinas and Gearey, is that they do not acknowledge that the legal system represents the dominant ideology of society and that before and after the meaning-giving act, law is force. Law's meaning coerces, they claim. It is naïve to present law as exclusively textual and ethical (Douzinas and Gearey 2005: 8–9). So, the basic critique, which has to be taken seriously, is that when stressing the ethics of legal interpretation we downplay the power, force and violence included in it. I will try to answer that critique in this chapter. It is evident that ethics immediately also opens up room for politics, and this is an idea that the two levels of the ethics of interpretation developed here takes into account. And even though I argue that legal interpretation includes a twofold ethicity, this does not lead to an absolution. As for the novelty of the approach of this book, the effort here is to elaborate the twofold nature of responsibility in a way that takes into account both the text and the situation.

By turning our attention to the second element of the ethics of reading, that is, the situation in which the reading takes place, we turn our attention to the where and when of interpretation. This element is no less important than the simple commanding 'I must' that shapes every reading. When we focus on *legal* interpretation with its special features, it may be that the connections of interpretation to places, times and legal cases are most important. What sets legal interpretation apart from other ways of reading is its role and function in society at large. The interpretation of legal texts has intensely concrete consequences. Here, the close relationship between interpretation and application also becomes apparent.

From this point of view, where interpretation is closely tied to historical, social and political factors, the question arises: Is the ethical nature of legal interpretation an always-present fact, something inevitable? The answer is twofold. As inscribed in the general structure of how language and communication work, interpretation is always ethical in the sense that an ethical attitude, a welcome, is the condition of possibility of meaning. However, this is simply a welcome towards what the text wants to say; it does not define meaning. The situational element of the ethics of reading imposes on the interpreter the difficult task of deciding on a certain meaning and deciding the case. This happening is also loaded with responsibility. It is conditioned by ethical demands that are at the same time political and social. Interpretation in this situational sense is a challenge that the interpreter has to face every time.

When we say that interpretation always means a choice, cannot we also assert that legal interpretation is only political, in the sense of being governed by power-play, the ideology of the strongest group, etc?[1] The twofold ethics presented here does not allow such an abrupt conclusion. Even though we connect legal

1 See for example, Duncan Kennedy in *A Critique of Adjudication*. He does not claim that all judges decide ideologically, but, according to him, it is plausible that many judges experience a role conflict between the idea of doing justice under law and the categorical exclusion of the personal, subjective and ideological considerations of the judge. These judges are aware that to decide questions of law means interpretation rather than mere application of rules to disputed facts. Moreover, they are aware that the law as it appears after the decision process is a function of that process (Kennedy 1997: 199–202).

interpretation with choices that are ethical, it need not imply subjective and arbitrary decisions. And just because there are power relations involved, it does not mean that legal interpretation is just politics. The text and the welcome are still there. Besides, theories that construct legal interpretation this way say too much. One can argue that if every decision is biased or subjective, then no decision is, and there is no way of criticising decisions on this ground. Thus the question of justice becomes impossible, or rather, justice disappears altogether. A theory of legal interpretation should be able to say something about how and on which conditions a particular act of legal interpretation is just or unjust or at least more just than another act. Of course this implies that the demand for justice is taken to be a built-in premise of law. This is not something that this book aims to prove. Rather, it is taken for granted as an axiom. Law should be just, and it is hard to see how any theoretical account of law could deny this.

The challenge that the demand for justice places on law is indeed great, as was seen already in the discussion of Levinas's theory. Throughout the practice of law this need for justice is echoed, from legislation to legal decision-making. The structure of the argument connected with justice in this book is that in order for legal interpretation to be able to take justice into account, it has to include ethical elements. It is ultimately through the idea of justice that interpretation gets its purpose. It is also through reference to justice that legal interpretations can be criticised.

For sure, legal interpretation is united with power and force. This chapter discusses these issues. There are scholars who think that there is no room for a belief in justice in the strategic power-play that law actually is. Others think that law simply cannot be just because of its general character. Interestingly enough, some of the discussions get their inspiration, at least partly, from Levinas. The idea is that law can never be like ethics, in which we are obliged to take full responsibility for the other person. This is a slightly different approach to law's tragic nature than the one presented above according to which the law always ends up being a violent system because language founds legal interpretation on emptiness.

## Justice and the force of law

In his classic essay on law and justice titled 'Force of Law: The "Mystical Foundation of Authority"', Derrida discusses the possibility of justice. This is an interesting text for many reasons. It has become important in critical legal theory and been an inspiration for critical and deconstructive accounts of law (see, for example, Cornell *et al.* 1992; Wolcher 1996; Hirvonen 2001; Goodrich *et al.* 2008a; de Ville 2009a).[2] Although the text has been commented a lot, it is nevertheless still enigmatic. There are some issues that are of particular interest to us here. Derrida starts by asking what deconstruction has to do with justice. Does it

2 Although many critical legal theorists have been interested in his work, Derrida has not been very popular in legal philosophy, especially in America (see Goodrich *et al.* 2008b: 8–9).

somehow insure, permit, or authorise the possibility of justice? Does it permit justice, or does it constitute a threat to law, right and justice? Perhaps what makes deconstruction problematic and even frustrating is that it deconstructs. It deconstructs things we would like to believe in. In the field of legal interpretation, it is precisely the absence of rules and clear criteria that contribute to the crisis of interpretation. Derrida agrees: deconstruction torments because of the absence of rules and definite criteria that would allow one to distinguish unequivocally between law (*droit*) and justice (Derrida 1992c: 4).

Derrida says that he cannot offer any response to the question of whether deconstruction permits or threatens justice. There cannot be an either/or answer. It is too simple to formalise the question in such a 'yes or no' way. What is interesting in Derrida's essay, and what makes it an important essay for our topic, is that he discusses language at length. He even says that the question of language and idiom is at the heart of the discussion (Derrida 1992c: 5). He maintains that deconstruction, at least in his own texts, has indeed been concerned with justice. Discourses on double affirmation, the gift beyond exchange and distribution, the undecidable, the incommensurable or the incalculable, or on singularity, difference and heterogeneity are through and through, although perhaps obliquely, discourses on justice. In fact, he reckons that deconstruction might be more at home in law schools than in philosophy or literature departments. Studies that tackle law and politico-institutional problems are, according to him, from a certain viewpoint most fertile and also most necessary. Deconstruction should not remain enclosed in a purely academic or theoretical discourse but intervene also in the *cité*, the *polis* and the world (Derrida 1992c: 7–9).

The expression 'force of law' implies that law always carries within itself the possibility of its being enforced, that is, applied by force. Even if there are laws that are not enforced, there is no law without enforceability. Applicability or enforceability is not some exterior supplement added to law but implied in the concept of law. Law is always connected to authorised force. How can we distinguish between this force of the law and an unjust force? What difference is there between a force that can be just and violence that is unjust? What is a just force? (Derrida 1992c: 5–6). Derrida says that the expression 'to enforce the law' reminds us that:

> [...] if justice is not necessarily law (*droit*) or the law, it cannot become justice legitimately or *de jure* except by withholding force or rather by appealing to force from its first moment, from its first word.
>
> (Derrida 1992c: 10)

We can distinguish between law and justice in the sense that justice requires force because there are also wicked people who do not follow justice if it is not enforced, and in the sense that law is not the same as justice, as one obeys laws because they have authority. There are two structures that can be discerned here. The first is the way law hides and reflects the economic and political interests of the dominant forces in society. The second, and which is more important, is another, more intrinsic structure beyond the first one. Derrida says:

> The very emergence of justice and law, the founding and justifying moment that institutes law implies a performative force, which is always an interpretative force: this time not in the sense of law in the service of force, its docile instrument, servile and thus exterior to the dominant power, but rather in the sense of law that would maintain a more internal, more complex relation with what one calls force, power or violence.
>
> (Derrida 1992c: 13)

Law implies an internal force or power when it justifies itself. This performative force is an *interpretative force*. Does this mean that there is always a structure of performative force or violence at play in legal interpretation?

The answer for Derrida is 'yes'. The moment when law is inaugurated and justified, the moment of the legal decision, is a moment of interpretative violence. It is interesting, however, that Derrida says that this violence is in itself neither just nor unjust. Nothing can justify, guarantee or validate a particular legal decision. This is what Derrida calls 'mystical' (Derrida 1992c: 13–14). There is silence around the legal decision. No previous judgment, no previous law, can validate this decision right here. The decision has no foundation, or, it is founded in a mystical silence. Also the origin of authority and the grounds of law cannot rest on anything but themselves. The authority of the law is simply that it has authority. It is violence without ground. This does not mean injustice in the sense of illegality. Law is neither legal nor illegal in its founding moment. The mystical silence appears at the origin of law, in its earlier conditions and conventions and also at the origin of its dominant interpretations.

Law is deconstructible because it is, on the one hand, founded – that is, constructed on interpretable and transformable textual material and, on the other hand, essentially unfounded. According to Derrida, this is not bad news. It may be a stroke of luck for politics and historical progress. Law can be studied, deconstructed and changed. Its legality, authority and legitimacy can be questioned. Law can be deconstructed, criticised and developed (Derrida 1992c: 14–15).

Justice is for Derrida an aporia in a slightly similar way that it is a problem in Levinas's theory to combine law and justice. Justice is an experience of the impossible. Every time that a good rule is applied to a particular case or an example according to a determinant judgment, law finds itself accounted for but certainly not justice, says Derrida. Here he holds on to the central, and difficult, distinction that law is not justice.

> Law is the element of calculation, and it is just that there be law, but justice is incalculable, it requires us to calculate with the incalculable; and aporetic experiences are the experiences, as improbable as they are necessary, of justice, that is to say of moments in which the decision between just and unjust is never insured by a rule.
>
> (Derrida 1992c: 16)

Let us pause here for a while. The beginning of the quote bears clear resemblance to Levinas in the way justice is seen as something incalculable. This idea is supported in Levinas's theory by his own metaphysics and ethics. Why is justice for Derrida something incalculable? If we combine this idea with the thought that law has no foundation, it seems that the foundation of law cannot be justice. The foundation of law is authority that has no foundation, and the legal decision is calculation. Justice, however, is not calculation but something else. We begin to see the complex ways in which Derrida connects and disconnects law and justice.

Derrida discusses the general nature of law. We can recall Levinas's problem of justice, which is that it demands singular decisions that pay attention to individuals and the specific characteristics of a case, that is, to the uniqueness of the other person, whereas law as rules or norms is general in nature. To respect singularity and otherness seems to be impossible in law because the idiom of law is that of the third party, not that of the other. Justice as right, which means justice the way it appears in law, implies universality (Derrida 1992c: 17). This problem might be exaggerated by the absoluteness of the way it is formulated.[3] There is no reason why in principle a general rule could not respect singularity. We could well have a legal norm that commands us to respect otherness, individuality and singularity. Why is this not enough? In Levinasian theory one could argue that it is not enough because it means that otherness is not really respected as otherness, but the problem is that if otherness is respected in a really ethical manner, as passivity in which the other takes me hostage, then this results in a law that is not able to do anything or to protect anybody.

Interestingly enough, from a Levinasian point of view it is not only law that has problems. The central question is how we are supposed to carry responsibility for everyone and if we do not, then how are we ever going to be able to justify only caring for certain people instead of others? It seems that inside the logic of responsibility there is a structure of irresponsibility because when we save one person, we sacrifice others. Derrida discusses this on many occasions. He gives his own cat as an example. How can he justify that he takes care of his own cat when so many other cats are suffering? This experience of irresponsibility haunts us in our everyday lives. It is a feature of the human condition (see Derrida 1995b, 2002; Miller 2009: 216–221). This is the problem that Levinas discusses in connection to the third. But it is not only a problem for law but for all action and decision-making. There is always violence, if violence means falling short of my responsibility to the other (Llewelyn 1995: 144). Absolute and boundless responsibility is impossible, and this goes for all life, not only legal. Or, as Marinos Diamantides puts it, Levinasian ethics results in the acknowledgement that one has to serve the other 'infinitely, that is, never well enough and to the unjustifiable neglect of other Others' (Diamantides 2007: 184).

3 On Derrida's habit of discussing things either–or, see Miller (2009: 214–215, 218).

It has to be noted at this stage that the affinities between Levinas and Derrida should not be exaggerated. Nevertheless, many commentators have read *Force of Law* from a strikingly Levinasian perspective. De Ville argues that this has become the 'orthodox reading' of this text of Derrida's and that it is both misguided and narrow. The reason for it being misguided, according to de Ville, is that although Derrida's thinking is in some parts affected by Levinas's ideas, major differences make it impossible to understand Derrida's justice as simply the same as a singular ethical relationship or an ethical response to the other. Some commentators have concentrated on debating whether Derrida's other refers to litigants that come to court or those that are oppressed in society. The other should here be understood in more abstract terms. We cannot equate Derrida's other with a particular human being who faces us, as in Levinas's ethics. De Ville argues that for Derrida there can be no direct access to the other (or the other's face). A belief that such access were possible represents for Derrida a metaphysics of presence. It is thus important to read *Force of Law* also in the context of Derrida's other writings. De Ville rejects the idea that Derrida's thinking would have undergone an ethical turn that would licence reading *Force and Law* and his other later texts without regard to his greater 'project' (see de Ville 2009a).

Derrida's text is unquestionably very complex, and many different interpretations of it can be productive. It is certainly interesting to read it in a manner that keeps in mind Derrida's other writings. This is an attractive approach especially for the questions posed in this book, as it includes the idea of the importance of language for questions of justice. But there is no point in distancing the text completely from Levinasian themes of responsibility either.

## Justice in despair

In a way justice is for Derrida something impossible, but he does not want to give it up. He keeps up hope for law and the tasks it should fulfil. Incalculable justice can lead to terrible things. Left to itself, it can go bad. And so justice requires us to calculate. We must calculate and negotiate the relationship between the incalculable, which is justice, and the calculable, namely law, politics, economics, ethics, literature, and so on (Derrida 1992c: 28). The relationship between law and justice has to be considered and reconsidered. Justice, for Derrida, is something that is always to come.

The idea of justice being never present but ever-elusive bears a resemblance to the way Derrida thematises meaning in his earlier work. We can call to mind the transcendental signified and the trace (see, also, Weber 2008: 179). As we recall, there is no transcendental signified that would be the thing itself in its self-presence. Logocentrism and the metaphysics of presence involve an impossible desire for such a signified. Likewise, there can be no access to 'justice itself' regardless of how much we would like such a reassuring presence. '[O]ne cannot speak directly about justice' (Derrida 1992c: 10). The trace is a possibility of meaning in Derrida's theory. The trace is the way the other (the thing) announces itself. It is not fully present but presents itself in the dissimulation of itself. The thing or the object that a sign refers to is always hidden behind the never-ending chain of signs.

The possibility of failure, of meaning getting lost or changing on the way, is a necessary characteristic of language. Perhaps it is so for justice as well. Just as the uncertainty of language is at the same time its possibility, we can think of justice as necessarily uncertain. Justice would not be just if it were easy.[4] But how can we live with empty and insecure justice? This problem is certainly one reason why many commentators have wanted to read *Force of Law* through Levinasian spectacles. Respect for the other would be a way to give some substance to the emptiness of Derrida's justice.

There is no way of defining justice. But this does not mean that there would not be possibilities for thinking anew questions of justice, such as property, the subject, the responsible subject or the legal subject (Derrida 1992c: 8). Legal concepts, practices and definitions can be reappraised and revalued. This is highly important also regarding the situational elements of the responsibility of legal interpretation.

We can find in *Specters of Marx* a comment that has bearing on the emptiness of justice. Here Derrida talks of absolute hospitality as justice and the messianic character of it. He says that it may seem strange and inhospitable that the promise of absolute hospitality is so impossible and so extremely poor, so unsure and anxious. This can lead to despair. But:

> [...] without this latter despair and if one could *count* on what is coming, hope would be but the calculation of a program. One would have the prospect but one would not longer wait for anything or anyone. Law without justice. One would no longer invite, either body or soul, no longer receive any visits, no longer even think to see. To see coming. Some, and I do not exclude myself, will find this despairing 'messianism' has a curious taste, a taste of death.
>
> (Derrida 1994: 169, emphasis in original)

Justice has a taste of emptiness. But consider the alternative: Ready-made justice? A justice already negotiated and easy to use? Justice the commodity?[5] This would be law *without* justice. Ultimately, it would mean that we would not even need to think. Would not this apathy have a sour taste as well, an alarming taste of death?

4 One important thing has to be noted in making this comparison between meaning and justice. Derrida deconstructs meaning, but he says explicitly that justice cannot be deconstructed. Deconstruction is justice. Justice is the act of deconstructing. Ari Hirvonen underlines in his reading of *Force of Law*, that deconstructive questioning of law has been one of the main 'genres' of deconstructive legal studies. Derrida sees this as very important, but Hirvonen points out that deconstruction takes place in the interval that separates the undeconstructibility of justice from the deconstructibility of law. This means that close-reading of law must take place in relation to the question of justice (see Hirvonen 2001). Hirvonen concentrates in his reading on Derrida's connections to Jewish jurisprudence.

5 In the context of *Specters of Marx*, this idea does not seem as outrageous as it might at first appear. Derrida discusses the commodity-form as a spectrality, something ghost-like.

## The problem of the universal and the particular

The above discussion on justice leads us to the problem, discussed already in connection to Levinas, that a legal decision is a situation in which the general (a rule) and the particular (a concrete situation in life) have to be combined. The tension between law and justice is portrayed in Levinas's thinking as the discrepancy between the ethical face-to-face relationship, which is singular and situational, and the moral, political or legal relationship between people, where things like equality and fairness matter and which comply for this reason with a general logic including comparisons and calculations. To simplify: the problem is that law is general whereas justice is singular and particular, which means that law can never be just. This has been described by Emmanuel Melissaris in the following way:

> What originated as a reaction against the levelling effect of legal formalism and was expressed as a demand for responsiveness and context-sensitivity in law tends in recent years, and especially with the increasing popularity of postmodern theory, to regress to a sort of fetishism of the particular. Very often this tendency goes as far as to even deny the possibility of achieving justice through the application of universal (or at least universalizable) norms or, indeed, the very existence of such norms.
>
> (Melissaris 2006: 129)

So law is doomed to be a failure; it cannot be compatible with ethics and justice.[6] The problem of merciful law can be seen as one version of the universal–particular dilemma. It is the very nature of law to operate through rules, which brings us the question of whether mercy as an ethical attitude towards people can ever be part of law. The definition of mercy is that it is always an exception (see Christodoulidis 1999). Because law functions in generalisations and operates through rules, law cannot be merciful. Law is general, justice is particular.

Aristotle notes this basic problem of justice. In *Nicomachean Ethics*, he discusses the interconnectedness of justice and equity. First, he remarks that they appear to be neither absolutely the same nor generically different. The same thing can be both just and equitable, but he notes that the equitable is superior. What is equitable is just but not legally just. It is a correction of legal justice. This is because 'all law is universal but about some things it is not possible to make a universal statement which will be correct' (Aristotle 1984: V.10). Law speaks universally and conforms to usual cases. When a case arises that is not covered by the universal statement, then it is right to make an equitable decision. This is a way of correcting the error

6 According to Scott Veitch, postmodern jurisprudence is unable to overcome the modernist dichotomy of law and ethics. That law is an autonomous field separated from morality and ethics is an idea that postmodern thinking has tried to question. This questioning has not been a complete success. In postmodern jurisprudence law is positioned ambiguously as both the protector and the enemy of justice (see Veitch 1997: 97).

that arises from the absoluteness of the universal speech of law. According to Aristotle, this is the nature of the equitable, a correction of law where it is defective owing to its universality. Here, the equitable functions as a mediator between universal law and particular justice. It is worth noting, however, that Aristotle's discussion concerns things about which it is impossible to lay down a law, or situations in which the legislator has failed and 'erred by over-simplicity'. In the latter cases it is necessary to correct the omission by saying what the legislator would have said and would have put into the law if he or she had known (Aristotle 1984: V.10).

For legal theories that stress the autonomy and the integrity of law, the conceived gap between law that has the form of rules and the real world that has the form of particulars is a serious problem. Different theorists, especially those labelled 'legal positivists', have tried to fill this gap with different intra-legal means, such as values (for instance fairness), principles or rights.[7] Universals and particulars have also been discussed in legal theory in connection to problems of justification. Here the question concerns the possibilities of justifying a decision by reference to universals, that is, to rules and principles. For instance, MacCormick argues for universalism and says that there is no justification without universalisation. Even though legal decision-making requires us to weigh particular reasons found among the facts and circumstances of the case, universalisation is essential to justification. This follows from the nature of practical reasoning (MacCormick 2006; see, also, Walker 2006). These varied legal theoretical discussions focus on legal reasoning and argumentation, but there is some resemblance to the Aristotelian problem described above, which is close but not identical to the aporetic nature of Derrida's law.

For the questions at hand regarding legal texts and their meaning, the tension between the universal and the particular has another dimension than the above-discussed ancient dilemma of general law and singular justice. Our primary concern is interpretation, which is not problematised, for instance, in Aristotle's discussion. It is simply assumed here that the content and meaning of 'the law' is known. It is not part of the problem that we would not know what the law commands, as the question is rather that what the law commands does not match the real world in all its manifoldness. It is interesting to look at the universal–particular dilemma specifically from the point of view of legal interpretation because in this context it appears slightly different.

According to Aristotle, law *speaks universally*. Law speaks. This implies that what it says is clear. Problems arise when a case does not fit the law's command. This book tries to locate the fundamental problem of legal decision-making on a deeper level in underlining that law does not speak by itself either universally or in any other manner. It only speaks with the mouth of interpreters, and depending on the meaning they give it, it can conform to usual or less usual cases.

7 See, also, Fernando Atria's discussion of how positivism has struggled with the problem of harmonising universal law with adjudication, which is particular in nature (Atria 2006).

Interpretation makes law dynamic and flexible. The content of law's statements is always negotiable to some degree.

Studying the moment before the application of a rule to a case, the juxtaposition between the universal and the particular can be rethought. In the interpretation process an oscillation occurs between the general and the situational. Understanding a text is a movement from generalisations to particulars and from the parts to the whole. On this level, we see that a sharp distinction between the universal and the particular does not hold. Every text is singular and has to be approached as such, but at the same time it contains something universal, rule-bound and general, which connected to our presuppositions makes understanding possible. As Gadamer points out, tradition is the background for understanding, but every text is nevertheless unique and the reader has to focus on what this particular and singular text says.

We can therefore question the generality law. If, according to the hermeneutic view, we hold that every understanding and interpretation happens in a hermeneutic spiral in which the text and what it commands are understood through the facts of a case (an actual case that the judge is deciding or historical or hypothetical ones) and the facts of the case chosen and considered with a certain text in mind, then an amount of particularity already exists at the level of understanding the text. The meaning of a text is not pure general normativity. Through always being interpreted with some facts or cases in mind, the meaning of legal texts includes both universal and particular features. (And vice versa. As the particulars of a case are considered in the legal context this means that the case always gets some universal features)

The idea of the twofold ethics of legal interpretation takes into account both the text and the situation. It includes both universality and particularity. It focuses on the real situation of the person interpreting the text and the choices that he or she makes on the meaning of it. The situation spreads to different contexts, but begins with and returns to the person who is face to face with the words of the text. The structure of this thought is similar to the way that Levinas's ethics is simultaneously individual but universal (see, for example, Ciaramelli 1991 on a discussion of this theme). Ethics is based on a radical asymmetrical responsibility which is mine, that is, something ultimately very individual. Yet it transcends into something universal as Levinas holds that this is the general foundation for ethics, first philosophy, and it binds us all.

According to this picture of legal interpretation, it is impossible to see law as simply universal and the facts, the case as particular. This way, as we question the way the opposition between the universal and the particular has been understood in legal theory as a situation in which the meaning of the law is *given*, we find that the opposition is mitigated, if not resolved completely. The classic problem described by Aristotle as the universal law that does not fit a singular situation thus changes as we turn our attention to meaning and how it is established. Also, if we accept that ethical elements are already internal to the interpretation of legal texts as it has been argued here, then a sharp conceptual distinction between law and justice (as responsibility) is impossible. The content of the law is only accessible through interpretation, which already contains ethical elements and there is no law before interpretation. Justice shapes law from within so that the meaning of a legal text is not first a rule that then has to be applied in a responsible way to a case. Meaning already carries with it elements of responsibility that derive from the twofold ethics of legal interpretation.

## Uncovering violence in legal interpretation

If the demand of justice that is the ultimate criterion of legal interpretation is related to responsibility, then what kind of responsibility are we talking about? We have to pay attention to the 'who' and the 'where' of legal interpretation. We have been discussing responsibility so far in an individualistic way as every human being's own. Does this really apply to law? If legal interpretation is about responsibility, then whose responsibility is it?

Of the many writers who connect law and injustice, Robert Cover is of seminal importance. He was one of the first scholars to claim that legal interpretation is intrinsically violent in nature. His perhaps best-known text, 'Violence and the Word', was published in 1986, but already in 1983 he had published an important article called 'The Supreme Court, 1982 Term – Foreword: Nomos and Narrative'. Cover's views on the violence of law are intriguing in many ways, but his main argument is quite simple. He claims that law is always connected with violence and pain, and that legal interpretation is necessarily violent. I will first present some of his arguments and then discuss possible objections to them and the importance of the issues he discusses in the context of the ethics of legal interpretation.

Cover's perspective on legal interpretation is a holistic one in the sense that he emphasises the roles and structures in which legal interpretation takes place. No judge acts alone, but the interpretation he or she does and the verdict he or she passes take part in a complex system in which word and deed come together. A judge does not carry out their verdicts, for instance. This is done with the help of lawyers, police, wardens and magistrates. For this reason it is misleading to see legal interpretation primarily as the mental acts of one person. It should rather be understood as the violent activity of an organisation of people (Cover 1986: 1628).

The trend in legal scholarship to compare legal interpretation with other forms of interpretation, say literary, was prominent at the time of Cover's writing.

> Legal interpretation takes place in a field of pain and death. This is true in several senses. Legal interpretive acts signal and occasion the imposition of violence upon others: A judge articulates her understanding of a text, and as a result, somebody loses his freedom, his property, his children, even his life. Interpretations in law also constitute justifications for violence which has already occurred or which is about to occur. When interpreters have finished their work, they frequently leave behind victims whose lives have been torn apart by these organized, social practices of violence.
>
> (Cover 1986: 1601)

Cover's strategy, then, is not to look at legal interpretation from the point of view of language, semiotics or hermeneutics. He does not start off by wondering what meaning is or how texts acquire and are given meanings. His description starts from a perspective that first situates the practice of legal interpretation in the field of law with its peculiar characteristics.

Cover says that the problem of meaning in law, or the problem of legal interpretation, is often associated with the narrow quest of finding out what the law commands. A decision must be made about the meaning of a legal text. He refers to the famous vehicle example discussed above, where it must be decided whether or not an airplane or a toy car is a 'vehicle' in the same sense as it is meant in the statute prohibiting vehicles from entering a park. These problems form one type of questions that are important, but they are not what Cover himself wants to concentrate on. He studies law as a normative universe held together by interpretive commitments. The commitments of officials, judges and ordinary people define what law means and how it is to be applied (Cover 1983: 6–7).[8]

There are many normative worlds. Different groups of people have different normative universes with their own laws and narratives. Laws are linked to discourses that supply, for instance, their history, explanation and purpose. Our apprehension of the normative world is fundamental for us, just as our apprehension of the physical universe. Cover says that to inhabit a *nomos* is to know how to live in it (Cover 1983: 4–8). The normative worlds of different communities clash, and the State's legal order imposes its own *nomos* on the other worlds. For Cover, the State order is not necessarily superior. But the government's norms are able to kill off the norms of other communities because they are backed by force and the power to suppress (see Minow *et al.* 1995: 9). The challenge to law is thus to come to terms with the plurality of normative worlds. This means for legal interpretation that the absence of one 'objective' interpretation leads to the situation in which a sense of legal meaning has to be maintained even though there can be no pretence of superiority of one *nomos* over others. Cover criticises state law because it exercises a brute force to shut down the creative hermeneutics of communities (Cover 1983: 44). The state imposes on others its normative universe with its particular discourses.

According to Cover, neither legal interpretation nor the violence it occasions may be properly understood apart from the other (Cover 1986: 1601–1602). Many a research has tried to cut legal interpretation loose from the situation in which it is done, and such research has often led to misleading results. We can see that the

8 Cover sees that, for instance, Dworkin's work is interesting because it does not concentrate on the traditional questions about how a particular word or phrase should be given effect in some particular context but studies the effort to impose meaning on the institution. Cover says that Dworkin 'has written the most elaborate and sophisticated jurisprudence which places the meaning giving, constructive dimension of interpretation at the heart of law' (see Cover 1986: 1602). However, Dworkin too concentrates mostly on the judge and their interpretation activity.

structure of Cover's argument is, first, to describe where and in what context legal interpretation takes place and from this draw conclusions on what it therefore has to be like. Legal interpretation must be distinguished from, for instance, interpretation of literature as well as political philosophy because although legal interpretation has political connections, it takes place in institutional modes of action. The text itself may be political, at least in its pedigree, but it is embedded in the institutional system that leads from the text to action. Legal interpretation is always played out in the field of pain and death (Cover 1986: 1607).

The violence in the act of legal interpretation can, according to Cover, be most clearly seen when we look at it from the defendant's perspective. This is why many who have wanted to downplay this violence have concentrated on the judge and their act of interpretation. However, if we try to put ourselves in the place of the defendant, we can clearly see the interconnections between violence and the word. Law constructs different interpretive categories such as 'blame' or 'punishment'. With the help of these, meaning is created and the judge's sentence and their role in the violence of law are justified to himself or herself and to others. Of course, these ideological justifications are not only the property of judges but part of the general culture. The ideology of punishment justifies the practices of law. Its importance is especially vital for judges who – unlike, for instance, people who take part in the general discourse or political debate – cause pain and even death (Cover 1986: 1608–1609).

Cover's argumentation is subtle because he explicitly says that judges do not *only* or *always* cause pain and death. However, their being part of the institutional structure of violence that is the law and a most important part in the actual deeds of the law, the connection between a judge's interpretation and pain has to be acknowledged. He says rather enigmatically: 'The judges deal pain and death. That is not all that they do. Perhaps that is not what they usually do. But they *do* deal death, and pain' (Cover 1986: 1609; see, also, Cover 1985–1986: 818, emphasis in original). So judges not only deal pain and death, but the fact that they sometimes do is so relevant that we cannot understand legal interpretation correctly without admitting it.

According to Cover, the three main characteristics of legal interpretation are that: (a) it is a practical activity; (b) that is designed to generate threats and actual deeds of violence; and (c) in an effective way (Cover 1986: 1610). Cover pays much attention to the fact that certain important roles are present in the practice of legal interpretation. A judge's interpretation becomes a deed because of other actors involved. Thus the word–deed bond is dependent on a system of social co-operation in which people have different roles and respective tasks (Cover 1985–1986: 822, 824). A hermeneutic link exists between the interpretation of the judge and the social organisation that is required to transform it into a reality. Legal interpretation requires and is shaped by an understanding of what other actors will do with their decision. The judge often adjusts the interpretation according to the institutionalised context (Cover 1986: 1612). So it is not only legal and social texts that are relevant in a case, or rather, their interpretation is shaped by the institutional context in which the interpretive act is done.

Cover claims that legal interpretation can never be free, whatever that may mean. It can never be only an understanding of the text. It must be able to transform itself into action and capable of massing a sufficient degree of violence. To be able to do this, it must be self-reflective. The meaning of the text is an important element, but it is potentially in tension with the need to generate effective action. Legal interpretation is in Cover's view always embedded in its context, and the considerations of the *word* (the legal text), the *deed* (the actions that the interpretation generates) and the *role* (the actor who interprets and their particular place in the system) are always present to some degree (Cover 1986: 1617–1618). All three are important.

What conclusions can be drawn from this? As regards the violence that law levels against different and competing world views, Cover recognises that there has to be some order, but he wants it to be such that it does not suppress and kill the normative worlds of different communities. He searches for a balance between order and plurality. Judges have a role to play in shaping the law, and Cover maintains that they are important for limiting the State's violence. Judges can use their interpretive acts to oppose governors and administrations that are too violent (Cover 1983: 57). He also says that if violence is to be a part of our society and political system, then it is a very good thing indeed that it is at the centre of law as well. The idea seems to be that there it is visible and at least in some ways manageable. The alternative would be unacceptable – that violence would be within our polity but outside the law, which, after all, consists of our collective rules and individual efforts to achieve outcomes through those rules (Cover 1986: 1628–1629). This is important because it shows how Cover still believes in law and judges' possibilities to limit violence at least to some extent. He also believes in rules.

Cover does not claim that the meaning of law would be easy or indisputable. The legal system, which includes words, roles and deeds, is important for the violence of the law to be both manageable and effective. Responsibility for violence must be shared. Law must operate through the acts of many different actors, who would otherwise be both unwilling to act and irresponsible in their violent acts. No single individual, even if he or she were a judge, can render an interpretation operative as law. But the relevant actors are unlikely to have a similar understanding of the meaning of law. There will always be a tragic limit to the common meaning of law because judges, officials, martyrs and convicts do not necessarily share a common vocabulary and philosophical framework. Cover says that the violence of law interferes between the idea and the reality of common and shared meanings (Cover 1986: 1628–1629). This means that even though some of the violence of the law can be limited, it nevertheless always implies an imposition of one normative world upon others.

Legal interpretation is, indeed, closely connected with pain and even death. This fact underlines the need to pay attention to the second level of the ethics of interpretation, the context in which it occurs. But it is argued here that this second element of the ethics of meaning is at least to some extent conditioned by the first one. It is the text that raises the whole question of interpretation. This is what post-semantics refers to. It is a necessary reconstruction of the importance of words. The more there are shifting meanings, the more an interpreter is needed and the more responsibility they therefore have, even though it is clear that everybody does not share their nomos. Legal interpretation places on the interpreter an almost impossible demand, and the scope of the heavy responsibility they have to carry is even widened by the fact that there is no way they can only refer to the 'ordinary meanings of words' or some other artificial argument of justification. The judge has to choose one meaning, and as Cover points out, this means simultaneously the choice of one normative universe over others.

We can compare Cover's views with Miller's on the ethics of reading. Cover explicitly says that we should not concentrate on the man or woman reading the pages. We can even simplify his vision of legal interpretation as all violence and no text. It is true that we should keep in mind the larger picture in which legal interpretation takes place. Law is violent, sometimes. But it does not have to be *only* violent, and it is through interpretation that some of the violence can be overcome. In a sense it seems almost trivial today to claim that law includes violence, as it is one of the very functions of law that it is a system of control and governance. What else would it be? But law is not all bad. It not only commands, forbids and punishes but protects and shelters as well. In order for law to able to do good, it has to be kept in check by insisting on justice. There are limits to legal interpretation, which restrict the power of law over people.

We have to move beyond theories that concentrate on traditional questions about how a particular word or phrase in a legal text should be given effect in some particular context. We have to take into account the meaning-constructing character of the practices of legal interpretation. There cannot be anything that could be called legal interpretation in the sense that it would concentrate only on the meanings of words because to concentrate on the meaning of words or phrases necessarily opens the door to a discussion of practice, meaning giving, choice and responsibility.[9] This is the new semantics that we have to live with. Cover says that legal interpretation can never be free because it can never be only the understanding of a legal text (in contrast with the interpretation done, for instance, when reading literature). But already through a discussion of Wittgenstein and Gadamer we find that there is no such thing as understanding a text cut out from life, society, tradition. Interpretation always entails more than a semantic study and legal interpretation even more so. Legal interpretation is always already conditioned by many factors, *one* being violence, which Cover so creditably describes.

Marianne Constable argues that the importance of Cover's analyses of legal violence lies not so much in the newness of their description of law, because even though many scholars at the time of Cover's writing were concentrating on

9 For a discussion on Cover and Levinas, see, also, Gibbs (2006).

interpretation, application and legal reasoning, they were hardly in need of a legal realist reminder. This is because at one level Cover's argument is indeed self-evident: legal interpretation takes place in the context of social coercion and power. Few researchers would deny this. Constable suggests that the significance of Cover's work lies in the questions it raises (Constable 2005: 132–134). The questions are similar to those that were raised in the above discussions of responsibility and justice.

It is important to consider what Cover understands by law. He states that modern law, by which he means State monopolised coercion, is essentially violent. The first problem today is that law is no more only a system of fully sovereign States. It includes both soft law and non-State law made and enforced by non-State organisations. The positive law of the State does not exhaust law (see Constable 2005: 134).[10] In addition, even though Cover speaks on a general level, his exposition raises the suspicion that what he first and foremost has in mind is criminal law, administrative law and other areas of law, where 'the citizen' is seen as being in a relationship with 'the State' which commands. But what about private law? Of course contracts, marriages and inheritances are also in many ways legally regulated and there is always the element of imposing one normative universe through law, but perhaps not to the same extent as with public law or criminal law. The coercion and violence here is different because it is up to the parties themselves to draw up at least some of the rules. An amount of pluralistic normativity can be seen here.

According to Constable, Cover argues that when social control and domination produce behaviour, both the acting self and its 'normative world' are lost. Persons can be responsible for action only when behaviour is not controlled by social or legal mechanisms such as rules, for instance. Thus it becomes uncertain if people, for instance judges, can be held responsible (see Constable 2005: 143). They are controlled and dominated just the way ordinary people are, and their self along with the possibility for them to carry responsibility for their action is lost. We will come back to this crucial question of the judge's freedom and responsibility later. Suffice it to say here that it is too straightforward to assert that *either* a person is totally free and can make responsible decisions *or* they are affected by rules and thus not responsible for their actions.

On Constable's reading of *Violence and the Word*, the limits of domination can be found, surprisingly enough, in language. The many people and the *many voices* that are required for domesticating violence allow responsibility for it to be shared. This way the system ensures that no single mind or will can generate the violent outcomes that follow from interpretation (Constable 2005: 143–144). Constable points out that language is already there, before the coercing law. All normative activity presupposes a belonging-together of persons in a world that appears to

10 See, also, Tuori on the present predicament of nation State law in Tuori 2011: 287–314.

them through their language, she says. 'The gathering, in (and to) a world, of persons-belonging-together is prior to the violent positive law of which Cover speaks' (Constable 2005: 147). I completely agree. Language as something shared is already there and it includes ethical elements.

Constable points out that Cover is silent about justice. She claims that an account of interpretation in the service of violence may be acceptable as a characterisation of modern law. But it underplays its correspondence to justice, which is a *prior* issue and irreducible to the 'modern language of law'. She concludes that Cover's silence on the issue of justice warns of the danger of forgetting justice (Constable 2005: 147–148). Indeed, it is interesting that Cover does not talk about justice, even though it is without doubt the most important question that his analyses lead to.

Whereas Constable goes on to search for alternative ways of approaching justice through discovering its silences, we need to focus on legal interpretation and certain issues that come up in Cover's discussion of it. Even though his understanding of law would be narrow and perhaps even outdated, his argument still carries force. The ethics of legal interpretation has so far been an attempt at reconceptualising legal interpretation through the notion of responsibility. But it is clear that responsibility is a highly complex thing.

## The irresponsibility of law

Where Cover's work underlines shared responsibility in the field of law, it can also be, however, that it is precisely this that leads to problems. When responsibility is shattered in the complex role structure of the law, it can disappear. Scott Veitch argues in his book *Law and Irresponsibility* that the traditional way of seeing law as a system that creates responsibility is misguided. According to him, law takes part in the production of irresponsibility. Legal institutions, practices, concepts and categories involve organised irresponsibility. This is seen especially clearly in massive human rights violations. Law produces suffering and irresponsibility.

Veitch's analysis is disturbing from the point of view of justice because he claims that even when law functions as it should, it is nevertheless unjust. He says that contrary to what is often assumed, it is not only unlawful acts that cause harm and suffering. Lawful acts that are accepted by the legal system can, and in fact do, cause massive suffering. Acts that do not break any legal rule can still do harm. In this way law makes irresponsibility possible. It is not a question of bad legal decisions, false interpretations of rules or corrupt politicians. It is in the nature of law that when it functions as it should, it results in irresponsibility anyway. Law itself has an irresponsible nature. The United Nation sanctions against Iraq in the 1990s are an example of this. These sanctions were lawful. They required legal practices, administration and implementation. They were legitimate from the law's point of view. And they were no mistake. From the point of view of the suffering people, the situation is totally different. Law was an accomplice (Veitch 2007: 12–24). Veitch's main point is that we should not see the production of suffering and irresponsibility as a mistake, as something that takes place when law fails, but as a natural consequence of the way law actually works. It is part of the normality of law.

Veitch draws a sketch of how law that is meant to organise responsibility paradoxically ends up organising irresponsibility. This happens through different processes. One of them is the disappearance of responsibility for legal decisions. When large-scale suffering is concerned, it is especially difficult to make any individual person accountable for it. The responsibility for the harm done is shattered in complicated organisations. It is impossible to find the person(s) guilty of producing harm (Veitch 2007: 29–34). Veitch's central claim is that responsibility is defined in different responsibility practices that all have their own origins and history. The reason why responsibility disappears is that responsibility practices are power practices. He writes:

> In order to understand the asymmetries between suffering and the ability to establish responsibility for it, we must understand how these very 'technologies of responsibility' themselves, as part of the broader social forms of power, also provide some of the major resources through which dispersals and disavowals of responsibility in society can occur. It is through analysing the complicitous relationship with these broader forms of power – in their diversions and distinctions, their priorities and interests – that we will come to a fuller understanding of the proliferation of irresponsibilities in the rise of responsibilities.
>
> (Veitch 2007: 41)

One of the examples that Veitch discusses is the truth and reconciliation process of South Africa. The South African Truth and Reconciliation Commission made findings of responsibility for the organisation of the old regime and for gross human rights violations committed or allowed by its agents. Many former State service operatives came forward to seek amnesty for crimes they confessed to and Veitch underlines that many were granted amnesty. He argues that the process leads to a situation where those who were most to blame got away with it. The people who had most responsibility for apartheid, who had established and delivered its policies, who had established the political, military and, to an extent, judicial establishment, were not punished. It turned out that the carefully assembled and tightly secured links in the chains of command quickly broke apart, became unidentifiable and disappeared. It became impossible to piece together responsibility and to establish a link between action and consequences then and now. Veitch uses this example to illustrate his main claim that there is an asymmetry between the production of suffering and establishing responsibility for it. This asymmetry always works in inverse proportion: the greater the suffering is, the less responsibility is established for it (Veitch 2007: 30–31).

What is the role of law in this? Veitch thinks that law is one of the responsibility practices that are most important in the production of irresponsibility. What is more, the meaning of legal irresponsibility is enhanced by the very strong role that the law plays in society. Other normative structures, for instance morality, are influenced by the ways in which responsibility is defined in law. In addition, in most societies law has invaded most social relationships, which means that they are now regulated by law at least to some extent. Non-legal activities are influenced by law. Instead of this being a sign of a responsible society, Veitch thinks that it rather shows how other responsibility practices have failed (Veitch 2007: 74–77).

Law produces irresponsibility through its concepts and definitions. In this way, legal normativity is a tool for escaping responsibility. The law makes, for instance, a distinction between different types of harm: there are illegal harms and there are legal harms. If an act is lawful, the harm usually goes unpunished. This means a shift in responsibility from the actor to the legal norm. It is actually the norm that carries responsibility, or to put it otherwise, the responsibility for suffering ends with the norm, it does not stretch to an actor. The same kind of abstractness concerns legal roles. A judge is seldom seen as personally responsible for their decisions. It is the law itself that carries the responsibility for the consequences of the decision. It is the legal argumentation that is to blame, not the judge (Veitch 2007: 85–95).

Veitch laments that there is no personal responsibility in law and that legal concepts and institutions make responsibility disappear.[11] But as with Cover, we must stop and ask what the law is that Veitch has in mind. Cover believes in the power of rules. We can see that Veitch, too, has faith in law and in legal

11 Veitch's description of law is quite depressing. One of his examples is Australia and the suffering of the Aboriginal people caused by the colonial regime. He says that Australian law has been founded on racist assumptions. Even if the society nowadays is committed to legal principles of equality, democracy and the rule of law, racial discrimination still occurs. He tries to show through the Australian High Court decision *Mabo v The State of Queensland (No 2)* how legal reasoning comes up against its limits. The case concerned land. When Australia was colonised by the British in 1788, the official doctrine held that the land was uninhabited. Even though the Aboriginals already lived on the land, their society was seen as inferior and lacking social organisation, which meant that the land could be colonised. In the *Mabo* case, the Meriam people claimed that they had native title to their land. The problem for the court was how to acknowledge principles of justice and equality when the Australian State itself and its law were founded on racist assumptions. The court recognised the people's native title to land for the first time in this case, but nevertheless Veitch finds many points of critique in the decision. For instance, it left the old racist doctrine and the founding act of the State intact. Thus the decision takes part in whitewashing responsibility for the damage caused by the invasion of Australia and produces ongoing discrimination. According to Veitch, we see here the power of common law reasoning to legitimate on the very grounds of equality, freedom and formal justice the ongoing dispossession and effective disavowal of the past. Veitch asks whether the law could be changed, for instance by a new case, so that it could redress what has until now been impossible to register as suffering. This would be inadequate because at the root of the problems lie the forms of sovereignty and property that are distinctive to Western legal conceptions. No new case can shake these foundations (see Veitch 2007: 99–114). Compare this with Manderson's claim that the Australian High Court went through a phase when it recognised proximity. Manderson connects this to the influential judgments of Justice William Deane. He was one of the judges who recognised native title in the *Mabo* case.

argumentation because for him, law is and does certain things. Law is a system, a structure, with its own logic and ways of functioning, almost as if it were an active subject. There is an ambivalence here. On the one hand, law is something definite, something clear, or at least sufficiently organised and systematic to produce miserable effects. On the other hand, Veitch seems to imply that legal actors, for instance judges, avoid their responsibility and should be held responsible for their large role in interpreting and shaping law. Veitch thinks that it is law that is irresponsible. But there are also legal actors who make irresponsible decisions. Irresponsibility therefore turns out to be fuzzy. How can *law itself*, if it is always subject to interpretation, be at fault? Moreover, how can legal actors be blamed if they apply categories and concepts that are already irresponsible? The question arises, what is the nature of the irresponsibility and whose irresponsibility is it?

Veitch says that law is bad by nature, not by accident or mistake. Veitch's examples mostly concern massive human rights violations and suffering on a large scale. But does Veitch really claim that even in smaller cases law is unable to function in a responsible way? Are all legal fields equally bad? He does not say that law is completely unable to ever hold any actors, institutions or States responsible. This way the scope of his accusation against law is somewhat unclear. Are there instances when law works well, responsibly and justly, and, if so, are all these mere mistakes?

Veitch's argumentation has a hint of extremism built into it. He condemns law, all law, on the basis of certain cases and (admittedly extensive) examples. His exploration threatens to end up with a verdict that law is irresponsible, full stop. The problem with this is that it makes it difficult to study the irresponsibilities of law in a way that would differentiate between more and less irresponsible. The arguments regarding the law's responsibility and lack thereof can be rather different. First, we can say that law is always violent, at least to some degree, because it is a system of power and control. This way, no matter how beneficial the results of law are in some cases, we can still argue that it is generally a structure of violence. Second, we can claim that law is violent because it produces suffering and pain. This is certainly not self-evident. Some of the results of legislation and legal decision-making have evidently good results and increase the well-being of people or society. Third, we can see law as a structure that constructs violence. It is here seen as a meaning-giving system in which violence is defined and created. We see that there are many ways of talking about the irresponsibility and the violence of law. Veitch's book includes elements of all these three ways of thinking, whereas Cover's can perhaps be categorised as belonging mostly to the first.

The most difficult thing in the image of law and legal interpretation drawn in Cover's and Veitch's analyses is that law is violent and irresponsible *as a system*. The actor perspective becomes problematic from this point of view. I have been arguing so far that the meanings of legal texts cannot be pinned down to anything secure or solid, and therefore a judge always has an amount of freedom when interpreting and applying law. At the same time he or she is, of course, conditioned by the law, its language, habits and traditions. Their legal education and the fact that they take part in and renew the practices of law make them a construct of the law. Where, then, should the emphasis be placed when speaking of responsibility: on individual judges, or on law as a system?

## Accountability of the subject and responsibility of legal interpretation

The argument about the two dimensions of legal interpretation emphasises the responsibility of the interpreter, but we have seen that responsibility is a difficult notion. What kind of responsibility are we talking about? Whose responsibility and for what? As the focus here is on legal interpretation in connection with legal decision-making, that is, on legal interpretation mostly done by judges, the issue has to be connected with questions about the judge and their identity. Cover's discussion shows that a judge never acts alone but in a field where the different actors have certain roles. This raises doubts whether individual judges can be held accountable for their interpretations. Veitch argues that often legal actors are not held accountable, but now the question that has to be discussed to more detail is to what extent individual legal decision-makers *can* be held accountable for their decisions.

How is responsibility affected by the fact that judges not only interpret and create law but are also themselves created by it? This question is a version of the intricate problem of freedom. One main disagreement between, for instance, structuralism and existentialism can be described as a disagreement concerning a person's freedom and whether their choices really are their own. In what sense can we say that a person is responsible for their actions if they are at the same time a product of their time and place and if their thinking and acting are influenced by something outside?

An interesting angle on this is provided by Judith Butler's ideas on accountability. She asks if a theory of subjectivity as it is represented in post-structuralism has undermined the possibility of responsibility. Is it so that the idea of a socially constructed subject cannot provide the basis for an account of responsibility? If we are always to some extent divided, ungrounded or incoherent, is it then impossible to ground a notion of personal or social responsibility? Butler argues against this impossibility as she tries to work out a theory that acknowledges the limits of our abilities to fully know and govern ourselves but nevertheless holds on to responsibility.

A judge is a subject and as such created in the many social and legal connections or discourses in which they have learned to become a judge. They renew their ways of being in their actions. They are created in a certain kind of legal order and a specific community, which dictate what being a judge means. Even when engaging in self-reflection, he or she is conditioned by their role as a judge. One could say that their own story of themselves always arrives late in the sense that a more general story of who they are has already been created.

> [...] I cannot be present to a temporality that precedes my own capacity for self-reflection. This means that my narrative begins *in media res*, when many

> things have already taken place to make me and my story in language possible. And it means that my story always arrives late. I am always recuperating, reconstructing, even as I produce myself differently in the very act of telling.
>
> (Butler 2001: 27)

This resembles Wittgenstein's idea of us always already being in a language with a grammar and always also taking part in certain ways of living. Many things come to us ready-made and are not produced by ourselves. A lot has to be available to us in language in order for us to be able to tell a story of ourselves.

A judge does not fully control themselves or their identity. They have been constructed in a legal world, which is only partially their own and for which they cannot give a complete account. Does this mean that the judge does not carry full responsibility for their decisions? Does it also mean that a theory of legal interpretation in which responsibility is ultimately seen as the only possible way of limiting legal meaning has a serious flaw? We are quickly ending up in a paradoxical situation in which a judge is both responsible and not. Butler tries to develop a theory of responsibility that takes into account the fact that we are not complete, autonomous and self-present persons but that our identities are constructed in different social contexts. It is an ethics based on our shared partial blindness about ourselves. She asks if it could be that it is precisely our opacity to ourselves that makes it possible for us to confer a certain kind of recognition on others? At least the realisation that one is not completely the same and that there is something for which one cannot give an account might induce patience towards others. One would not expect other people to be selfsame at every moment either (Butler 2001: 27). This ethics is based on the idea that when we know ourselves, that is, when we are aware that we can never know ourselves completely, then we realise that we cannot expect anything else from others.

To know the limits of one's self-knowledge is, according to Butler, a self-limiting act. This can constitute a disposition of humility and generosity since we need to be forgiven for what we cannot fully know or control and need to forgive others who are constituted in the same way. An ethical attitude towards another human being is thus that of patience and tolerance. The ethical encounter with the other is illustrated by the question 'Who are you?', to which no definite answer is expected. Butler says that by letting this question stay open we let the other live because life is exactly that which escapes all our efforts to define it (Butler 2001: 28). There is in this ethical structure that Butler describes the idea that ethics means encountering and recognising another person, but this recognition does not turn into a definition.

Butler turns on its head the idea about a subject that is opaque to itself and therefore not fully responsible for its actions. She says that the fact that we are always interrupted by alterity means that we are ethically implicated in the lives of others. Ultimately, when we are trying to tell the story of ourselves, the 'I' is always interrupted by otherness. This implies that the 'I' that I am is never anything without a 'you'. I cannot even begin to refer to myself without referring to other people at the same time. It is through my capacity of being in a relationship with another person that I become I in the first place. In accordance with Levinas, Butler says that I can speak of myself only because I have already been addressed by you (Butler 2001: 37; 2005: 83–92; see, also, Critchley 2007a: 11). The self is always, in a way, divided, and can never attain complete self-mastery.

Butler argues that the meaning of responsibility has to be rethought on this basis. Responsibility cannot be tied to the fantasy of a transparent and fully accountable subject. To take responsibility for oneself is to *accept the limits* of one's understanding of oneself. This can be taken as a Kantian thought, as the limits of reason are connected with our humanity. My foreignness to myself is the source of my ethical connection with others. The realisation that I am not complete and that I am what I am because of others can make me see the importance of ethics. This way the lack in my self-understanding is the source of ethics and the reason to pay attention to ethics. Of course, I need to know myself to some extent in order to act responsibly in relations with other people. But the fact that I am never fully myself means that I cannot think about ethics alone without a connection to others (Butler 2001: 37–38). This is very much in line with Levinas' approach in which the subject *qua* subject appears only after encountering the face of another person. It is the ethical encounter that makes us humans. The fact that we are never completely owned or defined by ourselves is not a problem for ethical responsibility in Levinasian theory.

We can try to apply this idea to legal interpretation. A judge can never know themselves fully, and what they are lies not completely in their hands. They are structured by others. The important others here are, first, the legal texts and the other legal actors that together form and uphold the legal tradition or practice, and, second, they are the people whose lives the law governs and who form society. A judge's responsibility is divided and even possibly in contradiction as regards these others. This responsibility can be conceptualised through the idea of twofold ethics of interpretation developed above. And even though the judge is not a master of themselves, their responsibility is not diminished. On the contrary: for the judge to take responsibility for their interpretation choices, they have to accept the limits of their power and understanding. What this ultimately leads to is humility, as the self-governing omnipotent judge is questioned.

Albeit a judge is a construction of the law that they interpret, they nevertheless have a freedom to make decisions. Through the fact that a decision can never be dictated by anything and because of the openness of meaning always haunting texts, there is something very personal in judging. Even if there are rules, decisions are never guaranteed by them. Judges take an active part in choice and production of meaning and the application of that meaning to people's lives. A judge is a person who chooses, even though their choices are not completely free. According to Butler reading Foucault, ethical agency is neither fully determined nor radically free (Butler 2005: 19), and this applies for legal decision-making as well.

Still, we want a government of law instead of a government of men, if by 'government of men' we mean a legal system that consists of arbitrary commands and despotic decisions of individual judges. But we have to accept that, strictly speaking, there can be no government of law. Law does not govern by itself. Legal decision-making includes the personal responsibility of the judge (and other actors as well), because there is no possibility for law to rule without the help of men and women who make the actual interpretation choices. Only through the choices of the legal interpreter do legal texts acquire meaning and become applied in certain ways. Subjective elements are present in these choices, but this does not necessarily mean that they are subjective through and through, or biased and partial.

Derrida also discusses the identity of a decision-maker and says that it is difficult to say *who decides*. If a decision-maker does not experience undecidability, then the decision would simply be application of a programme and not a proper decision. This way one can say that a decision always has to go through impossibility. The decision-maker does not know what to do but nevertheless a decision has to be made and responsibility for it has to be carried. This does not mean paralysis, but is the general structure of decision-making. Because of this, it is never certain *who* makes decisions. I can never know for sure that 'I' made a decision. As soon as I claim that 'I' am the master of a decision, it implies that I know what to do, and that I am certain (Derrida 1999a: 66–67).[12] A true decision, which is not just an application of a matrix, is always uncertain and foreign to the decision-maker, as it were. The decision is never owned by them, and this way they can never really call it theirs.[13] This does not mean, however, that he or she would not be accountable for it.

In Cover's picture of law as roles and deeds, the judge threatens to become a cog in a machine. Veitch also talks about the law as a *system* of irresponsibility, which implies that the judge's role is reduced to the minimal. But even if the judge always works inside a machine, their struggle with the norms governing its function is their own. Butler discusses the struggle with social norms through Foucault's later writings on ethics. Through a practice of care of the self, the subject has an amount of freedom to reflect on themselves and the ways in which they are produced and are producible (Butler 2005: 118–132). Critical thinking is an element in this. One of the most important ideas in Foucault's later work is that he recognised the freedom of critical thinking. Critical thought includes self-reflection and the possibility to change aspects of oneself. The subject can problematise its behaviour and beliefs and also the social field of which it forms part.

12 See, also, Wolcher (1996: 56–64). He points out that Derrida problematises the possibility of anybody saying 'I am just' or even 'I am unjust'. Interestingly, Wolcher underlines the impossibility of *saying* these things and compares it with a Wittgensteinian silence on ethics.

13 See, also, Badiou on the responsibility of a singular person in a concrete *situation*. The ethical subject (the decision-maker) is created in these situations. The subject becomes a subject in certain circumstances. It does not exist before ethical choices but is created through them (Badiou 2002: 40–44). See, also, Critchley (2007a: 42–47). Critchley emphasises that the subject and the event come into being at the same time.

Freedom is not only the ontological possibility of ethics, ethics as a practice is a practice of freedom. It means that the subject explores new ways of thinking and living. It consists in both creative activity as well as critical interrogation of the present (see Oksala 2005: 180–182, 188–190).

A judge's responsibility is *theirs*. It is a personal responsibility. Derrida says that even if a decision is never mine, it comes to me.

> The decision itself corresponds to the other, and [...] I am myself only from this infinite responsibility which the other places in me. The other who is in me is greater than I. I can only gain access to my selfhood [...], my egoity, etc., from this relation to the other in me, but the other in me can nevertheless not be incorporated or introjected – who is in me, greater than I. [...] Thus, the decision comes to me: there it is, it is a thought, a simple decision, a decision that comes to me. I must take responsibility for the decision that comes to me.[14]
>
> (Derrida 2000: 468)

Responsibility derives from the fact that I as decision-maker have to decide. I am singular and irreplaceable in the situation. This makes the responsibility of an interpretation mine even if I am not completely the master of the decision.

Thus the argument is that a judge belongs to a legal system and is constructed by it but at the same time has a responsibility of his or her own. This tension means that the decisions each makes are theirs but not completely – they do not own the system and the norms included in it. The foreignness of the judge to him or herself is not contrary to their responsibility because it is through being in a relationship with otherness that is the very source of their responsibility. Responsibility is born through an encounter with otherness and has two distinct and equally important elements. First, there are the texts of the legal system that constitutes and compels them. But there is another important other as well, the persons who appear before them and address them. These two very different forms of otherness make up the judge's responsibility. They correspond to the distinction made earlier between the textual and the situational dimension of the ethics of legal interpretation.

## Dissenting voices

Meanings are always open to debate. According to Cover, this ultimately means that a struggle occurs and the law reflects the choices of the strongest group. But a debate also means that there is room for disagreeing and arguing for and against meanings. Ideally, it is a discourse where no one has the final word or a voice above others. There is space for debate and contestation in the way meanings live

14 The other is here not just the other person but more abstractly understood otherness. That the decision corresponds to the other means that it corresponds to everything else than it is, its reverse side and its negation.

in practices and habits and in the community. The legal decision is influenced by its societal surroundings and also affects them. Let us now look more closely at the political dimension of legal interpretation as it is understood here.

The thought about the twofold nature of the ethics of legal interpretation implies that ethics immediately also opens up a space for politics. This theme is visible in Levinas's thinking. Ethical saying goes together with the said, and there can be no other without the immediate appearance of the third. The third is encountered in encountering the other.

Even though I have discussed an understanding of ethics that is most strongly opposed to totalising strategies, it may nevertheless be the case that the most severe objections that an ethics of legal interpretation has to face focuses on what emphasising ethics might lead to in a broader societal framework. There is a worry that law in the name of ethics turns into a performance that only bolsters up existing strategies and power-relations. For instance Jacques Rancière fears that 'ethics, Otherness and the infinite respect for Otherness thereby become a sort of "new Gospel" working to legitimate the practice and ideology of "liberal democracy", which is not political at all' (Rancière 2010: 60). Ethics, seen this way, is not open to politics or disagreement.[15] It can be flattened out to an abstract call for responsibility completely separated from socio-legal realities (Christodoulidis 2009: 16).[16]

The threatening result of this is a silencing of dissenting voices and an unacceptable blockade of critique. This threat is real. But the way we have perceived ethics here underlines that ethics includes not only infinite responsibility for others, but also a concrete demand that is most urgently political and social.[17] The distinction between ethics and politics is not stable. Immediately where there is ethics, there is room for politics as well. Emphasis on responsibility does not close off dissenting voices, nor does it deny the possibilities of resistance. On the

15 It is difficult to see how ethics as it is understood here inspired by the super demanding sense in which it is developed in Levinas's work could be flattened out. But, generally speaking, the risk always exists that ethics is reduced to mere morality, a systematised order of norms, instead of a creative living challenge. This is perhaps a Nietzschean way of thinking, which can be compared to Arendt's idea of the dangerousness of people who are secure in their moral beliefs. People like this are most easily turned to another normative system. The activity of thinking and re-thinking, not relying on normative systems, can be seen as a condition against evildoing (Arendt 2003: 160, 178). In connection to a discussion of Socrates, she says that thinking also has an undermining effect on established criteria for good and evil and our customs and rules of conduct (Arendt 2003: 176).

16 He says that against 'the ethical turn of critical legal theory, against the recourse to the ungraspable other, but also against a certain emancipatory mysticism that sees the "return of the repressed" in the inexhaustible opportunities of under-determination, excess and the rest, I have argued that resistance to the order of capital requires resituating it as political, not ethical or mystical, and rethinking it in terms of the now seemingly outmoded category of strategy' (Christodoulidis 2009: 22).

17 Compare with Nick Smith's reading of Levinas and Adorno. He accuses them of being too vague on practical and political issues. They 'deny us any means of drawing comfortable distinctions between the justifiable and the unjustifiable' (Smith 2009: 71). I would like to draw the reader's attention to the word 'comfortable' here, which is interesting in this context.

contrary, it is by definition openness to difference and sensitivity to otherness. The very moment of responsibility arises out of the restlessness and hesitation of choice. This is the core of an ethics of legal interpretation.

Let us look at the critique against ethics more closely together with Rancière, who is deeply sceptical of an ethics of the other. He makes the well-known distinction between politics and the police (policing), where politics refers to a logic of conflict, disagreement and dissensus. The police defines, counts and classifies.

> The police is not a social function but a symbolic constitution of the social. The essence of the police lies neither in repression nor even in control over the living. Its essence lies in a certain way of dividing up the sensible.
>
> (Rancière 2010: 36)

Police logic is a division of the sensible. It governs the visible and the sayable by dividing up the world and people. It is the symbolic constitution which includes, excludes and separates people into subjects and groups. Politics, in contrast, is always an intervention. It puts definitions, exclusions and separations into question by claiming something new, something different from what is known and accepted. This way the essence of politics is disagreement.

There are always those who claim to speak correctly, the masters of classification. They want to retain their power and do this by denying others the capacity to speak. Political subjectivity means in this theory the ability to reconfigure, to contest the sayable and the visible (see Rancière and Panagia 2000: 115). According to Rancière, we should not understand politics as a space where certain subjects communicate and understand one another. This presupposes that people come together because they understand one another. It also requires that both speakers and the objects about which they speak are already preconstituted. Politics as Rancière sees it is possible only as disagreement. In his view, there can be politics only when there is no pre-established agreement, not only regarding the objects of debate but, more importantly, regarding the speakers.

> The principle of political interlocution is thus disagreement; that is, it is the discordant understanding of both the objects of reference and the speaking subjects. In order to enter into political exchange, it becomes necessary to invent the scene upon which spoken words may be audible, in which objects may be visible, and individuals themselves may be recognized.
>
> (Rancière and Panagia 2000: 116)

Politics has to do with the radical equality of people. Equality is the principle of politics, the idea underlying it. Politics presupposes the equality of all speaking beings, which contradicts the police definition of subjects who are put in their place and given certain roles. Rancière says that equality cannot consist in any form of social bond. It cannot have place in the social or State organisation, or it immediately turns into inequality (Rancière 1999: 33–34).

For Rancière, equality and democracy are connected. Politics is democratic, because it is action of the demos that takes equality for granted (see May 2008: 52–53). Democracy is politics' way to be. He says that democracy as he understands it is a name for the disruption of an order of distribution of bodies, that is, the disruption of police order. Democracy is not a regime (Rancière 1999: 101). It consists of forms of expressions that oppose the logic of the police by arguments of equality. 'Consensus democracy', which is the form of government that prevails in many Western societies today, Rancière calls 'postdemocracy'. It is a version of policing, a mechanism for allocating parts and shares in the society that makes democracy proper disappear (see Rancière 1999: 102; see, also, Hewlett 2007). What has to be kept in mind here, however, is that politics and the police should not be understood simply as different orders or areas of the social. They are different kinds of logic that coexist.

We can compare the idea of disagreement with Cover's conception of different and competing normative worlds. Making legal decisions means choices of meaning that can suppress the normative understandings of people or groups. Legal interpretation involves having to maintain one legal meaning even though there can be no pretence of superiority of one *nomos* over others. Granted, law can be criticised because it imposes one normative world and one way of interpreting on others. But the space offered by the legal text to the decision-maker can enable them to navigate between normative worlds and reach decisions that do not kill off the norms of others. Justice demands that we do not downplay, ignore or omit the perspectives of those who suffer the consequences of legal decisions and this is a possibility that the openness of language gives us (see, also, Etxabe 2010: 140). Judges can and should take differing normative worlds into account.

There is always a risk that ethics is misused. It can mean the subsumption of all forms of discourse and practice beneath the same indistinct point of view (Rancière 2010: 184). In this malformed version, ethics ends up in closing points of view instead of opening them. Here we come to the fundamental discrepancy between a Rancièrian political theory and Levinasian ethics. Rancière is suspicious of ethics because it can be anti-political. It can be used in ways that delimit and silence politics, thus becoming a way of suppressing disagreement and justifying the prevailing division of the sensible. This threat is serious, but on the basis of the discussion above that is not the kind of ethics we are thinking about here.

Considering legal decision-making, there is an interesting section in Rancière's *Hatred of Democracy*. He talks about the duality of man and citizen connected to human rights (or the rights of man) and says that the political subject is something that disrupts and questions identities, be they defined by social relations or juridical categories. 'Man' (as in human rights) and 'citizen' are names that can always be contested by the political subject. Politics is the questioning of names and categories. It *contests the meaning of juridical texts* (see Rancière 2009: 59). 'Man' and 'citizen' are terms whose extension and understanding are *litigious* and which, for that reason, lend themselves to political objections that test which subjects these names are applied to and what power they bear (Rancière 2006: 301; see, also, Rancière 2009: 59). This way, Rancière seems to agree that legal interpretation can sometimes provide a possibility for politics. We have seen through our reading of theories of language and interpretation. The meaning of all words can be contested. Meaning is litigious.

Rancière aptly says that the space of politics 'is constituted in the abstract literariness of the law and through polemics over its interpretations' (Rancière 2010: 102). The *abstract literariness of the law* clears up a place for disagreement. It leaves room for arguments on meanings, definitions and classifications. Law can offer a place where new ideas are presented and fought for, often also having high visibility in society. And I argue that it is especially because of legal interpretation being what it is that law has a chance of staying open to politics. Language can diminish the gap between law as coercion and politics as contestation.

For Rancière, equality is disagreement in the sense that it always questions and disrupts and can therefore never be implemented. Thus the legal definitions of equality are never sufficient but always lacking because as definitions they uphold the police and not equality. 'Intellectual emancipation accordingly cannot be institutionalized without becoming instruction of the people, in other words, a way of organizing the eternal minority' (Rancière 1999: 34). We see that law understood as an order and an institution can never uphold equality. It includes classifications and definitions, even when it strives at emancipation. But the legal decision is a certain kind of rupture of the order. As we have seen, it is never completely guaranteed by the system and its rules. It includes openness, partly because of the nature of language. We can compare politics as intervention with the idea of interpretation being an interruption, arresting the chain of signification. The decision is made on the basis of the text but never dictated by it. In addition, it includes an openness that derives from the situation where the decision takes place. Rancière's way of understanding disagreement fits this picture, as it does not concern only the meaning of words. The situational element of legal interpretation includes disagreement connected with the situation itself, with the object that is under dispute and even the parties of the case and their role in it.

When the legal decision functions as a rupture in the logic of the police, we have to remember that immediately after the decision has been made, law is no longer contestation but has become the tool for upholding a certain way of dividing the sensible. A new decision can contest this again, but also this decision, when it has been made, turns into a definition, a new conception, a new division of the sensible that is the police. Derrida speaks of a similar operation when he says that:

> performativity for me is – I have this impression more and more – that which produces events, all institutions and acts in which responsibility is to be assumed; but it is also that which neutralizes the event, that is to say, what happens [...]. Wherever there is the performative, whatever the form of communication, there is a context of legitimate, legitimizing, or legitimized convention that permits it to neutralize what happens, that is, the brute eventness

> of the arrivant [...]. Put another way, if in a certain manner performativity encounters the event produced by language, it is also that which neutralizes the eventness of the event.
>
> (Derrida 2000: 467)

The event, the rupture that contests and puts into question always also includes its negation that normalises and solidifies and thus nullifies the exceptionality of the event.

If politics can occur at a meeting point between police logic and egalitarian logic, then the legal decision can be a place for politics (Rancière 1999: 34). Politics makes visible that which had not been seen. Rancière on several occasions discusses the French feminist Olympe de Gouges, who opposed the way in which women were denied the rights of citizens. Women's activities were seen as belonging to the sphere of domestic life. They lacked a will of their own and could not be political subjects. De Gouges argued that since women were qualified to mount the scaffold, they should be regarded as citizens. Her argumentation disrupted the definition of citizen, as she claimed that on the scaffold everyone was equal, man or woman. The death sentence as an enemy of the Revolution was universal and made no distinction between public and domestic life. This way, women could affirm their rights as citizens (Rancière 2010: 56–57). This is an example of political action where the logic of the police is put into question. The place and the setting where this kind of contestation happens can be law, where people can through acting inside the order also change that same order.

According to Rancière's way of thinking, politics has no proper place. For instance, a public demonstration is not automatically political. 'A demonstration is political not because it occurs in a particular place and bears upon a particular object but rather because its form is that of a clash between two partitions of the sensible' (Rancière 2010: 39). Could a clash like this not happen in law? In *Disagreement: Politics and Philosophy* (1999), Rancière implies that the legal decision *could* be a place for political action but seldom is. Law functions as a way of legitimising State power, and in these operations politics does not stand a chance. Three phenomena can be recognised: the spread of law; the practice of generalised expertise; and the practice of the eternal opinion poll (see Rancière 1999: 112). However, difficult legal decisions are those that bring us to the boundaries of law. The difficulty is caused by clashes of different ways of defining the world and ways in which the legal decision can cope with this. I argue that a legal decision can be political. A legal conflict can be a place where those who have been excluded can make themselves visible and audible and where the unsayable can be said. Law is not only coherence and consensus. It is also a place of contestation, where categories and definitions can be put into question. This is made possible by the uncertainty of legal interpretation.

Rancière seems to admit as much in this passage, where he explains why democracy cannot consist in a set of institutions.

> The reason for this is that one and the same constitution and set of laws can be implemented in opposing ways depending on the sense of the 'common' in which they are framed. They can circumscribe the sphere of the political and restrict political agency to an activity performed by definite agents endowed with the appropriate qualifications; or *they can give way to forms of interpretation and practice that are democratic, which invent new political places, issues and agents from the very same texts.*
>
> (Rancière 2010: 54, emphasis added)

Democracy is not a set of institutions, because the same institutions, the same laws can be interpreted according to police logic or in political ways. The difference between the police and democratic politics lies not in the way the laws are written but in the way they are *interpreted.* Police logic tends to shrink the sphere of the political by limiting it in a biased way, for instance, in the name of the universality of the law (Rancière 2010: 54). Universality, as an argument for equal treatment, as in 'like cases should be treated alike', can in practice cause inequality and the continuing exclusion of certain people or groups.

This brings us again to the question of justice. It seems that in order for politics to get a chance, justice has to be understood as an open predicate in the sense that it has to be negotiated and renegotiated over and over again. Justice has to be open to dispute in a democratic society. Democracy is dissensus, not consensus. Justice is produced in difference and the uncertainty or contestability of meanings. It is here that equality can have a chance, but it is also a reason why justice has a chance. We see that this idea of disagreement can help us come to terms with the alleged crisis of legal interpretation, according to which law is in trouble. It is not a crisis but something that we indeed want to uphold: openness is needed for disagreement and equality. And the emptiness of justice is not the tragedy of law.

We can consider another case in addition to De Gouges. This is another of Rancière's examples of politics happening, and also has close links to law. The example is Rosa Parks, who in 1955 refused to give her seat on the bus to a white person (Rancière 2009: 61). This case illustrates the possibility of law to be something other than policing. Law can be a place for political action that produces equality. Parks's own act as she remained sitting in her seat was a one-woman political protest, active participation and contestation of the division of the sensible. By remaining sitting, she questioned the way people were defined as black and white and the subsequent rights that they had. But her act inspired other people and wide protests were held. After this the conflict became legal, as human rights activists and lawyers decided to argue cases against racial discrimination in various courts. Finally, the decision in *Browder v Gayle* ended racial discrimination on buses.[18] We can understand this example of Rancière's as an indication of

18 The case was argued with reference to *Brown v Board of Education of Topeka* from 1954.

the possibility for law to be open to politics as disagreement. Parks's and other active persons' protests gave rise to a legal decision that came to have a great impact on the partition of the sensible.

Of course, a legal case can be a contestation and a way of making oneself heard even if one loses the lawsuit. If it is disruption and disagreement that we want, then even the fact that a party argues his or her case can be a rupture of the police logic of the time.[19] Many trials are political in the sense that through them a political message can be spoken and heard.

For sure, law includes classifications and definitions, even when it is used to emancipate or to give a voice to those who have no voice in society. It operates through naming and determining the roles of things, facts, and persons.[20] But the legal decision is a certain kind of rupture. It is never guaranteed by the system and its rules. It includes openness, partly because of the nature of language. On the first level, the ethics of legal interpretation means a basic 'I must'. This spreads to an openness connected with the situation where the decision takes place and the demand for justice. The situational element of legal interpretation includes a possibility for disagreement connected with the situation itself, with the object that is under dispute and even the parties to the case and their role in it.

## Uncertainty, despair and consolation

The uncertainty of language is a possibility and an opening for justice. The possibility of failure, of meaning getting lost or changing on the way, is a necessary characteristic of language and also a feature of the interpretation of legal texts. Because of the unstableness of meaning, interpretation never stops. But there can still be better or worse interpretations, because we can assess the choices of the interpreter in ethical terms and by reference to justice.

This approach can be criticised for leaving too much open. What does it mean in practice to say that the judge faces the challenge of respecting both the text and the situation? How is this done? Even though justice (which is the ultimate aim of legal interpretation) is something empty and does not permit a definitive answer, certain issues should be emphasised. The argument is, first, that there cannot be

19 Consider, for example, the issue of the 'fox girls', animal rights activists in Finland, who were convicted because they let foxes loose from fur farms in the 1990s. This situation can be seen as a question of 'a clash between two partitions of the sensible'. But the situation is complicated in the light of Rancière's theory because, unlike de Gouges and Parks, these people were not striving at recognition or better conditions for themselves but for animals. Rancière's idea of politics as dissensus is difficult when it comes to animals, as he underlines the division between speech and noise. He does not count animals as relevant, which means that he continues the unreasonable and biased way of philosophising about man and animals that Derrida warns of (see Derrida 2002).

20 Constable says that the language of law reveals worlds. She takes as an example the notions of 'consumer' and 'service user'. A politics of association, where everybody is already situated in relations and dependencies with others 'goes to the very matter of modern law' (Constable 2005: 22–23).

any clear criteria for how the text and the demands of the case could be balanced. There cannot be such criteria and therefore we should not explicate such criteria. There is virtue in not trying to, because this would necessarily lead to failure and a relapse into dogmatism, which has to be refuted as an unfruitful approach. Second, that justice as the ultimate criterion for legal interpretation is left open can be understood as a positive thing. This is the argument against despair. Even though we cannot and should not define justice, this does not lead to silence or inaction. Following the discussion of Rancière above, we can argue from a politically informed point of view that openness and precisely the lack of definite criteria are conditions of possibility for justice.

The instance of a decision not ensured by a legal text is a promise, which includes the potential of contestation, change and resistance. This is not contrary to the claim that decisions of legal meaning should be responsible. Focusing on legal interpretation as situational practice, we can find some leeway between politics and ethics as they have been understood here. Rancière's politics is punctual, a claim spoken, a voice raised. Likewise, legal interpretation is something temporal and occasional. And it is in the uncertainty of the decision in which responsibility is required that we can hear the questions: responsibility for whom and how?

Responsibility as situational is always open and never predetermined as protection of a certain group or a particular way of life. Even protection of suffering persons can be questioned and rethought: suffering is not only an ethical question but political as well, and we have to argue about what suffering is and how much suffering is too much. We can recall here the Levinasian problems of law: Why should we care for others and how much? The first question gets an ethical answer but the second transcends immediately to the political sphere.[21] This means exactly calculating the incalculable. Justice as the meaning of law is always empty or we can also see it as too full. But this does not make justice less important for legal interpretation. Even if we cannot and do not want to define justice and have to contend that it has a taste of death, it should not lead to despair. On the contrary, openness is a prerequisite for dissenting voices to be heard.

## What kind of judgments do we want?

What is argued here is not that we would not know what legal texts mean but that they often mean too much, and a decision has to be made on one meaning over others to be applied in a particular case. Post-semantics is a way of understanding interpretation after the experiences of both a critical view of literal meaning and the idea that no correct interpretation of any text is provided by hermeneutics and deconstruction. Meaning, interpretation and the criteria for interpretation have to be

21 Christodoulidis at the Critical Legal Conference at Utrecht University in September 2010. See, also, Rancière 2010: 60: 'There is not one infinite openness to otherness, but instead many ways of inscribing the part of the other'.

rethought. What deconstruction really teaches us is not to give up reading and interpreting but to read more, and better. Deconstruction is not sceptical about meaning in the sense that it would give up interpretation. On the contrary, by focusing on the spectres of meaning, the way meaning shifts and reflects through different textual and other strategies, deconstruction urges the reader to look more closely, to pay more attention, to study not only every word but also every pause. Everything could be significant! So there is not less meaning, but more. Deconstruction does not really imply indeterminacy but too much determinacy (see Derrida 1999a: 79). And semantics is one of the most important things here. Words are important. The play of signification is a serious matter, not something to be taken lightly. Derrida, when asked in an interview, if we will ever act if we engage in a close reading that is potentially infinite (because there is no final truth to be found, said):

> At some point, and perhaps you were trying to provoke me, you said that if we practice close reading we will never act. On the contrary, I would assume that *political, ethical and juridical responsibility requires a task of infinite close reading*. I believe this to be the condition of political responsibility: politicians should read.
>
> (Derrida 1999a: 67; emphasis added)

Derrida does not here mean that we should spend our time at the library reading books but urges us, for instance, to read events, analyse situations and criticise the media. Reading is required for justice. The responsibility to read well is the ultimate responsibility of a decision-maker.

We have above discussed theories, many of which share a resistance to dogmatism. This resistance also argues for resistance to any criteria for legal interpretation. Because legal interpretation is what it is, such lists cannot work. Therefore, we should not try to construct them. We notice that the criteria fail and yet the reaction is often to try to think of other, better ones to do the trick. In line with Derrida this can be criticised, because drawing up criteria or rules for legal interpretation carries the risk of nailing it down to something definite, and thus the risk of dogmatic slumber. Justice and responsibility are – and have to be – in a certain sense unanswered questions. The question 'What is a correct interpretation?' cannot get a rule-governed response. It can be responded to only by deciding something every time, but no permanent responses can be given. We can have no good conscience. In Wittgensteinian terms, we can argue more or less the same thing. Dogmatic claims include the danger of injustice. Such theorising is not able to fully appreciate the manifoldness of things, different cases, exceptions and individual characteristics of the things studied. Or, we can think as Miller does, that whatever model of interpretation we adopt, this still requires a meticulous close reading of the text itself. But resistance to dogmatism should not be understood as only a methodological standpoint. As the discussion on dissenting voices shows, the absence of criteria is good as it can give room to multiplicity, different forms of life and the contestation of categories and names.

Legal interpretation frequently includes difficult choices, but they cannot be facilitated. Justice is precisely undecidability, suspension. The moment of responsibility arises out of restlessness and hesitation. This opens up new ways of looking at and also criticising law. Ethics comes in, responsibility comes in, and justice as the ultimate goal is underlined.

# Conclusion

This book has tried to answer the challenge posed on theories of legal interpretation by the openness of language. The aim has been to search for a middle ground between theories that see openness as a reason why law ultimately turns into power-play and violence, and those who are not willing to let go of the belief in the certainty of language. A way of understanding the politics of legal decisions in positive terms has also been explored. The thought is that we have to abandon our trust in exact and determinate language but that this is not a cause for despair. And it does not lead to the conclusion that anything goes.

I have argued that interpretation is a process without end. It is always possible that a new interpretation of a text will replace an old one, and thus interpretation is never complete or certain. This idea causes confusion in the field of law, where the self-understanding of lawyers and legal theorists alike includes that legal decisions are bound by the law. How can they be bound by the law if the law allows for several different meanings? It is important that it is somehow possible to decide what a legal norm allows and what it forbids. In this way, there have to be some kind of limits to legal interpretation. These limits have above been sought in hermeneutics and in the philosophy of Wittgenstein. We have studied how these theories do not provide any definite limits and how they are in fact compatible with deconstruction, where the question of limits is taken further.

None of the philosophy of language, hermeneutics or deconstruction can offer a definite account of what ultimately makes meaning and understanding possible. The paradoxical nature of this problem is that all these theories take for granted that language works and that we are able to make distinctions between meanings of texts, but they are not able to explain how this happens. This dead end, which is related to the crisis of legal interpretation, has to be answered in a different way, if it can be answered at all. We must redirect our search to something other than the definition of words. We must turn our thinking beyond language, semantics and linguistics. I have argued here that the bridge that can take us over the abyss of meaning, over the gap that always exists between texts and meaning, is ethics.

By focusing on the ethical dimensions of legal interpretation, it is not claimed that interpretation is always ethical in the sense that it would be moral or benevolent. The argument about the ethics of interpretation is twofold. First, there has to be a certain attitude of the interpreter towards the text in order for the interpreter to be able to understand at all. This attitude can best be described as ethical. It has been called 'textual responsibility'. Second, especially in the field of law, where interpretation is inscribed in the demand for justice, there is the challenge of every interpretation taking place in a particular time and place. This amounts to what has been called 'situational responsibility'. The idea is that by being responsible *this* interpretation of *this* text in *this situation* is also right and correct, that is, as correct as it can be. Ultimately, no other criteria are to be found for a correct interpretation of a legal text.

I argue that the fact that meaning is open-ended does not necessarily lead to arbitrary or uncontrollable interpretations. The crisis of legal interpretation is not a crisis after all. On the contrary: admitting vagueness in language is a possibility for ethical interpretative decisions and responsible applications of the law, as it opens up the space in which the interpreter moves and compels them to make choices and carry responsibility for them. Acknowledging vagueness and open-endedness forces the interpreter to deliberate and to decide while comprehending their own responsibility for the meaning of the text. A reason why we need judges and courts in the first place is that meaning has to be decided in every case. Law does not reveal meaning easily, like a lamp that can be turned on and off. The vagueness and open-endedness of meaning result in the responsibility of an interpreter that cannot be shifted anywhere. The less we believe in the power of language to draw clear definitions, the more we have to actively aim for justice. There is no logical necessity that leads from the indeterminacy of language to legal decisions being a wanton free play or only an unjustified exercise of power. Rather, the situation is the other way around: the more indeterminacy and freedom to decide, the more responsibility and the stronger the call of justice.

By way of concluding, three general claims of this book can be summarised. They can also be seen as three stages in the argument. First, I have tried to show that language and communication require a being together with other people. A community of speakers is necessary for language to work. This does not, however, mean that a community decision ultimately defines the meanings of words. It is only claimed that meaning is made possible by ethics as being together. Ethics is the condition of possibility for meaning. In order for us to be able to understand we have to want to understand. We have to say 'yes' to the other and be open to what he wants to say. The way ethics is meant here should not be understood too broadly but is referred to in a rather specific sense.

Why is interpretation not fundamentally arbitrary choice? The reason is that ethics precedes meaning. Ethics does not define meaning, but it structures meaning. Even before suppression, violence, lying and deceit there must be communication and the possibility for people to understand one another. Understanding is enabled by the ethics of language. This way, interpretation is never completely arbitrary or free. Respect for the text and its uniqueness structures the meaning of it and limits its interpretation. Ethics provides a space in which the interpreter can move and limits the freedom of the judge who has to decide what the legal text commands. That is the second point of this book.

However, if we simply said that the legal text limits the freedom of the judge, or that interpretation should always respect the text (and its wording), then this would contain the idea that founds the correctness of legal interpretation on fidelity towards the text. It has hopefully become clear that the argument in this book does not end in such a position. It moves further by concentrating on the interpretation situation with its political, social and legal consequences, and, in this connection, by emphasising how legal interpretation is always organised around a demand for justice. This is the third point of the book.

So, according to the argumentation put forward here, it is the ethics of legal interpretation including its situational aspect with an in-built reference to justice that overcomes the crisis of legal interpretation. The demand for justice is ultimately what sets *legal* interpretation apart from other practices of interpretation. I suggest a view of legal interpretation that is in many ways similar to deconstructive reading. It includes a meticulous close reading of the text combined with an analysis of hidden structures, ideologies and operational concepts that the text relies on. But legal interpreters cannot, and should not, only read texts and follow them blindly but try to do justice both to them *and* to the situation. This is the way law as text and law as life are brought together: it happens with the help of an interpreter who translates between these two. A reading of a legal text requires sensitivity towards what the text says and what a case demands. This way legal interpretation is at its best an oscillation between respect for the text (and with it the law as a system) and care for the parties in the case. Justice is ultimately singular in nature, a just decision in *this case* with regard to people and the time and place of the decision.

I have hopefully been able to show that the theory of ethics of legal interpretation developed here moves beyond proclamations made by many nowadays about the need for law to be responsible. This incontestable longing is often announced in the name of Levinas. He is the new authority who has been referred to again and again. 'Law should respect otherness!' Sure, but we need to go further and ask what it means and what risks are involved in such refrains. Law should be responsible, but how? The last part of the book has sought to uncover the possibilities and also the pitfalls of law and tried to formulate an understanding of responsibility with content.

Immediately where ethics and responsibility are present, there, too, calculating, comparing and thus politics are also to be found. But the text is still there. Legal interpretation is not merely empty force, nor is it simply imposition of one normative world on others. Law can do good, not only cause suffering. And because of the openness of legal interpretation, legal decision-making has the potential also to be a place of contestation and emancipation.

The structure of the argument of the book is similar to the way Derrida discusses iterability and also resembles Butler's discussion of accountability. Derrida shows that iterability, which is something negative, a weakness in language because it makes meaning uncertain, is also a strength in the sense that it enables meaning in the first place. Like *pharmakon*, it is the poison and the cure. Butler's argument for ethical accountability of the subject has an analogous structure. A subject is never fully present for him or herself and thus seems to be unable to give a full account of themselves. But the fact that something is always missing in their story of themselves contributes to their possibility of being ethical because it leads to humility and sensitivity towards others. So what can be seen as a negative thing is also something positive and even necessary at the same time. The argument put forward here is similar. Language is something we share but cannot control. Meaning never returns to us and is never fully present. It escapes our grasp. This is a problem for legal interpretation but also its redemption. The fact that language lends law a degree of openness is good because it gives room for responsibility and also disagreement. Openness means possibilities for dissenting voices and for sensitivity to otherness. Justice is produced in the uncertainty or contestability of meanings.

This book began with the description of a crisis and the threat of nihilism, a sense of meaninglessness. The task set out was to resist this despair and find ways of coping with meaning being lost. But has any real consolation been given? It is clear that even though this analysis has proven that there is no reason for a crisis, some readers are nevertheless left with a sense of disappointment as no proper guidelines for legal interpretation have been drawn up. But things are left open because they have to be left open if we are to stay true to the argument. Justice can be defined but then it is at the same time already open for redefining. And there is no just decision without openness and the insecurity that goes with it. Does the whole argument thus end up in emptiness? Yes and no. I have searched for a middle ground between words having definable meanings and empty tragic judgments. I have argued that legal interpretation is not guaranteed by language, nor is it simple brute force causing suffering. The understanding of justice developed here means that we need openness and undecidability in order for law to be just. We do not want a tool-box for interpretation, we want responsible interpretations. And in order for law to not succumb to becoming only a totalising structure of force, there has to be room for contestation and disagreement.

# Bibliography


Agamben, G. (1991) *Language and Death: The Place of Negativity*, Minneapolis, MN and Oxford: University of Minneapolis Press.

Arendt, H. (2003) *Responsibility and Judgment*, New York, NY: Schocken.

Aristotle (1984) *Nicomachean Ethics: Volume 2 of The Complete Works of Aristotle*, electronic edition, revised Oxford translation, J. Barnes (ed.) Princeton, NJ: Princeton University Press.

Atria, F. (2006) 'Adjudication and the Particular', in Z. Bankowski and J. MacLean (eds) *The Universal and the Particular in Legal Reasoning*, Aldershot and Burlington, VT: Ashgate, pp 69–83.

Attridge, D. (1992) 'Introduction to Ulysses Gramophone: Hear Say Yes in Joyce', in J. Derrida (ed.) *Acts of Literature*, New York, NY and London: Routledge, pp 253–254.

Badiou, A. (2002) *Ethics: An Essay on the Understanding of Evil*, London and New York, NY: Verso.

Badiou, A. (2009) *L'antiphilosophie de Wittgenstein*, Caen: Nous.

Baker, G.P. and Hacker, P.M.S. (1988) *Wittgenstein: Rules, Grammar and Necessity*, Oxford: Blackwell Publishers.

Bankowski, Z. (2006) 'In the Judgement Space: The Judge and the Anxiety of the Encounter', in Z. Bankowski and J. MacLean (eds) *The Universal and the Particular in Legal Reasoning*, Aldershot and Burlington, VT: Ashgate, pp 25–40.

Bankowski, Z. and MacLean, J. (2006) 'Introduction', in Z. Bankowski and J. MacLean (eds) *The Universal and the Particular in Legal Reasoning*, Aldershot and Burlington, VT: Ashgate, pp xi–xx.

Bengoetxea, J. (1993) *The Legal Reasoning of the European Court of Justice: Towards a European Jurisprudence*, Oxford: Clarendon Press.

Bouwsma, O.K. (1961) 'The Blue Book', *The Journal of Philosophy*, 58(6): 141–164.

Butler, J. (2001) 'Giving an Account of Oneself', *Diacritics*, 31(4): 22–40.

Butler, J. (2005) *Giving an Account of Oneself*, New York, NY: Fordham University Press.

Caputo, J. (1989) 'Gadamer's Closet Essentialism: A Derridean Critique', in D.P. Michelfelder and R.E. Palmer (eds) *Dialogue and Deconstruction: The Gadamer-Derrida Encounter*, Albany, NY: State University of New York Press, pp 258–264.

Caputo, J. (2002) 'Good Will and the Hermeneutics of Friendship: Gadamer and Derrida', *Philosophy & Social Criticism*, 28(5): 512–522.

Cavell, S. (1979) *The Claim of Reason: Wittgenstein, Skepticism, Morality, and Tragedy*, Oxford and New York, NY: Clarendon Press.

Cavell, S. (1995) *Philosophical Passages: Wittgenstein, Emerson, Austin, Derrida*, Oxford: Blackwell Publishers.

Cavell, S. (2000) 'Excursus on Wittgenstein's Vision of Language', in A. Crary and R. Read (eds) *The New Wittgenstein*, London: Routledge, pp 21–37.

Christodoulidis, E. (1999) 'The Irrationality of Merciful Legal Judgement: Exclusionary Reasoning and the Question of the Particular', *Law and Philosophy*, 18(3): 215–241.

Christodoulidis, E. (2009) 'Strategies of Rupture', *Law and Critique*, 20(1): 3–26.

Ciaramelli, F. (1991) 'Levinas's Ethical Discourse between Individuation and Universality', in R. Bernasconi and S. Critchley (eds) *Re-Reading Levinas*, Bloomington, IN and Indianapolis, IN: Indiana University Press, pp 83–105.

Constable, M. (2005) *Just Silences: The Limits and Possibilities of Modern Law*, Princeton, NJ and Oxford: Princeton University Press.

Cornell, D., Rosenfeld, M. and Carlson, D.G. (eds) (1992) *Deconstruction and the Possibility of Justice*, New York, NY: Routledge.

Cover, R.M. (1983) 'The Supreme Court, 1982 Term – Foreword: Nomos and Narrative', *Harvard Law Review*, 97: 4–68.

Cover, R.M. (1985–1986) 'The Bonds of Constitutional Interpretation: Of the Word, the Deed and the Role', *Georgia Law Review*, 20: 815–833.

Cover, R.M. (1986) 'Violence and the Word', *The Yale Law Journal*, 95: 1601–1629.

Critchley, S. (1999) *The Ethics of Deconstruction: Derrida and Levinas*, 2nd edn, Edinburgh: Edinburgh University Press.

Critchley, S. (2002) 'Introduction', in S. Critchley and R. Bernasconi (eds) *The Cambridge Companion to Levinas*, Cambridge: Cambridge University Press, pp 1–32.

Critchley, S. (2007a) *Infinitely Demanding: Ethics of Commitment, Politics of Resistance*, London and New York, NY: Verso.

Critchley, S. (2007b) 'Five Problems in Levinas's View of Politics and a Sketch of a Solution to Them', in M. Diamantides (ed.) *Levinas, Law, Politics*, London and New York, NY: Routledge-Cavendish, pp 93–105.

Critchley, S. (2008) 'The Reader: Derrida Among the Philosophers', in P. Goodrich *et al.* (eds) *Derrida and Legal Philosophy*, Basingstoke and New York, NY: Palgrave Macmillan, pp 21–32.

Critchley, S. (2009) 'Anarchic Law', in D. Manderson (ed.) *Essays on Levinas and Law: A Mosaic*, Basingstoke and New York, NY: Palgrave Macmillan, pp 203–211.

Dallmayr, F. (1989) 'Prelude: Hermeneutics and Deconstruction: Gadamer and Derrida in Dialogue', in D.P. Michelfelder and R.E. Palmer (eds) *Dialogue and Deconstruction: The Gadamer-Derrida Encounter*, Albany, NY: State University of New York Press, pp 75–92.

Davidson, D. (1973–1974) 'On the Very Idea of a Conceptual Scheme', *Proceedings and Addresses of the American Philosophical Association*, 47: 5–20.

Davidson, D. (1990) 'The Structure and Content of Truth', *The Journal of Philosophy*, 87(6): 279–328.

Derrida, J. (1976) *Of Grammatology*, Baltimore, MD and London: The Johns Hopkins University Press.

Derrida, J. (1978) *Writing and Difference*, Chicago, IL: University of Chicago Press.

Derrida, J. (1981a) *Positions*, Chicago, IL: University of Chicago Press.

Derrida, J. (1981b) *Dissemination*, Chicago, IL: University of Chicago Press.

Derrida, J. (1982) *Margins of Philosophy*, Chicago, IL: University of Chicago Press.

Derrida, J. (1984) 'Dialogue with Jacques Derrida: Deconstruction and the Other', in R. Kearney (ed.) *Dialogues with Contemporary Continental Thinkers*, Manchester and Dover, NH: Manchester University Press, pp 107–126.

Derrida, J. (1986) 'But, beyond... (Open Letter to Anne McClintock and Rob Nixon)', *Critical Inquiry*, 13(1): 155–170.

Derrida, J. (1987) *The Post Card: From Socrates to Freud and Beyond*, Chicago, IL: University of Chicago Press.

Derrida, J. (1988a) *Limited Inc*, Evanston, IL: Northwestern University Press.

Derrida, J. (1988b) 'Letter to a Japanese Friend', in D. Wood and R. Bernasconi (eds) *Derrida and Différance*, Evanston, IL: Northwestern University Press, pp 1–5.

Derrida, J. (1989a) 'Three Questions to Hans-Georg Gadamer', in D.P. Michelfelder and R.E. Palmer (eds) *Dialogue and Deconstruction: The Gadamer-Derrida encounter*, Albany, NY: State University of New York Press, pp 52–54.

Derrida, J. (1989b) 'Interpreting Signatures (Nietzsche/Heidegger): Two Questions', in D.P. Michelfelder and R.E. Palmer (eds) *Dialogue and Deconstruction: The Gadamer-Derrida Encounter*, Albany, NY: State University of New York Press, pp 58–71.

Derrida, J. (1992a) *Acts of Literature*, New York, NY and London: Routledge.

Derrida, J. (1992b) 'Passions: "An Oblique Offering"', in D. Wood (ed.) *Derrida: A Critical Reader*, Oxford: Blackwell Publishers, pp 5–35.

Derrida, J. (1992c) 'Force of Law: The "Mystical Foundation of Authority"', in D. Cornell, M. Rosenfeld and D.G. Carlson (eds) *Deconstruction and the Possibility of Justice*, New York, NY: Routledge, pp 3–67.

Derrida, J. (1994) *Specters of Marx: The State of the Debt, the Work of Mourning, and the New International*, New York, NY and London: Routledge.

Derrida, J. (1995a) *Points... Interviews, 1974–1994*, Stanford, CA: Stanford University Press.

Derrida, J. (1995b) *The Gift of Death*, Chicago, IL: University of Chicago Press.

Derrida, J. (1999a) 'Hospitality, Justice and Responsibility: A Dialogue with Jacques Derrida', in R. Kearney and M. Dooley (eds) *Questioning Ethics: Contemporary Debates in Philosophy*, London and New York, NY: Routledge, pp 65–83.

Derrida, J. (1999b) *Adieu to Emmanuel Levinas*, Stanford, CA: Stanford University Press.

Derrida, J. (2000) 'Performative Powerlessness: A Response to Simon Critchley', *Constellations: An International Journal of Critical and Democratic Theory*, 7(4): 466–468.

Derrida, J. (2002) 'The Animal That Therefore I Am (More to Follow)', *Critical Inquiry*, 28: 369–418.

Derrida, J. (2004) 'Uninterrupted Dialogue: Between two Infinites, The Poem', *Research in Phenomenology*, 34: 3–19.

Derrida, J. (2005) '"Justices"', *Critical Inquiry*, 31(3): 689–721.

Diamantides, M. (2000) 'The Subject May Have Disappeared but *Its* Sufferings Remain', *Law and Critique*, 11(2): 137–166.

Diamantides, M. (2007) 'Levinas and Critical Legal Thought: Imbruglio, Opera Buffa, Divine Comedy?', in M. Diamantides (ed.) *Levinas, Law, Politics*, London and New York, NY: Routledge-Cavendish, pp 179–215.

Douzinas, C. and Gearey, A. (2005) *Critical Jurisprudence: The Political Philosophy of Justice*, Oxford and Portland, OR: Hart Publishing.

Douzinas, C. and Warrington, R. (1991) '"A Well-Founded Fear of Justice": Law and Ethics in Postmodernity', *Law and Critique*, 2(2): 115–147.

Eco, U. (1990) *The Limits of Interpretation*, Bloomington, IN: Indiana University Press.

Eco, U. (1992) *Interpretation and Overinterpretation*, Cambridge: Cambridge University Press.

Eco, U. (2000) *Kant and the Platypus: Essays on Language and Cognition*, London: Vintage.

Endicott, T. (2000) *Vagueness in Law*, Oxford and New York, NY: Oxford University Press.

Enwald, M. (2004) *Displacements of Deconstruction: The Deconstruction of Metaphysics of Presence, Meaning, Subject and Method*, Tampere: University of Tampere.

Eriksson, L. *et al.* (1998) 'Introduction: A Polytical Manifesto', in A. Hirvonen (ed.) *Polycentricity: The Multiple Scenes of Law*, London, Sterling: Pluto Press, pp 1–10.

Etxabe, J. (2010) 'The Legal Universe After Robert Cover', *Law and Humanities*, 4(1): 115–147.

Gadamer, H.-G. (1979) *Truth and Method*, London: Sheed and Ward.

Gadamer, H.-G. (1989a) 'Destruktion and Deconstruction', in D.P. Michelfelder and R.E. Palmer (eds) *Dialogue and Deconstruction: The Gadamer-Derrida Encounter*, Albany, NY: State University of New York Press, pp 102–113.

Gadamer, H.-G. (1989b) 'Letter to Dallmayr', in D.P. Michelfelder and R.E. Palmer (eds) *Dialogue and Deconstruction: The Gadamer-Derrida Encounter*, Albany, NY: State University of New York Press, pp 93–101.

Gadamer, H.-G. (1989c) 'Hermeneutics and Logocentrism', in D.P. Michelfelder and R.E. Palmer (eds) *Dialogue and Deconstruction: The Gadamer-Derrida Encounter*, Albany, NY: State University of New York Press, pp 114–125.

Gadamer, H.-G. (1989d) 'Text and Interpretation', in D.P. Michelfelder and R.E. Palmer (eds) *Dialogue and Deconstruction: The Gadamer-Derrida Encounter*, Albany, NY: State University of New York Press, pp 21–51.

Gadamer, H.-G. (2006a) 'Looking Back with Gadamer Over his Writings and their Effective History: A Dialogue with Jean Grondin (1996)', *Theory, Culture & Society*, 23(1): 85–100.

Gadamer, H.-G. (2006b) 'Classical and Philosophical Hermeneutics', *Theory, Culture & Society*, 23(1): 29–56.

Gadamer, H.-G. (2006c) 'Language and Understanding', *Theory, Culture & Society*, 23(1): 13–27.

Garver, N. (1994) *This Complicated Form of Life: Essays on Wittgenstein*, Chicago, IL and La Salle, IL: Open Court.

Gasché, R. (1986) *The Tain of the Mirror: Derrida and the Philosophy of Reflection*, Cambridge, MA and London: Harvard University Press.

Gehring, P. (2008) 'The Jurisprudence of the "Force of Law"', in P. Goodrich *et al.* (eds) *Derrida and Legal Philosophy*, Basingstoke and New York, NY: Palgrave Macmillan, pp 55–70.

Gibbs, R. (2006) 'Verdict and Sentence: Cover and Levinas on the Robe of Justice', *Journal of Jewish Thought and Philosophy*, 14(1/2): 73–89.

Goodrich, P. *et al.* (eds) (2008a) *Derrida and Legal Philosophy*, Basingstoke and New York, NY: Palgrave Macmillan.

Goodrich, P. *et al.* (2008b) 'Introduction: A Philosophy of Legal Enigmas', in P. Goodrich *et al.* (eds) *Derrida and Legal Philosophy*, Basingstoke and New York, NY: Palgrave Macmillan, pp 1–18.

Greisch, J. (1991) 'The Face and Reading: Immediacy and Mediation', in R. Bernasconi and S. Critchley (eds) *Re-Reading Levinas*, Bloomington, IN and Indianapolis, IN: Indiana University Press, pp 67–82.

Grondin, J. (2002) 'Gadamer's Basic Understanding of Understanding', in R.J. Dostal (ed.) *The Cambridge Companion to Gadamer*, New York, NY: Cambridge University Press, pp 36–51.

Hacker, P.M.S. (1993) *Wittgenstein: Meaning and Mind*, Oxford and Malden, MA: Blackwell Publishers.

Hart, H.L.A. (1958) 'Positivism and the Separation of Law and Morals', *Harvard Law Review*, 71: 593–629.

Heller, A. (1992) 'Rights, Modernity, Democracy', in D. Cornell, M. Rosenfeld and D.G. Carlson (eds) *Deconstruction and the Possibility of Justice*, New York, NY: Routledge, pp 346–360.

Hertzberg, L. (1994) *The Limits of Experience*, Acta Philosophica Fennica Vol 56, Helsinki: The Philosophical Society of Finland.

Hertzberg, L. (2001) 'The Sense Is Where You Find It', in T. McCarthy and S.C. Stidd (eds) *Wittgenstein in America*, Oxford: Clarendon Press, pp 90–103.

Hertzberg, L. (2002) 'On the Need for a Listener and Community Standards', in M. Gustafsson and L. Hertzberg (eds) *The Practice of Language*, Dordrecht, Boston, MA and London: Kluwer Academic Publishers, pp 247–266.

Hewlett, N. (2007) *Badiou, Balibar, Rancière: Re-thinking Emancipation*, New York, NY: Continuum.

Hintikka, J. (2004) 'Ludwig Wittgenstein – Lainsuojaton Filosofi', *Ajatus,* 61: 7–24.

Hirvonen, A. (2001) 'Promising Justice: Derrida with Jewish Jurisprudence', *Law and Critique*, 12(2): 159–183.

Kaarto, T. (2008) *Jacques Derrida and the Question of Interpretation: The Phenomenological Reduction, the Intention of the Author, and Kafka's Law*, Frankfurt am Main: Peter Lang.

Kauppinen, J. (2000) *Apologies of Derrida: Philosophy, Law and Literature*, Helsinki: The Department of Philosophy, University of Helsinki.

Kennedy, D. (1997) *A Critique of Adjudication (fin de siècle)*, Cambridge, MA and London: Harvard University Press.

Klatt, M. (2008) *Making the Law Explicit*, Oxford and Portland, OR: Hart Publishing.

Kripke, S. (1982) *Wittgenstein on Rules and Private Language*, Oxford: Blackwell Publishers.

Kuusela, O. (2006) 'Do the Concepts of Grammar and Use in Wittgenstein Articulate a Theory of Language or Meaning?', *Philosophical Investigations*, 29(4): 309–341.

Levinas, E. (1969) *Totality and Infinity: An Essay on Exteriority*, Pittsburgh, PA: Duquesne University Press.

Levinas, E. (1982) *Ethique et Infini: Dialogues avec Philippe Nemo*, Paris: Fayard.

Levinas, E. (1984) 'Ethics of the Infinite', in R. Kearney (ed.) *Dialogues with Contemporary Continental Thinkers*, Manchester and Dover, NH: Manchester University Press, pp 49–70.

Levinas, E. (1995) *Alterité et Transcendance*, Saint Clément de rivière: Fata Morgana.

Levinas, E. (1996a) *Basic Philosophical Writings*, Bloomington, IN and Indianapolis, IN: Indiana University Press.

Levinas, E. (1996b) *Proper Names*, London: The Athlone Press.

Levinas, E. (1998) *Otherwise than Being: Or Beyond Essence*, Pittsburgh, PA: Duquesne University Press.

Levinas, E. (2000) *Entre Nous: On Thinking-of-the-other*, London: Athlone.

Lindroos-Hovinheimo, S. (2009) 'Retracing One's Steps: Searching for the Ethics of Legal Interpretation', *International Journal for the Semiotics of Law*, 22(2): 163–178.

Llewelyn, J. (1985) *Beyond Metaphysics?: The Hermeneutic Circle in Contemporary Continental Philosophy*, Atlantic Highlands, NJ: Humanities Press International.

Llewelyn, J. (1995) *Emmanuel Levinas: The Genealogy of Ethics*, New York, NY: Routledge.

Llewelyn, J. (2002a) *Appositions of Jacques Derrida and Emmanuel Levinas*, Bloomington, IN: Indiana University Press.

Llewelyn, J. (2002b) 'Levinas and Language', in S. Critchley and R. Bernasconi (eds) *The Cambridge Companion to Levinas*, Cambridge: Cambridge University Press, pp 119–138.

Lyons, D. (1999) 'Open Texture and the Possibility of Legal Interpretation', *Law and Philosophy*, 18: 297–309.

MacCormick, N. (2005), *Rhetoric and the Rule of Law: A Theory of Legal Reasoning*, Oxford and New York, NY: Oxford University Press.

MacCormick, N. (2006) 'Pariculars and Universals', in Z. Bankowski and J. MacLean (eds) *The Universal and the Particular in Legal Reasoning*, Aldershot and Burlington, VT: Ashgate, pp 3–22.

MacCormick, N. (2007) *Institutions of Law*, Oxford: Oxford University Press.

MacCormick, N. and Summers, R.S. (1996) 'Interpretation and Justification', in N. MacCormick and R.S. Summers (eds) *Interpreting Statutes: A Comparative Study*, Aldershot: Dartmouth, pp 511–544.

Malcolm, N. (1954) 'Wittgenstein's Philosophical Investigations', *The Philosophical Review*, 63(4): 530–559.

Malcolm, N. (1986) *Nothing is Hidden: Wittgenstein's Criticism of his Early Thought*, Oxford and New York, NY: Basil Blackwell.

Malcolm, N. (1993) *Wittgenstein: A Religious Point of View?*, London: Routledge.

Manderson, D. (2006) *Proximity, Levinas, and the Soul of Law*, Montreal, Kingston, London and Ithaca, NY: McGill-Queen's University Press.

Manderson, D. (2007) 'Here I am: Illuminating and delimiting responsibility', in M. Diamantides (ed.) *Levinas, Law, Politics*, London and New York, NY: Routledge-Cavendish, pp 145–164.

Manderson, D. (2009a) '"Current Legal Maxims in which the Word Neighbour Occurs": Levinas and the Law of Torts', in D. Manderson (ed.) *Essays on Levinas and Law: A Mosaic*, Basingstoke and New York, NY: Palgrave Macmillan, pp 111–127.

Manderson, D. (2009b) 'Response', in D. Manderson (ed.) *Essays on Levinas and Law: A Mosaic*, Basingstoke and New York, NY: Palgrave Macmillan, pp 212–216.

Marmor, A. (2008) 'The Pragmatics of Legal Language', *Ratio Juris*, 21(4): 423–452.

May, T. (2008) *The Political Thought of Jacques Rancière: Creating Equality*, Pennsylvania, PA: Penn State Press.

Melissaris, E. (2006) 'Diachronic Universalization and the Law', in Z. Bankowski and J. MacLean (eds) *The Universal and the Particular in Legal Reasoning*, Aldershot and Burlington, VT: Ashgate, pp 129–141.

Michelfelder, D.P. and Palmer, R.E. (1989) 'Introduction', in D.P. Michelfelder and R.E. Palmer (eds) *Dialogue and Deconstruction: The Gadamer-Derrida Encounter*, Albany, NY: State University of New York Press, pp 1–18.

Miller, J.H. (1987) *The Ethics of Reading*, New York, NY: Columbia University Press.

Miller, J.H. (2009) *For Derrida*, New York, NY: Fordham University Press.

Minow, M. *et al.* (1995) 'Introduction: Robert Cover and Law, Judging, and Violence', in M. Minow *et al.* (eds) *Narrative, Violence, and the Law: The Essays of Robert Cover*, Ann Arbor, MI: The University of Michigan Press, pp 1–11.

Mouffe, C. (2001) 'Wittgenstein and the Ethos of Democracy', in L. Nagl and C. Mouffe (eds) *The Legacy of Wittgenstein: Pragmatism or Deconstruction*, Frankfurt am Main: Peter Lang, pp 131–138.

Mouffe, C. (2005) *The Democratic Paradox*, London, New York, NY: Verso.

Mulhall, S. (2001) 'Seeing Aspects', in H.-J. Glock (ed.) *Wittgenstein: A Critical Reader*, Malden, MA and Oxford: Blackwell Publishers, pp 246–267.

Naas, M. (2003) *Taking on the Tradition: Jacques Derrida and the Legacies of Deconstruction*, Stanford, CA: Stanford University Press.

Nancy, J.-L. (2000) *Being Singular Plural*, Stanford, CA: Stanford University Press.

Norris, C. (1986) 'Review: Deconstruction against Itself: Derrida and Nietzsche', *Diacritics*, 16(4): 59–69.

Norris, C. (1990) 'Review: Limited Think: How Not to Read Derrida', *Diacritics*, 20(1): 16–36.

Oksala, J. (2005) *Foucault on Freedom*, Cambridge: Cambridge University Press.

Overgaard, S. (2007) 'The Ethical Residue of Language in Levinas and Early Wittgenstein', *Philosophy & Social Criticism*, 33(2): 223–249.

Palmer, R.E. (2006) 'Introduction to Four Key Essays from the Gadamer Lesebuch', *Theory, Culture & Society*, 23(1): 1–12.

Paunio, E. and Lindroos-Hovinheimo, S. (2010) 'Taking Language Seriously: An Analysis of Linguistic Reasoning and Its Implications in EU Law', *European Law Journal*, 16(4): 395–416.

Perpich, D. (2009) 'Getting Down to Cases: Can a Levinasian Ethics Generate Norms?', in D. Manderson (ed.) *Essays on Levinas and Law: A Mosaic*, Basingstoke and New York, NY: Palgrave Macmillan, pp 21–38.

Petrilli, S. and Ponzio, A. (2005) *Semiotics Unbounded: Interpretive Routes through the Open Network of Signs*, Toronto, Buffalo and London: University of Toronto Press.

Pihlström, S. (2006) 'Shared Language, Transcendental Listeners, and the Problem of Limits', in S. Pihlström (ed.) *Wittgenstein and the Method of Philosophy*, Helsinki: The Philosophical Society of Finland, pp 185–221.

Putnam, H. (2001) 'Rules, Attunement, and "Applying Words to the World": The Struggle to Understand Wittgenstein's Vision of Language', in L. Nagl and C. Mouffe (eds) *The Legacy of Wittgenstein: Pragmatism or Deconstruction*, Frankfurt am Main: Peter Lang, pp 9–23.

Rancière, J. (1999) *Disagreement: Politics and Philosophy*, Minneapolis, MN and London: University of Minnesota Press.

Rancière, J. (2006) 'Democracy, Republic, Representation', *Constellations: An International Journal of Critical and Democratic Theory*, 13(3): 297–307.

Rancière, J. (2009) *Hatred of Democracy*, London and New York, NY: Verso.

Rancière, J. (2010) *Dissensus: On Politics and Aesthetics*, London and New York, NY: Continuum.

Rancière, J. and Panagia, D. (2000) 'Dissenting Words: A Conversation with Jacques Rancière', *Diacritics*, 30(2): 113–126.

Risser, J. (1989) 'The Two Faces of Socrates: Gadamer/Derrida', in D.P. Michelfelder and R.E. Palmer (eds) *Dialogue and Deconstruction: The Gadamer-Derrida Encounter*, Albany, NY: State University of New York Press, pp 176–185.

Rosenfeld, M. (1992) 'Deconstruction and Legal Interpretation: Conflict, Indeterminacy and the Temptations of the New Legal Formalism', in D. Cornell, M. Rosenfeld and D.G. Carlson (eds) *Deconstruction and the Possibility of Justice*, New York, NY: Routledge, pp 152–210.

Rosenfeld, M. (1998) *Just Interpretations: Law Between Ethics and Politics*, Berkeley, CA, Los Angeles, CA and London: University of California Press.

Rosenfeld, M. (2008) 'Derrida's Ethical Turn: The Case of Terrorism', in P. Goodrich *et al.* (eds) *Derrida and Legal Philosophy*, Basingstoke and New York, NY: Palgrave MacMillan, pp 71–98.

Schroeder, S. (2001) 'Private Language and Private Experience', in H.-J. Glock (ed.) *Wittgenstein: A Critical Reader*, Malden, MA and Oxford: Blackwell Publishers, pp 174–198.

Searle, J.R. (1969) *Speech Acts: An Essay in the Philosophy of Language*, Cambridge: Cambridge University Press.

Smith, N. (2009) 'Questions for a Reluctant Jurisprudence of Alterity', in D. Manderson (ed.) *Essays on Levinas and Law: A Mosaic*, Basingstoke and New York, NY: Palgrave Macmillan, pp 55–75.

Staten, H. (1985) *Wittgenstein and Derrida*, Oxford: Basil Blackwell.

Staten, H. (2001) 'Wittgenstein's Deconstructive Legacy', in L. Nagl and C. Mouffe (eds) *The Legacy of Wittgenstein: Pragmatism or Deconstruction*, Frankfurt am Main: Peter Lang, pp 43–62.

Taylor, C. (2002) 'Gadamer on the Human Sciences', in R.J. Dostal (ed.) *The Cambridge Companion to Gadamer*, New York, NY: Cambridge University Press, pp 126–142.

Tilghman, B. (2001) 'Morality, Human Understanding, and the Limits of Language', in T. McCarthy and S.C. Stidd (eds) *Wittgenstein in America*, Oxford: Clarendon Press, pp 237–249.

Tuohimaa (Enwald), M. (1999) 'Exteriority and Interiority of Interpretation', in A. Haapala and O. Naukkarinen (eds) *Interpretation and its Boundaries*, Helsinki: Helsinki University Press, pp 180–191.

Tuori, K. (2011) *Ratio and Voluntas: The Tension Between Reason and Will in Law*, Farnham and Burlington, VT: Ashgate.

Uschanov, T.P. (2006) 'On Ladder Withdrawal Symptoms and One Way of Dealing with Them', in S. Pihlström (ed.) *Wittgenstein and the Method of Philosophy*, Helsinki: The Philosophical Society of Finland, pp 131–167.

Veitch, S. (1997) 'Law and "Other" problems', *Law and Critique*, 8(1): 97–109.

Veitch, S. (2007) *Law and Irresponsibility: On the Legitimation of Human Suffering*, London: Routledge-Cavendish.

de Ville, J. (2008) 'Sovereignty Without Sovereignty: Derrida's Declarations of Independence', *Law and Critique*, 19(2): 87–114.

de Ville, J. (2009a) 'Derrida and Legal Scholarship: A Certain Step Beyond. Book review of Goodrich et al. (eds): Derrida and Legal Philosophy', *International Journal for the Semiotics of Law*, 22: 141–156.

de Ville, J. (2009b) 'Rethinking the Notion of a "Higher Law": Heidegger and Derrida on the Anaximander Fragment', *Law and Critique*, 20(1): 59–78.

Waldenfels, B. (2002) 'Levinas and the Face of the Other', in S. Critchley and R. Bernasconi (eds) *The Cambridge Companion to Levinas*, Cambridge: Cambridge University Press, pp 63–81.

Walker, N. (2006) 'The Burden of Universalism', in Z. Bankowski and J. MacLean (eds) *The Universal and the Particular in Legal Reasoning*, Aldershot and Burlington, VT: Ashgate, pp 53–67.

Weber, E. (2008) 'Deconstruction is Justice', in P. Goodrich *et al.* (eds) *Derrida and Legal Philosophy*, Basingstoke and New York, NY: Palgrave Macmillan, pp 177–182.

Wild, J. (1969) 'Introduction', in E. Levinas (ed.) *Totality and Infinity: An Essay on Exteriority*, Pittsburgh, PA: Duquesne University Press, pp 11–20.

Wilhelmsson, T. (2001) *Senmodern ansvarsrätt*, Helsinki: Kauppakaari.

Williams, M. (2001) 'The Etiology of the Obvious: Wittgenstein and the Elimination of Indeterminacy', in T. McCarthy and S.C. Stidd (eds) *Wittgenstein in America*, Oxford: Clarendon Press, pp 62–89.

Wittgenstein, L. (1958) *Philosophical Investigations*, 2nd edn, Oxford: Basil Blackwell.

Wittgenstein, L. (1965) 'A Lecture on Ethics', *The Philosophical Review*, 74(1): 3–12.

Wittgenstein, L. (1967) *Zettel*, Oxford: Basil Blackwell.

Wittgenstein, L. (1969) *The Blue and Brown Books: Preliminary Studies for the 'Philosophical Investigations'*, 2nd edn, Malden, MA, Oxford and Victoria: Blackwell Publishing.

Wittgenstein, L. (1974) *Philosophical Grammar*, Berkeley, CA and Los Angeles, CA: University of California Press.

Wittgenstein, L. (1975) *On Certainty*, Malden, MA, Oxford, Melbourne and Berlin: Blackwell Publishing.
Wittgenstein, L. (1980) *Culture and Value*, Chicago, IL: University of Chicago Press.
Wolcher, L.E. (1996) 'The Man in a Room: Remarks on Derrida's Force of Law', *Law and Critique*, 7(1): 35–64.
Wolcher, L.E. (2003) 'Ethics, Justice, and Suffering in the Thought of Levinas: The Problem of Passage', *Law and Critique*, 14(1): 93–116.
Wolcher, L.E. (2008) *Law's Task: The Tragic Circle of Law, Justice and Human Suffering*, Aldershot: Ashgate.
von Wright, G.H. (1957) *Logik, Filosofi och Språk*, Helsinki: Söderström.
Wyschogrod, E. (2002) 'Language and Alterity in the Thought of Levinas', in S. Critchley and R. Bernasconi (eds) *The Cambridge Companion to Levinas*, Cambridge: Cambridge University Press, pp 188–205.
Zerilli, L.M.G. (2001) 'Wittgenstein: Between Pragmatism and Deconstruction', in L. Nagl and C. Mouffe (eds) *The Legacy of Wittgenstein: Pragmatism or Deconstruction*, Frankfurt am Main: Peter Lang, pp 25–41.

# Index

Page numbers with 'n' following represent footnotes

www.ingramcontent.com/pod-product-compliance
Ingram Content Group UK Ltd.
Pitfield, Milton Keynes, MK11 3LW, UK
UKHW011014180926
475701UK00004B/740
* 9 7 8 0 4 1 5 7 2 0 1 9 9 *